IMAGES
of America

AROUND OVID

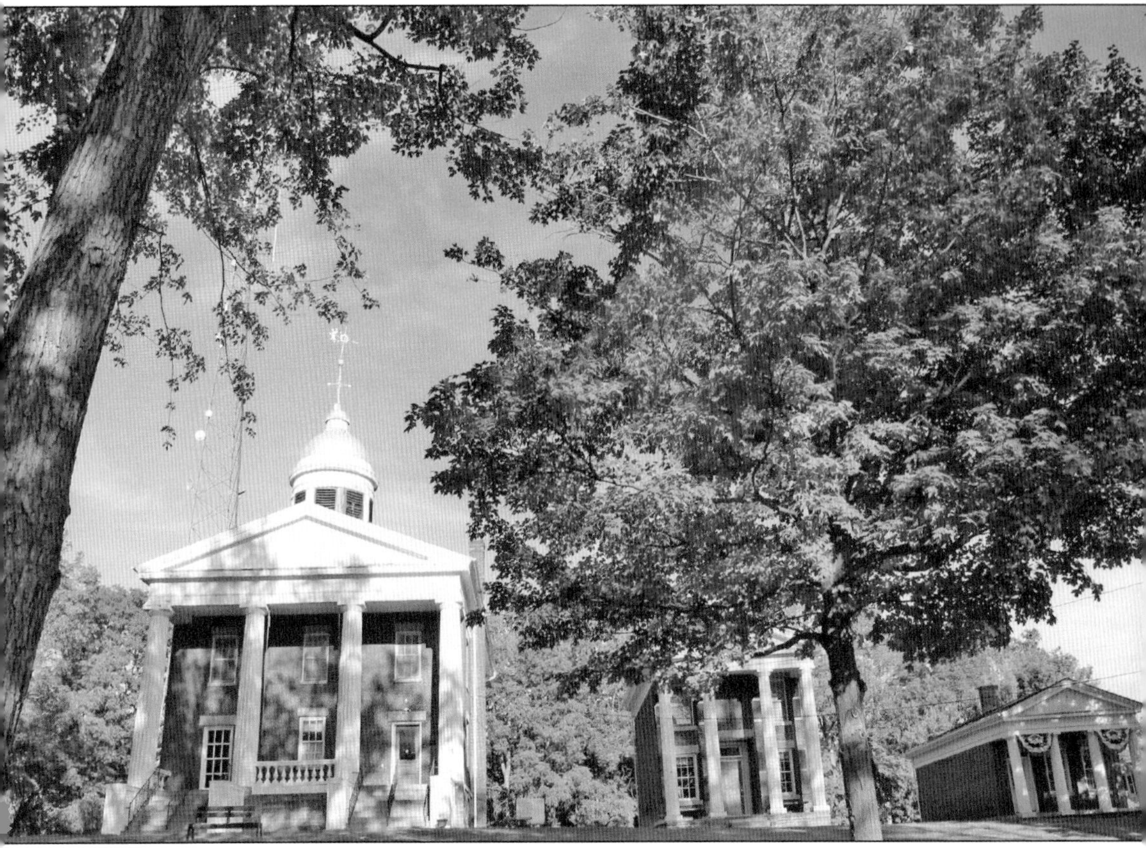

Shown here is an image of the most iconic buildings in Ovid. Completed in 1860, the so-called Three Bears—Papa, Mama, and Baby Bear—originally served as the town of Ovid's courthouse complex. For a period of their history, these three historic structures were the site of the Seneca County seat, which was a great honor for the town. And now this family of bears houses the Town of Ovid municipal offices. The Three Bears are the most beloved piece of local history. (Courtesy of Jane Braunig.)

On the Cover: Ovid is a town rich in rural and agricultural history. This evaporator and its crew likely represented the livelihood of a local family and a valuable cog in the town's young economy. In the early years of the town's history, Ovid's borders were significantly larger. This evaporator was once upon a time located in Ovid. Due to the area's evolution throughout the generations, the evaporator (still standing today) is now located in the neighboring town of Interlaken. (Courtesy of the Ovid Historical Society.)

IMAGES
of America

AROUND OVID

Ovid Historical Society

ARCADIA
PUBLISHING

ISBN 978-1-4671-1624-4

Published by Arcadia Publishing
Charleston, South Carolina

Printed in the United States of America

Library of Congress Control Number: 2015953460

For all general information, please contact Arcadia Publishing:
Telephone 843-853-2070
Fax 843-853-0044
E-mail sales@arcadiapublishing.com
For customer service and orders:
Toll-Free 1-888-313-2665

Visit us on the Internet at www.arcadiapublishing.com

This book is dedicated to the early settlers, those of us here now, and those who will be here in the future.

Contents

ACKNOWLEDGMENTS

The Ovid Historical Society encouraged the many residents of Ovid and the surrounding areas to share their photographs and postcards. With great enthusiasm, they responded to our plea for the pictures. They told great stories and contributed to the information that was used for writing the captions.

The society museum has a large collection of postcards and photographs from which we could draw. Some very interesting examples were those that were brought in to be scanned. The family photograph collections included a wide variety of subject matter that was quickly incorporated into the different chapters. Unless otherwise noted, all pictures in this book are from the Ovid Historical Society collection.

A huge thank-you is extended to all of the people, businesses, groups, and organizations that contributed to our book project. This includes those that gave us written and verbal material, as well as those that contributed their prints.

A special thank-you is extended to our Arcadia title manager, Henry Clougherty. His patient guidance and encouragement were sincerely appreciated. Without him, the work would have been much more difficult.

The members of the Ovid Historical Society book committee wish to extend our sincere thanks to all who made this book possible: Muriel Akers, Jane Braunig, Naomi Brewer, David Eastman, James McKee, William Sebring, and Gail Snyder.

Our thanks go to the following people for the special contributions that made this book: Muriel Akers, Peter Allen, Phyllis Betzler, Betty Boyce, William Braunig, Naomi Brewer, Pamela Tripp Coleman, Edwin Compton, Peter Depew, Mary Diamond, David Eastman, Kelly Fiske, Carol Franklin, Walter Gable, Roger Getman, David Griffith, Patricia Guinan, Dorothy Hicks, Interlaken Historical Society, Kate Lynch, Thomas Martin, Paul McPherson, Patricia Morrison, LeConte and Ruth Myer, William Palmer, Eugene C. Reigle, William Sebring, Carol Serling, Lucille Slike, Allen Smith, Ronald Steve, Florence Varguson, Frances Wickham, Jack Wickham, Kevin Wilkins, and Robert Zimmer.

INTRODUCTION

In 1779, Gen. John Sullivan was ordered by Gen. George Washington to remove the American Indians from the Finger Lakes region of New York State. The Indians had sided with the British during the Revolutionary War.

Between 1792 and 1795, several counties were reorganized. Albany County included all of the land to the west. Montgomery County was carved from Albany County in 1772; Herkimer County, in 1791; and Onondaga County, in 1794. Cayuga County was organized from Onondaga in 1799, and Seneca County was taken from Cayuga County in 1804. Seneca County, located on the ridge between Seneca and Cayuga Lakes, was divided into four towns— Junius, Fayette, Romulus, and Ovid.

Andrew Dunlap came from Pennsylvania in 1789. He was the first settler in the town of Ovid. John Seeley, the pioneer of the village of Ovid, arrived in 1792. The village of Ovid was founded in 1794. In 1804, Seeley gave the land for a wooden courthouse and jail to be built.

Settlers came to the area to farm. Sawmills and gristmills were built, and the number of businesses in the village increased. Churches and schools were added. Farmers took their grain to the various landings on the lakes to be shipped to customers in the cities. Passengers traveled on the ferryboats and steamers on the lakes.

This book of photographs leaves the reader with an overall impression of the rural character of the area. It shows the advancement, growth, and pride of the citizens during the first 200 years of the town and village of Ovid.

One

CHURCHES

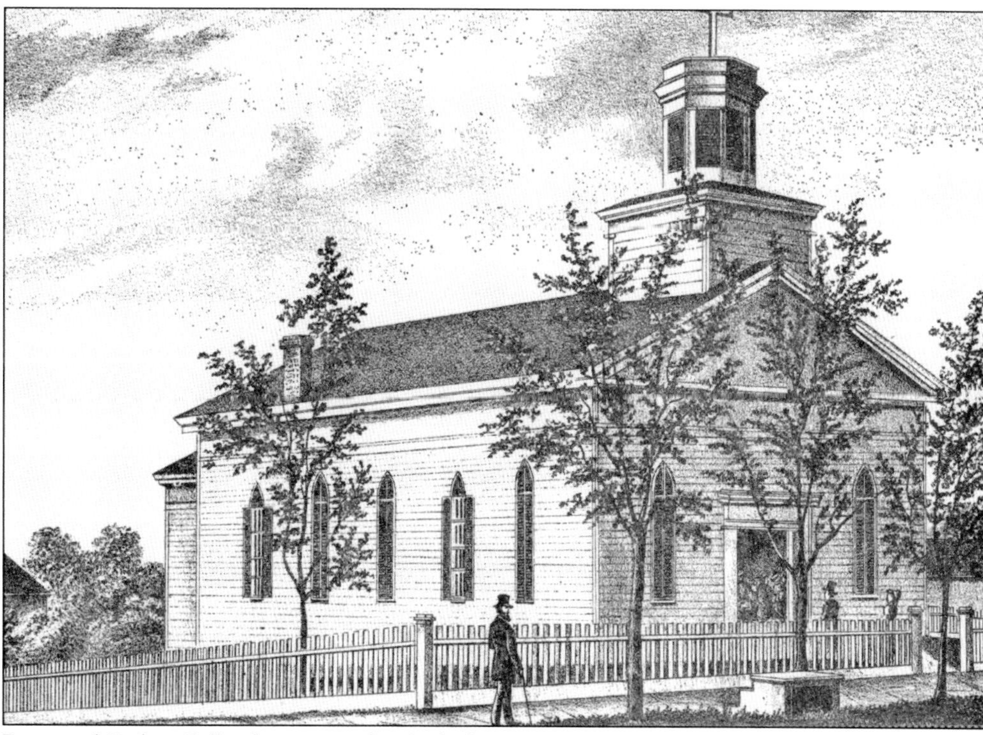

Reverend Father Gilbride organized a Catholic congregation in 1849. Mass was held in private homes before this church was built in 1850 on a 40-by-50-foot plot at the corner of South Main and Chapman Streets. The wooden building was destroyed by fire on October 25, 1907.

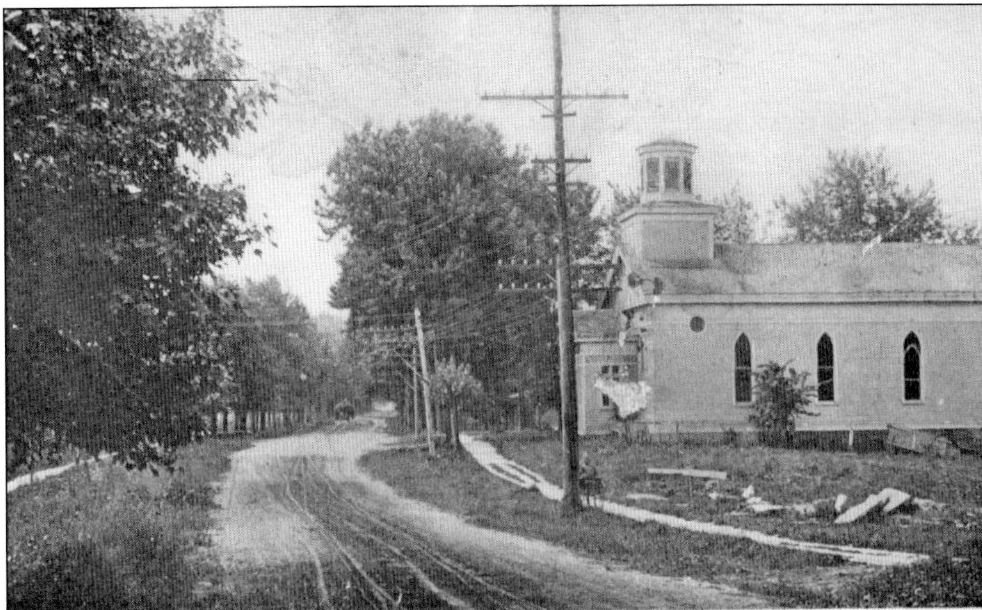

Columbus Hall, Ovid, N. Y. Destroyed by Fire Oct. 25, 1907.

Columbus Hall replaced the original wooden church to become the second Catholic church building in Ovid. It was doubled in size to hold an increased membership. When the new brick church was built, the hall continued in use for various functions until it was purchased by the Trumansburg Home Telephone Company.

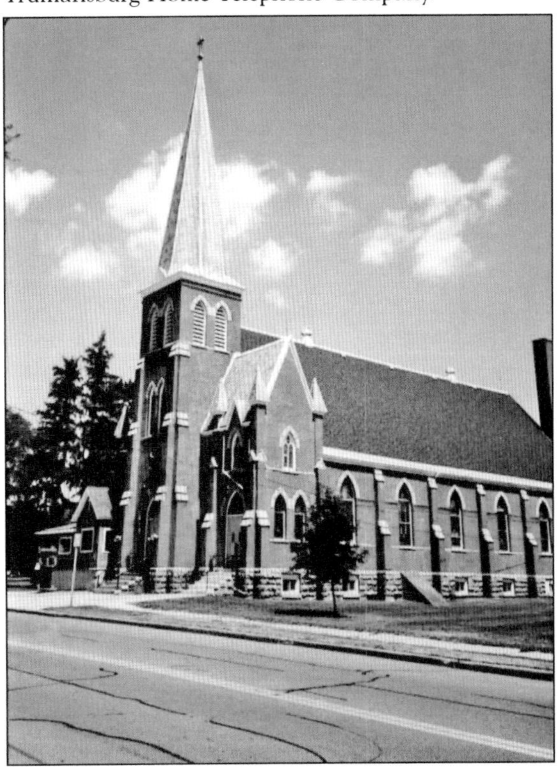

With the continued growth of the community, it was decided to build a new Holy Cross Catholic Church on property diagonally across Main Street from Columbus Hall. The brick structure has a center spire, Gothic arch windows, and Ruskinian Gothic details. Major renovations were made in 1961.

The Ovid Presbyterian Church was formed when 20 people joined together and held services either in the courthouse or high school. Many others joined them, so this brick church was erected about 1817. There were fires and reconstruction until this building was demolished and replaced by the Ford Municipal Building. In 1956, the members of the Presbyterian and Methodist churches combined, and their new Ovid Federated Church was built on the old Ovid High School grounds.

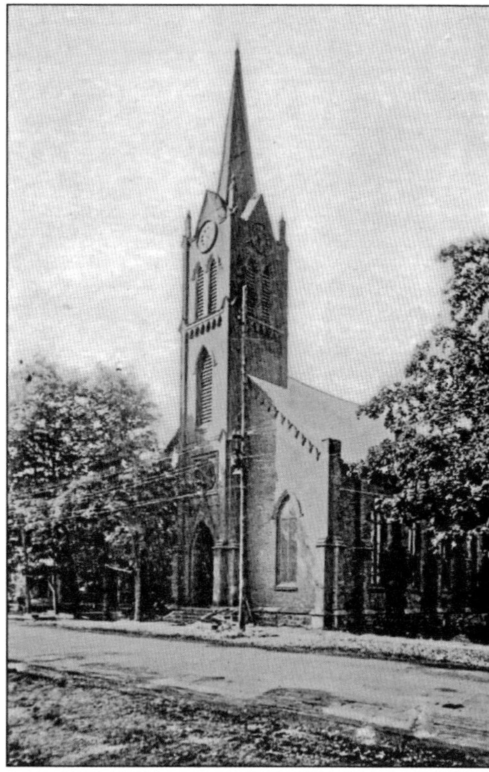

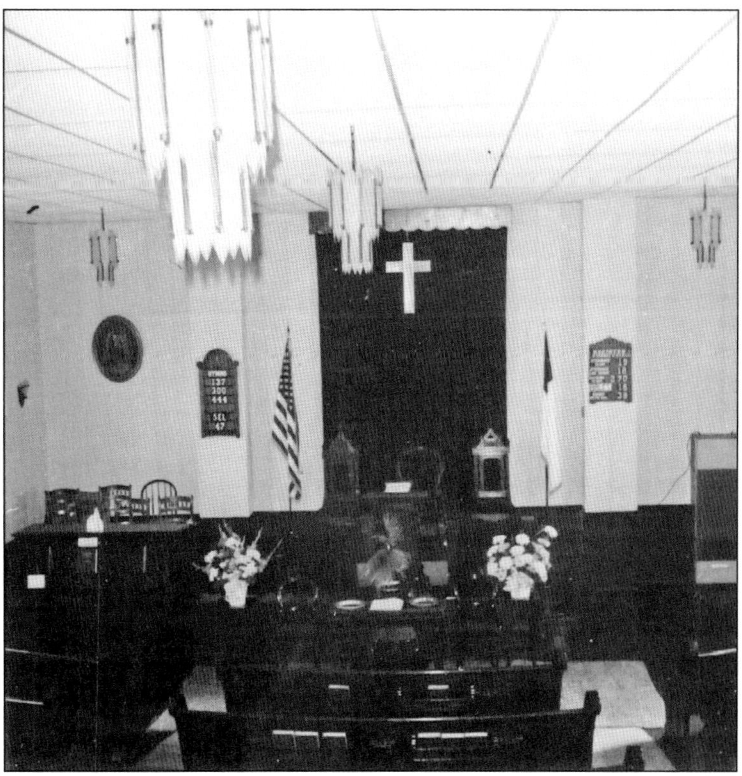

The interior of the Presbyterian church is shown with newly completed renovations. A dropped ceiling, chandeliers, and a lighted cross were installed. Along with the church flag, a new American flag with the correct number of stars graces the pulpit.

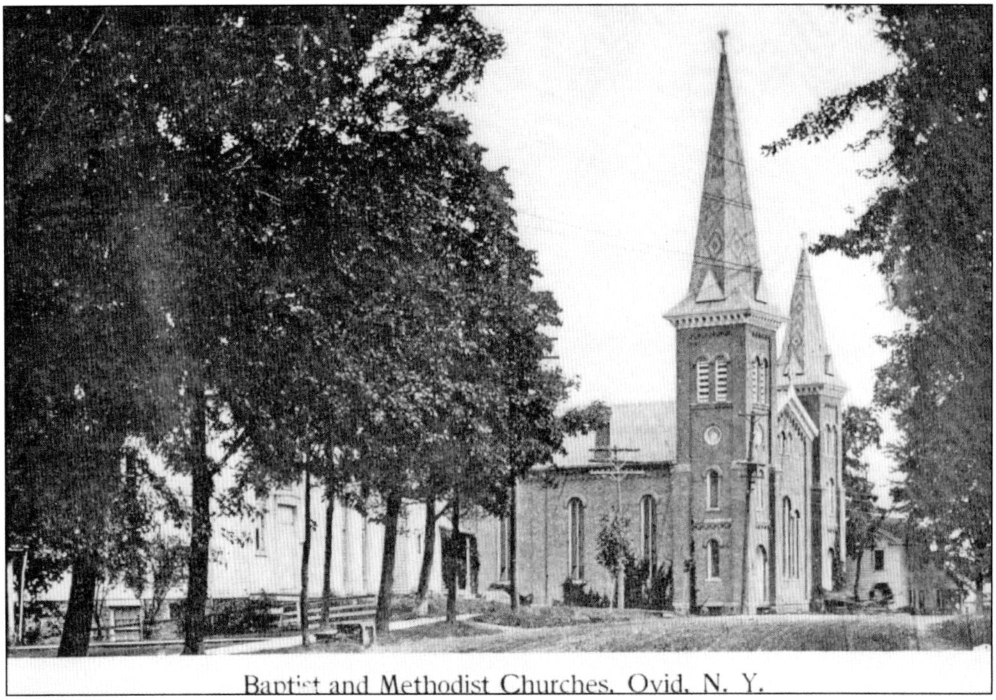

The Methodist church began before 1820 as a part of the Seneca Circuit, with James Smith as the first preacher in 1793. The two spires made the identity of the church unmistakable on the northwest comer of North Main and Brown Streets. It served the community for the 99 years, from 1870 to 1969.

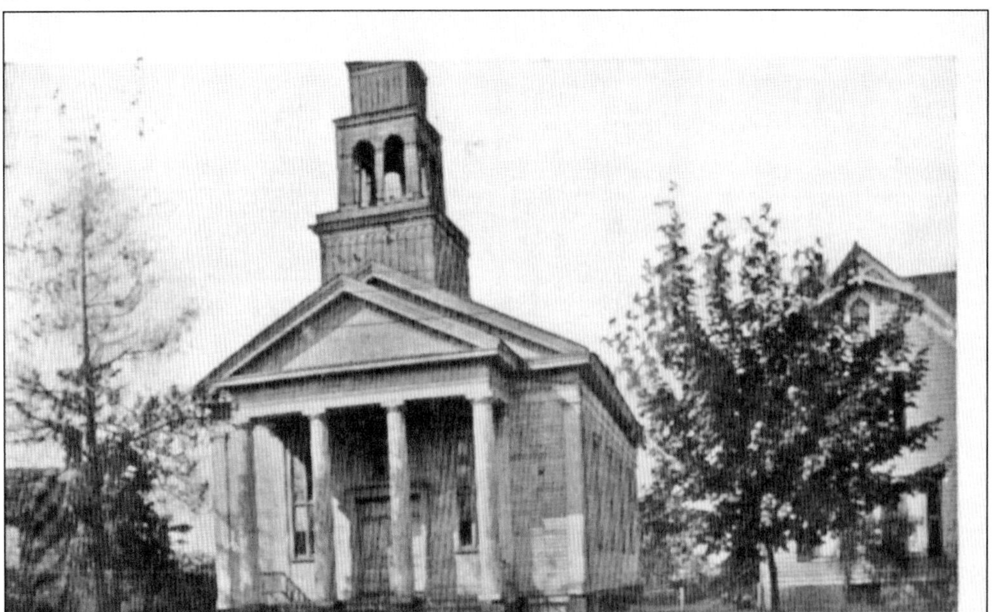

The Ovid Baptist Church was built in 1902 on North Main Street. It closed as a church and became known as the Franklin Town Hall. Eventually, it was used as the Ovid Grange Hall. In the 1970s, the building was bought by Lloyd Koke for his furniture and appliance store.

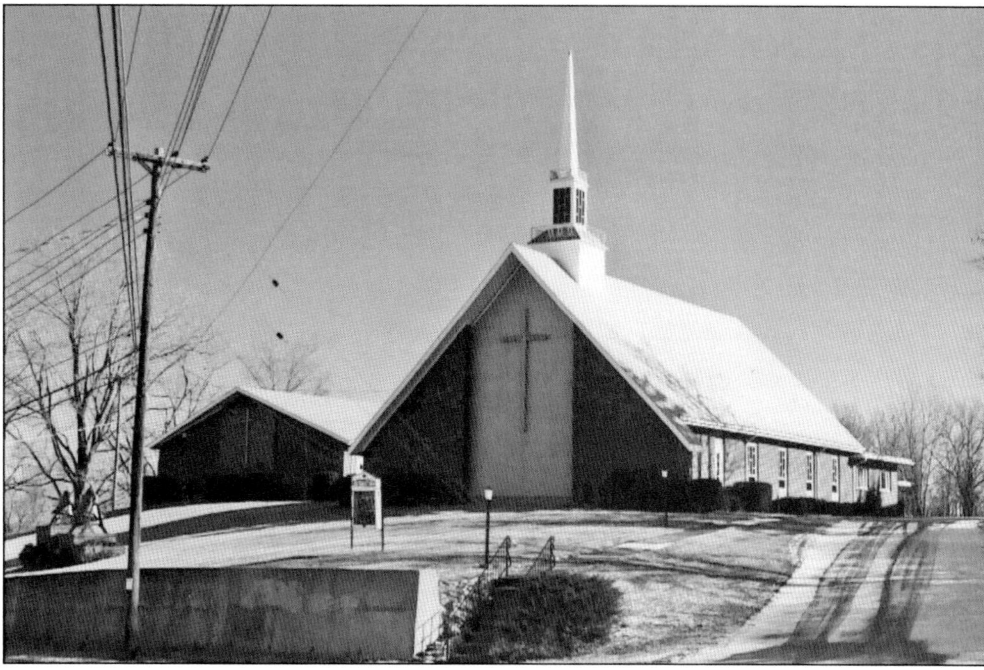

The Ovid Federated Church building was started in 1963, when the Sheldon Fellowship Hall portion was used for services and the remaining area housed the education hall. These were constructed on the site of the old Ovid High School. The main sanctuary was built last, with the first church service held on Mother's Day, May 14, 1967.

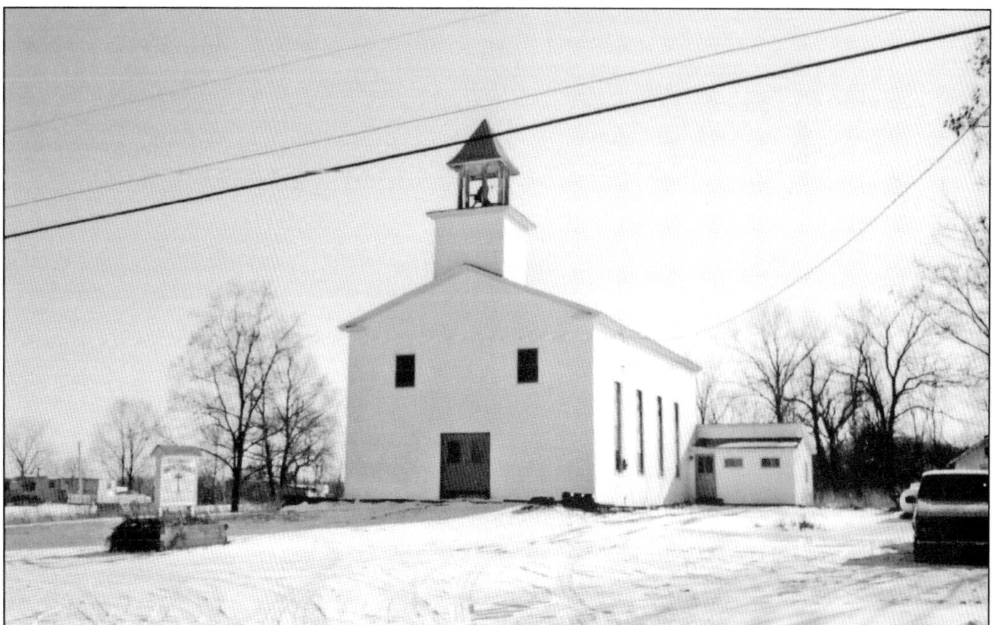

A group met at the home of Kezia Scott in Ovid Center to organize a Baptist conference. In 1830, the Ovid Center Baptist Church was built halfway between Ovid and Interlaken. The church bell in the steeple is the same one installed in 1830. The members were still very active in 1990, but the membership declined, and the church soon closed.

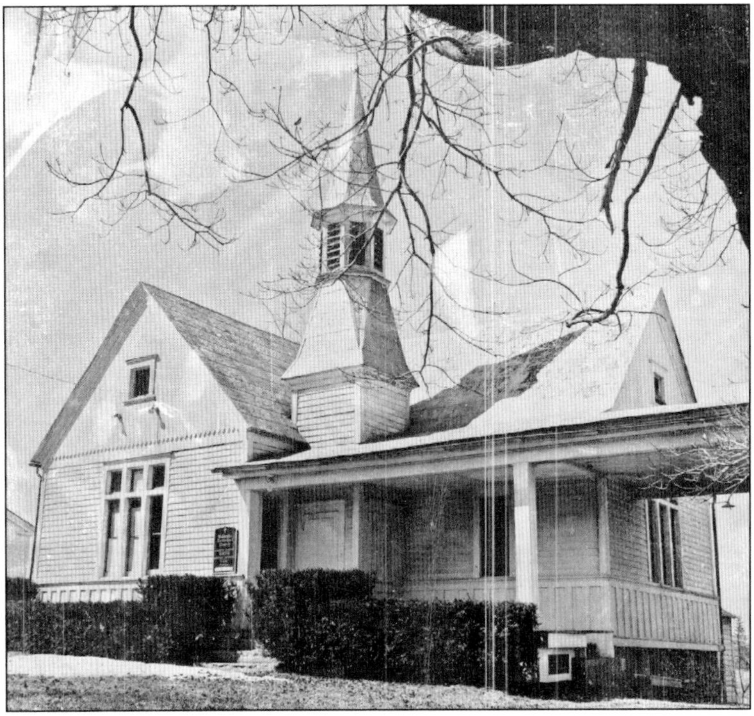

The Methodist church in Sheldrake was struck by lightning and burned to the ground in 1919. Mrs. John McDonald of Kidders gave the congregation this chapel from her estate. It was loaded on rollers and was pulled by John T. Hunt's team of horses. They transported it the three miles from McDonald's home to the present Sheldrake Church site. The building has since become a private home.

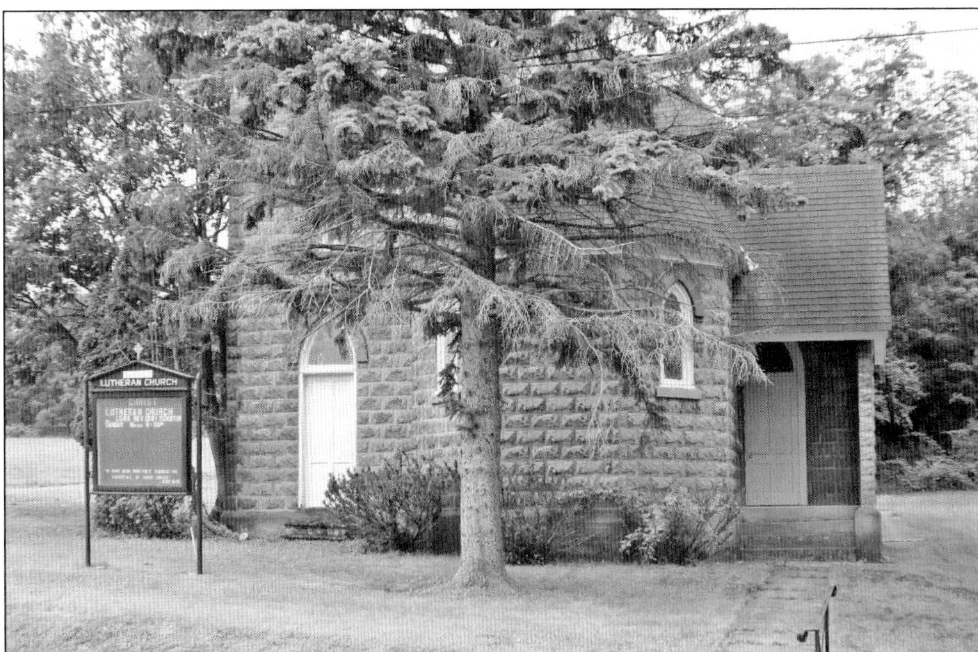

Christ Lutheran Church at Kidders was first built in 1880 as All Saints Episcopal Church. The land was given by Myron R. Cole, the owner of the Cole Hotel. In 1911, the church was struck by lightning and burned. It was rebuilt in 1912, and church services were continued with circuit ministers. It became idle, and a group of Lutherans acquired the property in 1958. Their church is still active.

Two

Schools

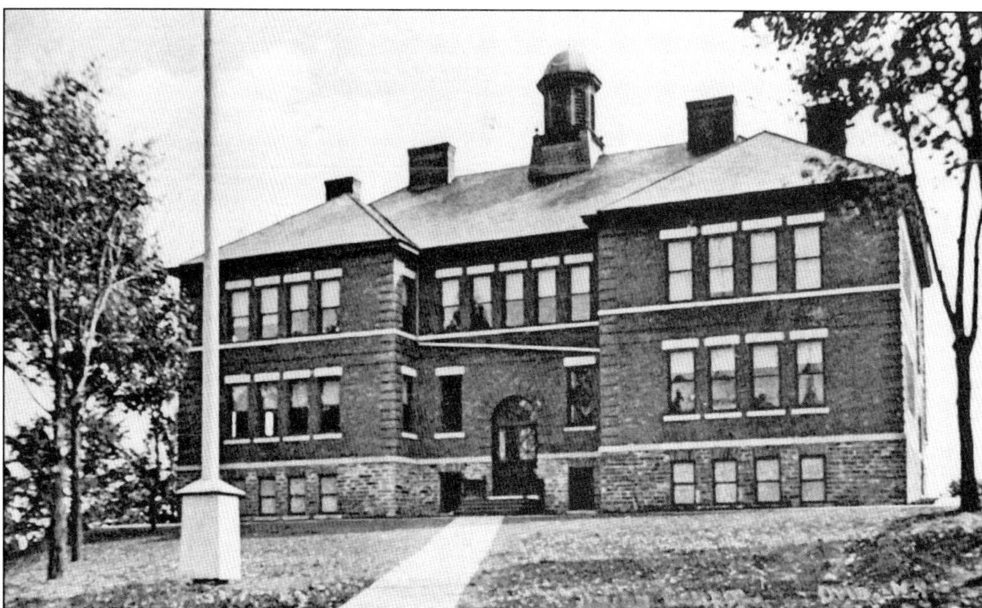

The Ovid High School was built in 1905, when the original Ovid Academy became overcrowded. Teachers had to be four-year college graduates. Crowded conditions required that gym classes be held in Columbus Hall, and varsity basketball games were at the Grange hall across the street. Commencement was held at Columbus Hall when the school closed in 1937.

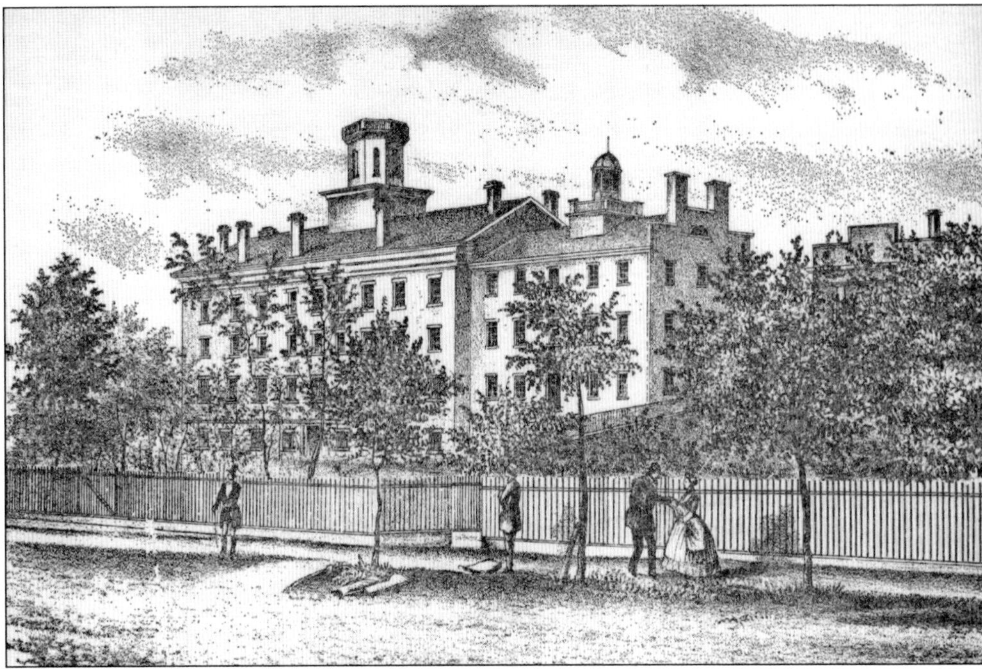

This is a sketch of the combined original educational buildings in Ovid. The three-story portion on the right is the Ovid Academy, which functioned from 1826 until 1854. The four-story addition made the following year is the Seneca Collegiate Institute. In 1864, the school became the East Genesee Conference Seminary. It was active for only one year, because many of the teachers and students enlisted in the Civil War.

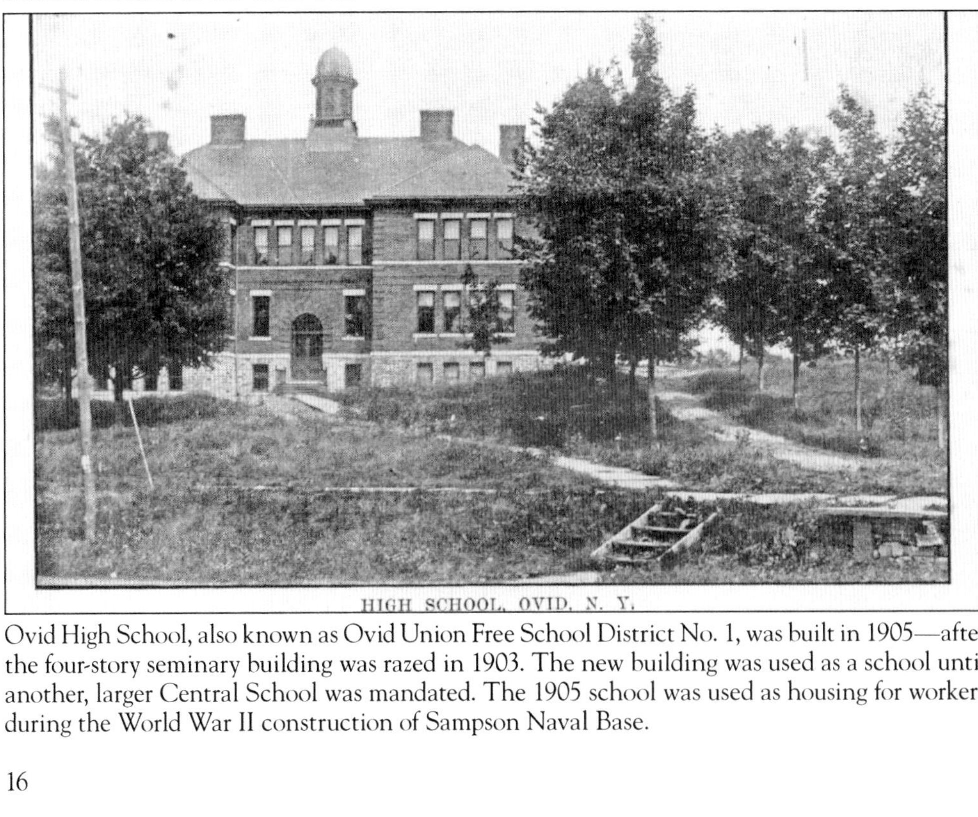

Ovid High School, also known as Ovid Union Free School District No. 1, was built in 1905—after the four-story seminary building was razed in 1903. The new building was used as a school until another, larger Central School was mandated. The 1905 school was used as housing for workers during the World War II construction of Sampson Naval Base.

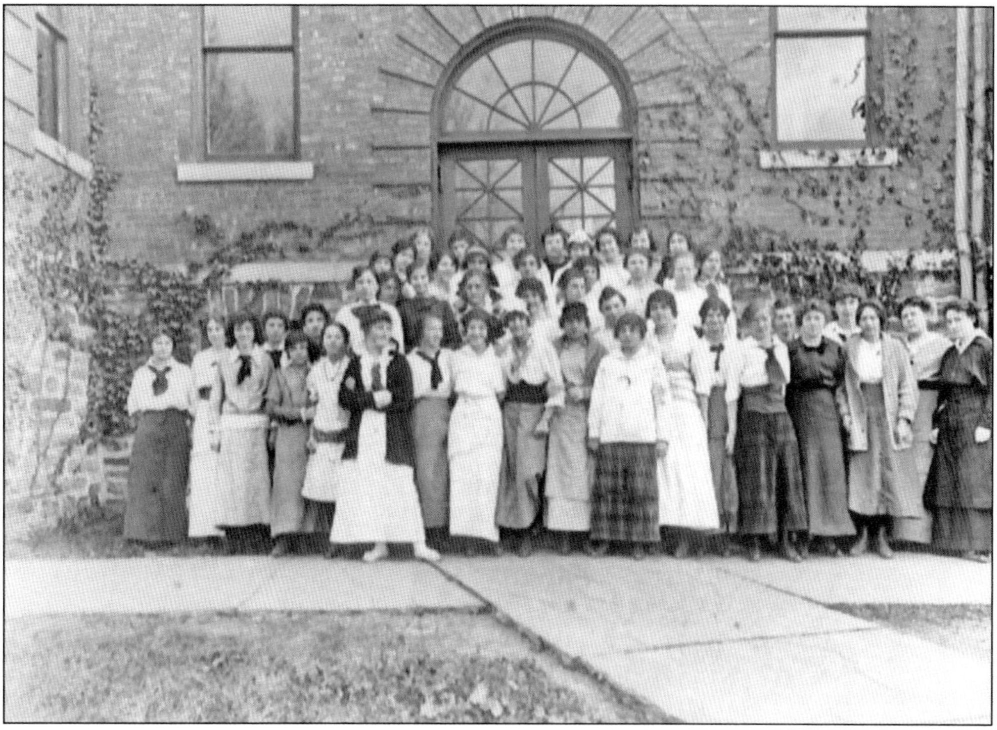

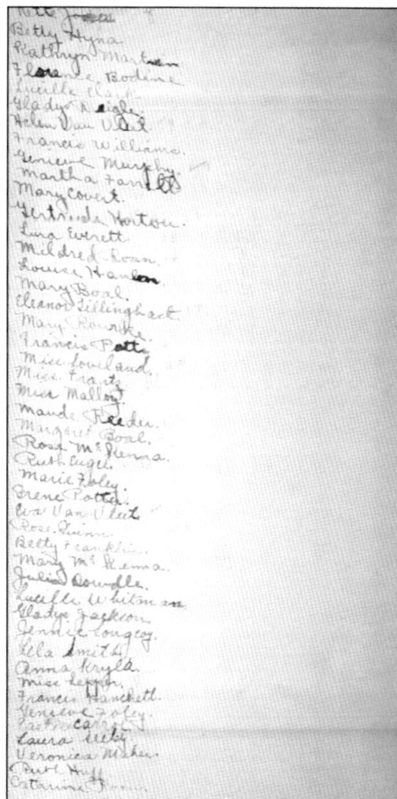

The Ovid High School Class of 1917 consisted of females when the males joined the armed forces during World War I. The class was one of the largest to graduate from the crowded school. The names of the girls and teachers have been preserved and can be seen at right. The names are not in order of placement, but some students may be identified from the list. The names of the girls pictured above are as follows: Nettie Jones, Betty Hyna, Kathryn Martin, Florence Bodine, Lucille Clark, Gladys Reigle, Helen Van Vleet, Francis Williams, Genevieve Murphy, Martha Farrell, Mary Covert, Gertrude Horton, Lura Everett, Mildred Roan, Louise Hanlon, Mary Boal, Eleanor Tillinghast, Mary Rourke, Francis Potts, Miss Loveland, Miss Frantz, Miss Malloy, Maude Reader, Margaret Boal, Rose McKenna, Ruth Engel, Marie Foley, Irene Potter, Eva Van Vleet, Rose Quinn, Betty Franklin, Mary McKenna, Julia Dowdle, Lucille Whitman, Gladys Jackson, Jennie Longcoy, Lela Smith, Anna Kryla, Miss Lepper, Francis Hanchell, Genevieve Foley, Esther Carroll, Laura Seeley, Veronica Maher, Ruth Huff, and Catherine Roan.

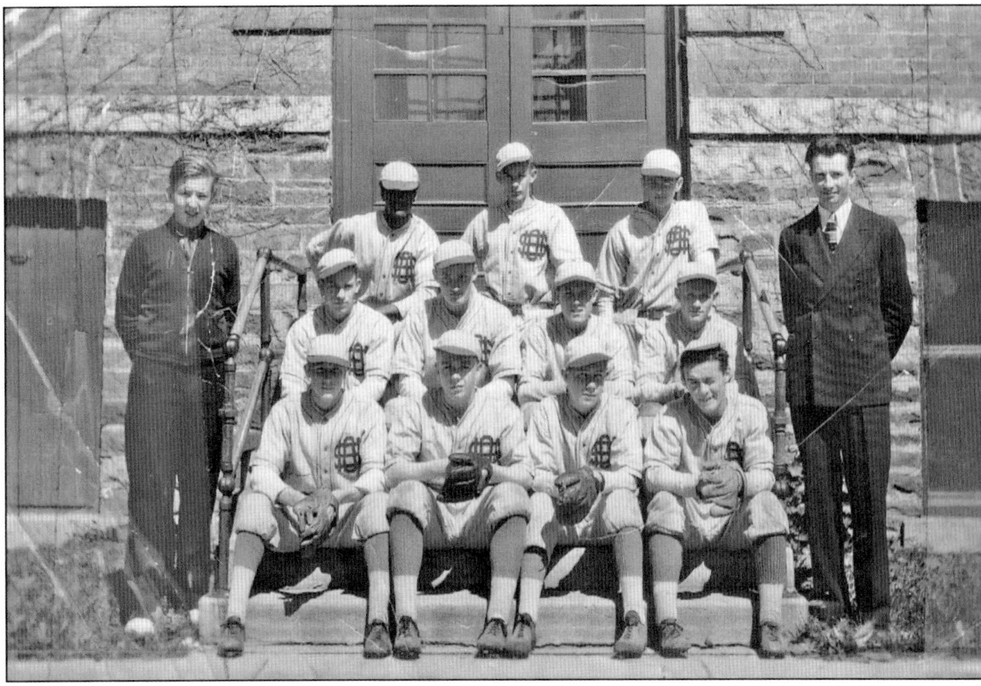

Ovid High School baseball players pose here, with the large school letters OHS on their jackets. They must have been very good ball players, since the team had only two substitutes. The uniforms were very complete, with gloves and cleated shoes. The manager is appropriately dressed, but the coach probably did not wear a suit and tie for practice.

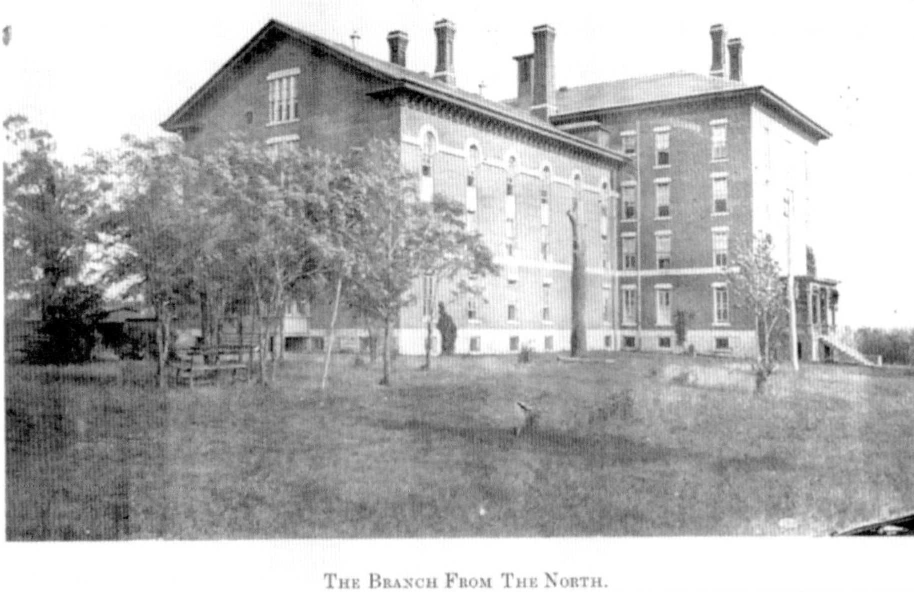

THE BRANCH FROM THE NORTH.

The New York Agricultural College at Ovid was the first chartered agricultural college in New York State and opened in 1860. It closed in 1862 due to students enlisting in the Civil War. Ezra Cornell arranged the transfer of the college to Ithaca's Cornell University in September 1864.

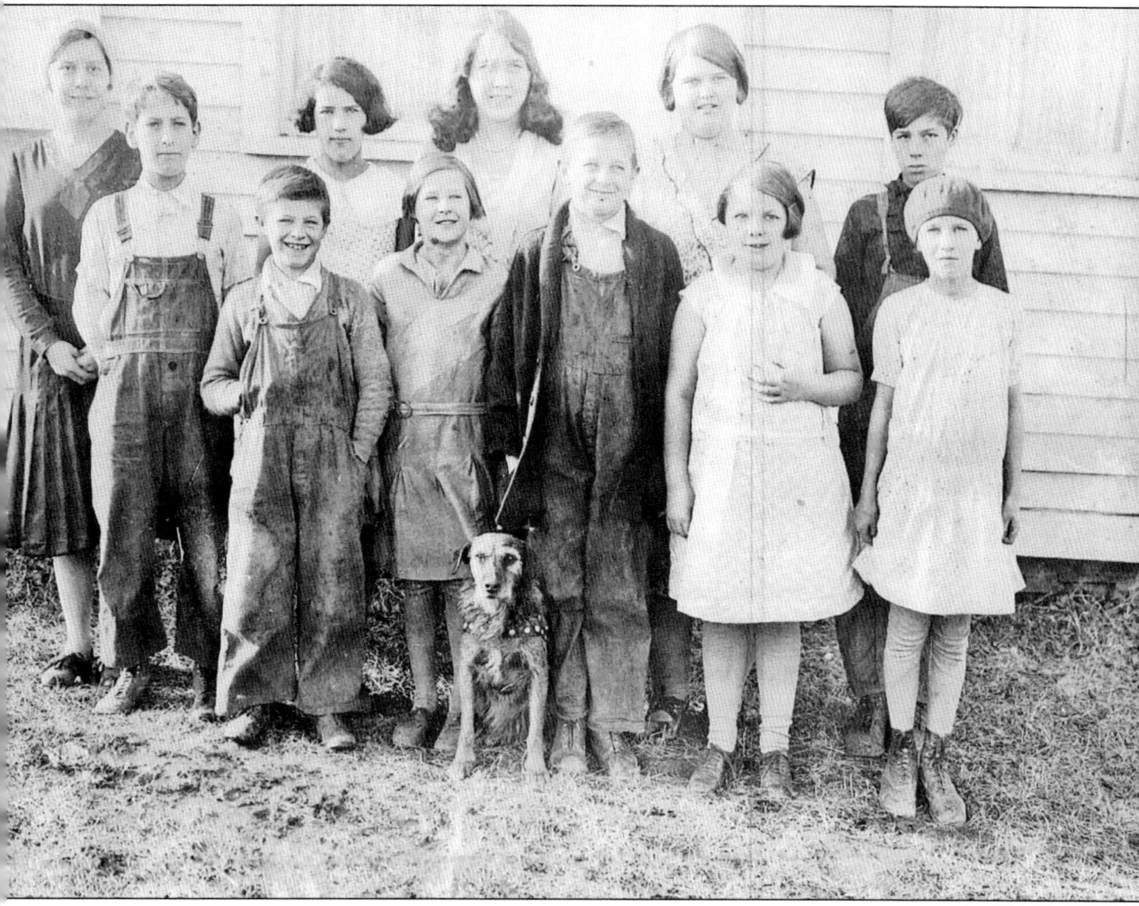

This photograph was taken in the 1930s at the Sheldrake School in District No. 3. Pictured are, from left to right, (first row) Steven Graber, Helen Graber, Stanley Graber, Eleanor Auten, and Helen Terry; (second row) teacher Theresa Kile Whittier, Earl Terry, Edna Terry, Irene Bradford, Frederika Ditmars, and William Bradford. (Courtesy of Marjorie Clark.)

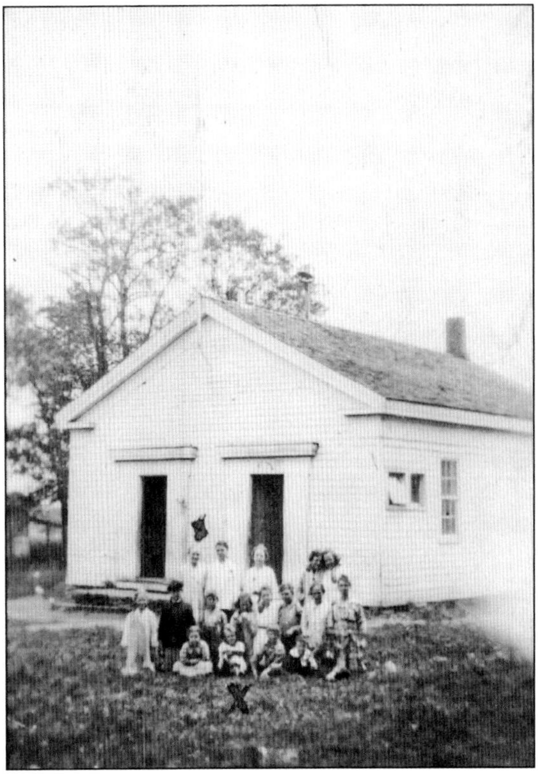

Sheldrake School District No. 3 is shown with unidentified students and teacher in the front yard. The two doors were designated one for boys and the other for girls. The school closed in 1938, and students were bused to the Interlaken Central School. The building and property reverted back to the Harold Wyckoff family and then were sold to Seymour Diamond and used to store farm machinery. The teacher and students pictured are unidentified.

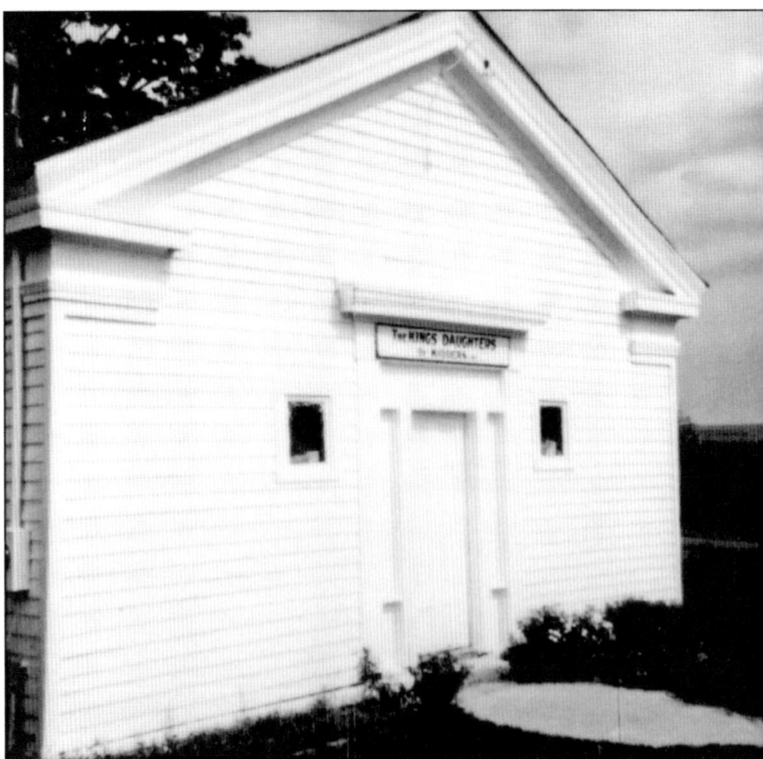

The Kidders School District No. 4, built in 1858, was a joint school for the towns of Ovid and Covert. After schools were centralized in 1938, the church group Kidders Kings Daughters held its meetings there. The women made quilts and aprons and did much to help the poor. Many years later, the building was sold and became a private residence.

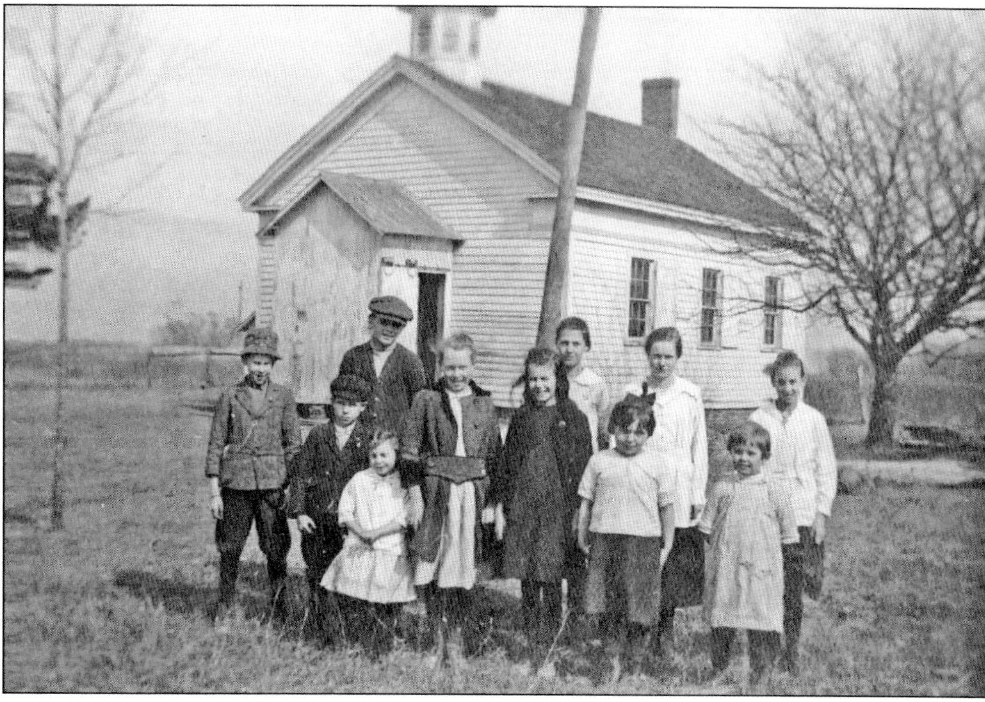

Starrett District No. 5 School was on the southwest corner of Hall and Munson Roads. One of the last rural schools to close, it became a private home. This early photograph was taken in the fall when all of the leaves were gone. The teacher and students are unidentified.

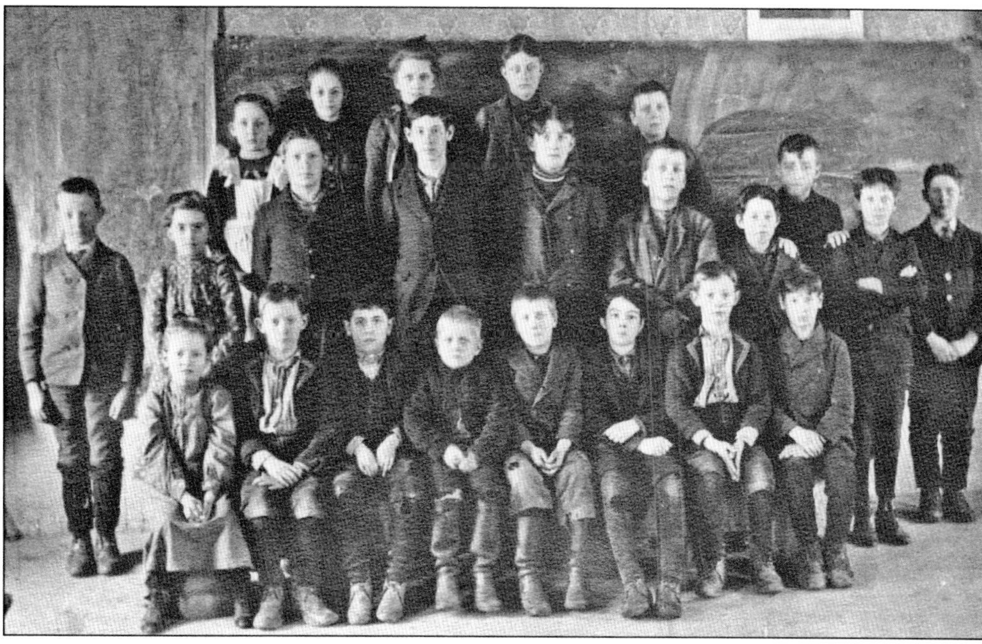

This 1919 photograph of unidentified teachers and students was probably taken in the winter, when it was too cold to take the usual outside pictures. The number of students has increased and so has the amount of clothing they are wearing. In the wintertime, the children were not needed to help with full chores on the farms.

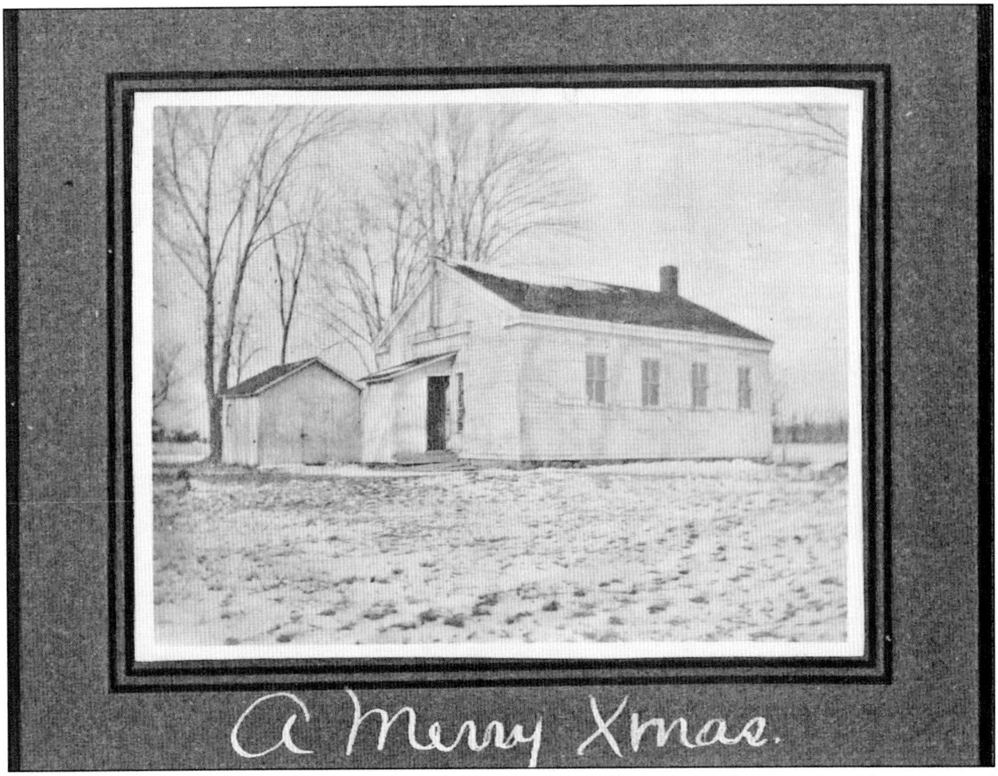

Coshun School District No. 6 was a joint district with Ovid and Lodi. It was one mile north and two miles east of Lodi, at the northeast comer of South Town Line and Townsendville Roads. The entry room was probably added as protection from the winter weather.

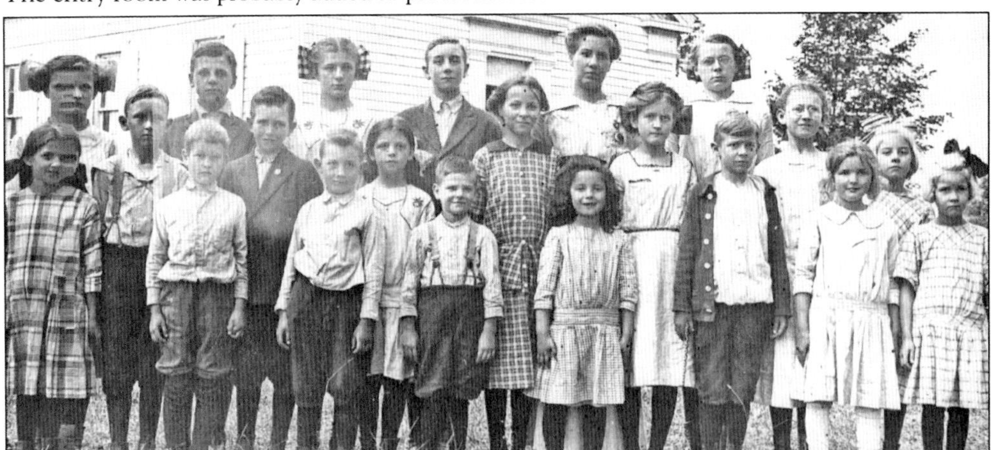

Coan District No. 7 School was built in 1855 south of Ovid. The Eastman family gave the land and money to build the school. When it closed, the property reverted to them. This postcard of the class of 1915 shows students Lena Mathews, Emma Burnha, Matie Mathews, Anna Boyce, Doris Colony, Esther Eastman, Hazel Whiteford, Alma Close, Helen Brown, Charlotte Barnes, Alice Longcoy, Evelyn Brown, Arthur Mathews, Carman Barnes, Howard Longcoy, Francis Updike, Glenn Boyce, Claude Stewart, William Eastman, and Lewis Whiteford. The teacher is not identified.

Combs District No. 8 School was located on the corner of Combs Road and the Upper Lake Road, which later became County Road 131. The original school was built in the 1850s. After it burned in 1881, a new brick schoolhouse was constructed. When no longer used as a school, it became the home of the Trim family. Eventually, it was torn down.

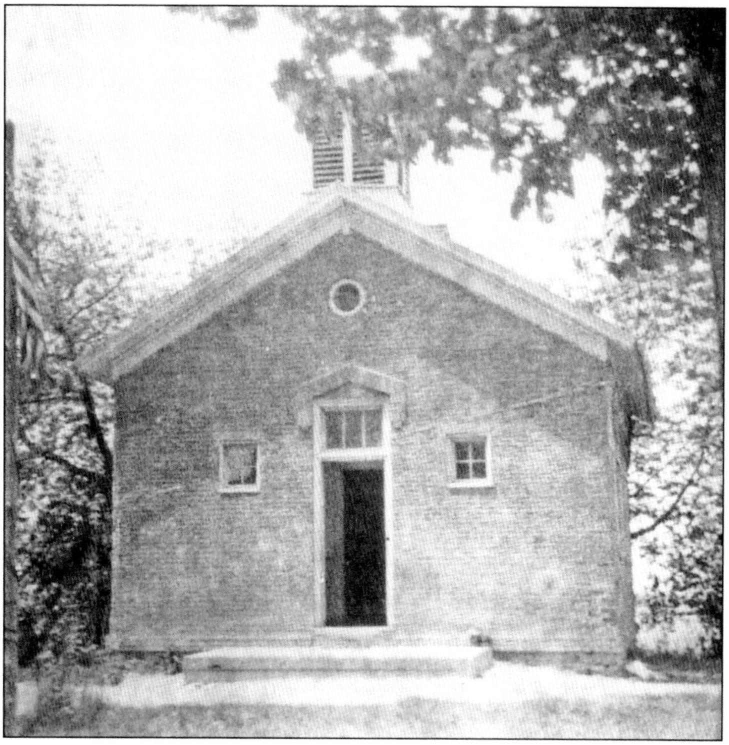

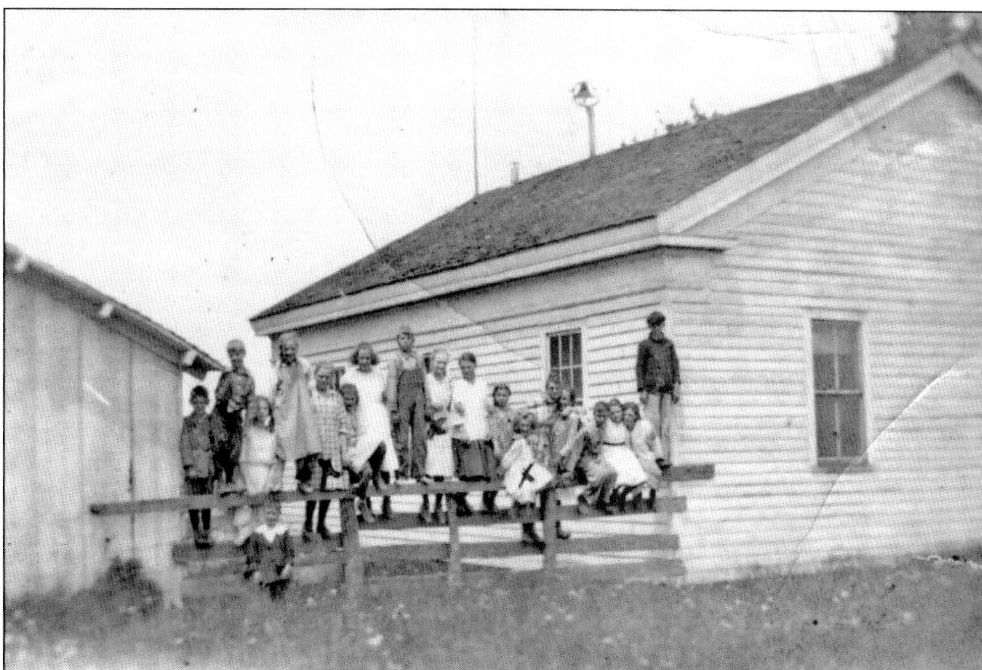

Scotts Corners District No. 9 School was southeast of Ovid on a turnpike that is known as County Road 139. It closed in 1936, became a private home, and later burned down. In this photograph, taken about 1925, teacher Ruth Akins is on the left and Naomi Akins is identified with an X. All others are unidentified. (Courtesy of Interlaken Historical Society.)

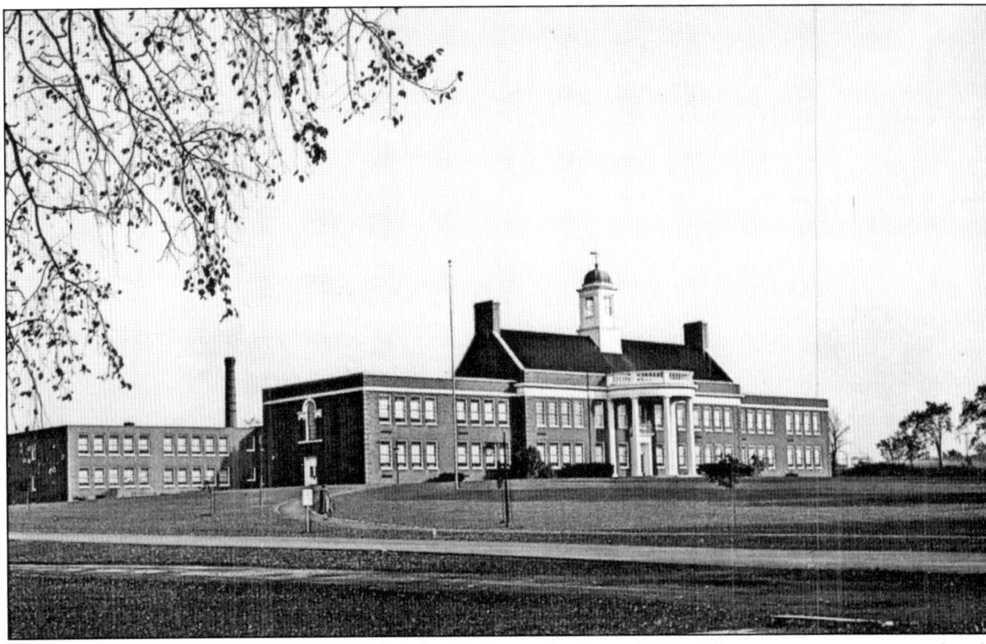

This postcard shows Ovid Central School, which was built in 1938. All one-room country schools in the town of Ovid were closed, and the students were bused here. The building had elementary classrooms on the first floor, while middle and high school students were on the second floor. The cafeteria and auditorium-gymnasium were also located on the ground floor. Classrooms and a new gymnasium were added in 1954.

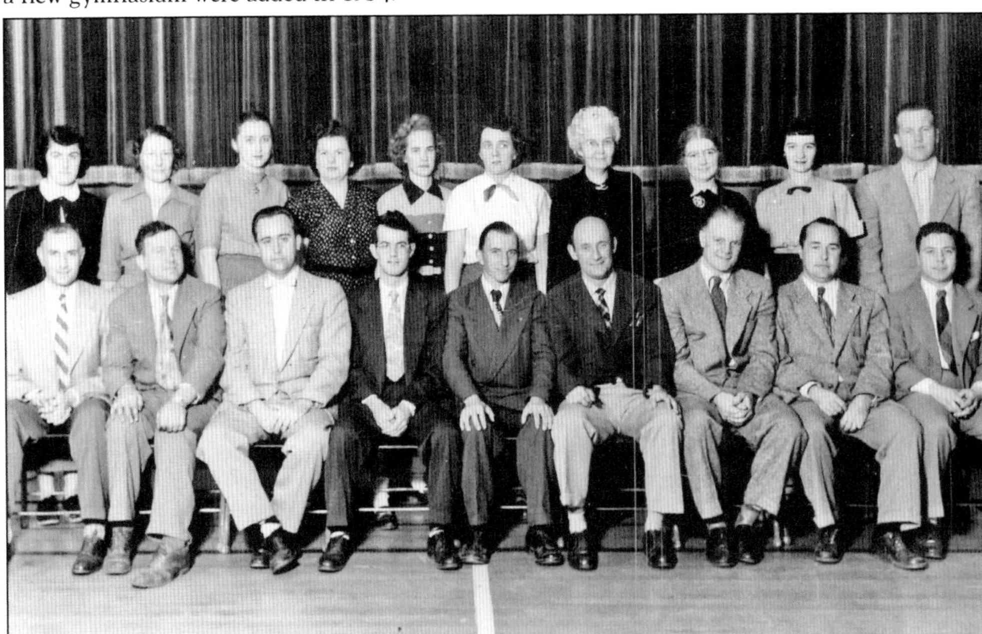

The Ovid Central School high school staff in 1951 is shown. Pictured are (first row) Mr. Meyer, Ralph Whitehead, Frederick Shaw, Mr. Hoppe, David Wilson, Thomas Blank, Mr. Edwards, Robert Jacoby, and Philip Natoli; (second row) unidentified, Lena Ditmars, Mrs. Rice, Dorothy Vangalio, Miss Russell, Lillian Edds, Clara Depew, Corine Lee, Miss Moyer, and Anthony Kay.

Three

FARMING

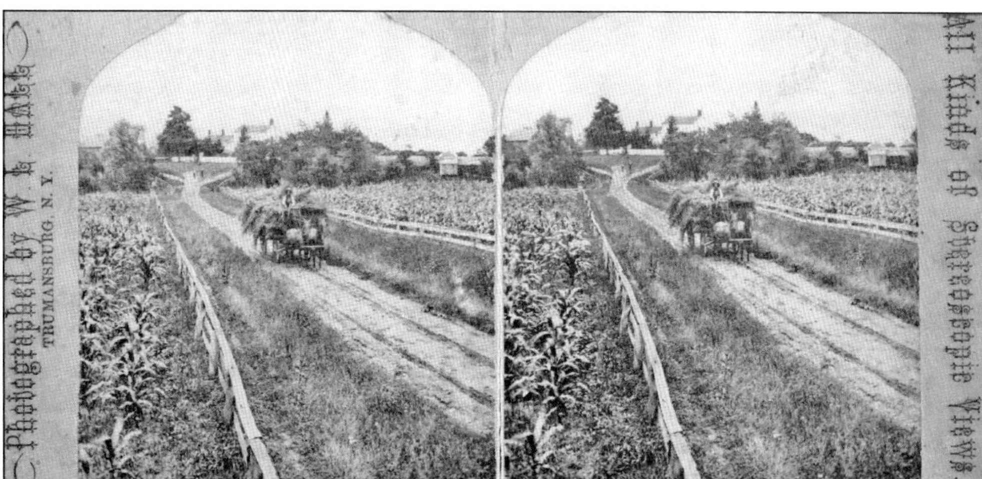

Sylvester D. Thomas and his wife, Rebecca, operated their farm east of Ovid. Sylvester was born in 1815, the son of Jonathan and Nancy Scott Thomas of Sheldrake. Sylvester was the Ovid supervisor for seven years and excise commissioner for five years. He participated in many community activities to improve the town and village.

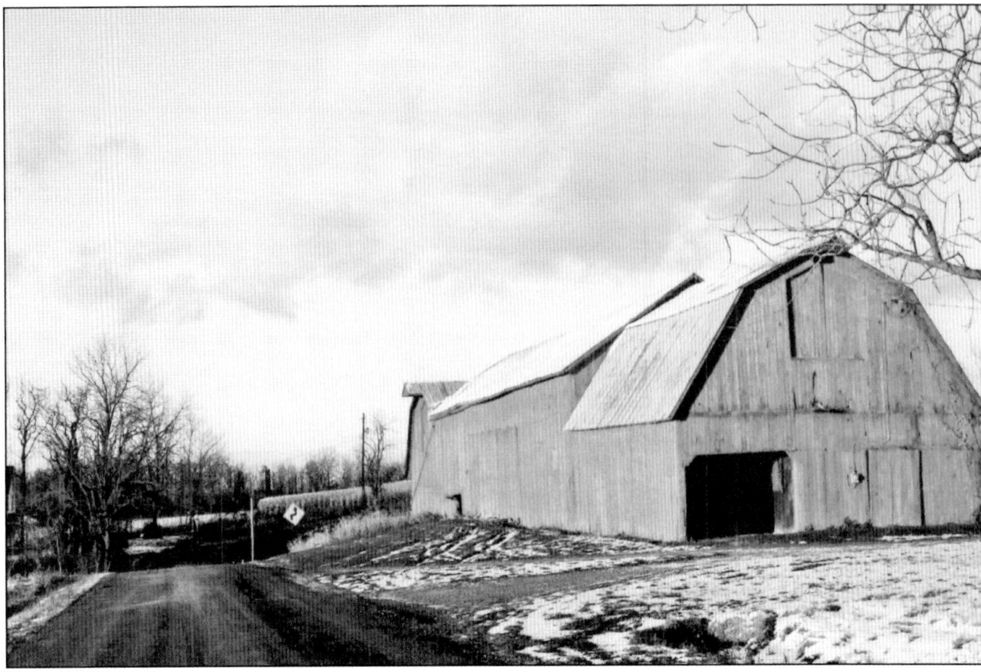

In 1789, Andrew Dunlap came with his family from Bucks County, Pennsylvania. He settled on Lot Eight southwest of Ovid. The middle portion of his barn was where the first court was held. The barn additions at the ends and the original barn are still standing. (Courtesy of Kate Lynch.)

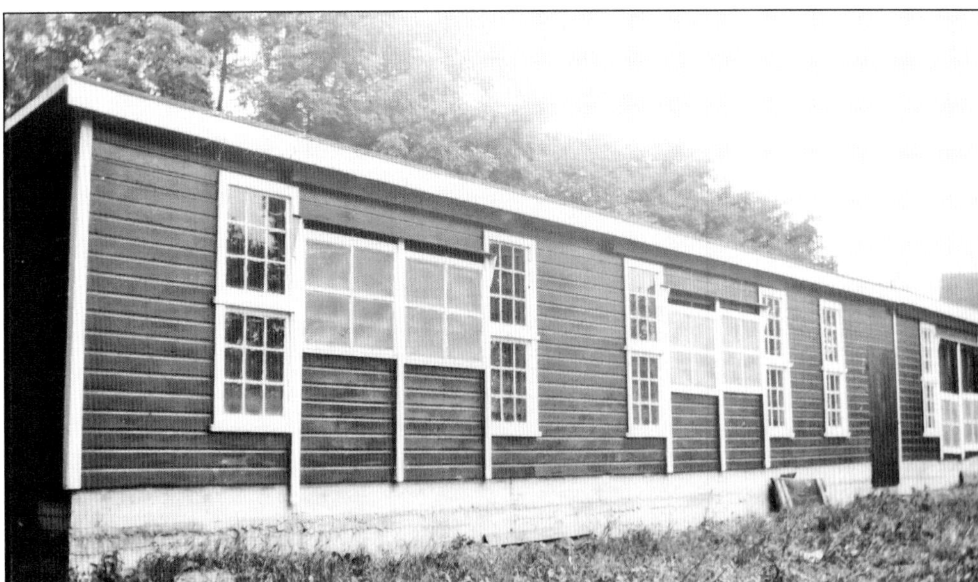

Few farms could boast the fine chicken house located on this property. The windows provided a good amount of light and fresh air, since they could be opened, as seen in the farthest set of windows. The enclosed yard behind the building provided a place for the hens and roosters to get exercise.

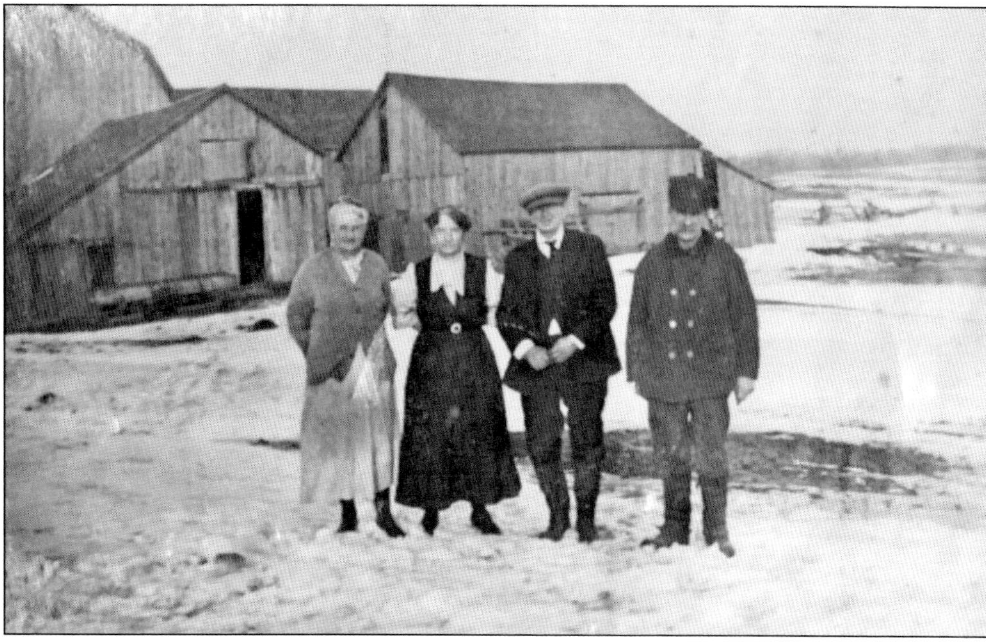

Arthur and Margaret McLaughlin Varguson bought this farm on Rock River Road and Center Road southeast of Ovid in 1919. In the early 1940s, their son Charles and his wife, Florence Lisk Varguson, came to live with them. Margaret (left) is proudly showing her siblings, from left to right, Betsy, Walter, and William McLaughlin the farm they just acquired. (Courtesy of Florence Varguson.)

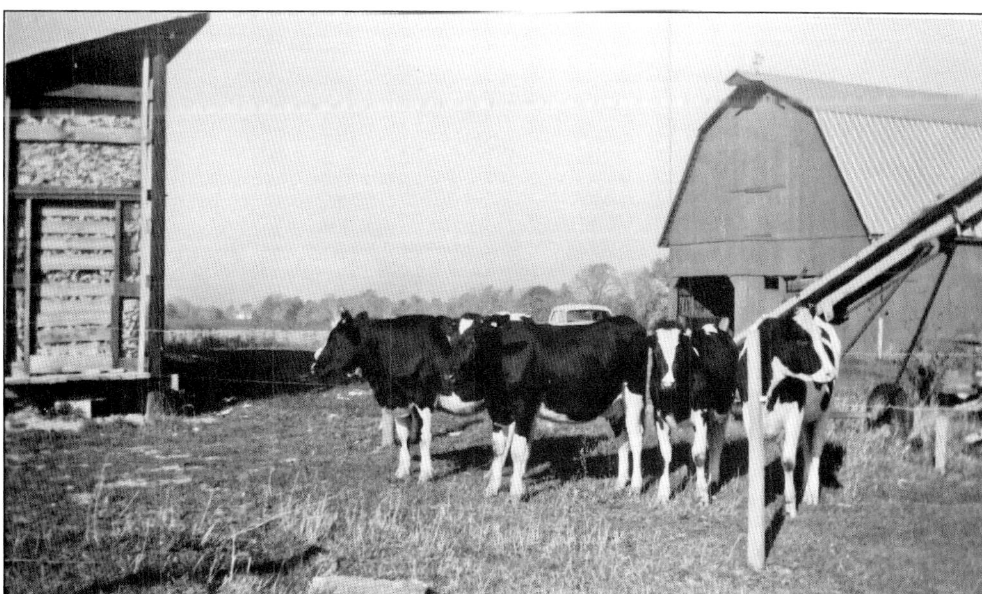

Many farmers became so familiar with the animals on their farm that they named each one. Some of them responded when their names were called. These four Holsteins are, from left to right, Andy, Nig, Beffy, and Ann.

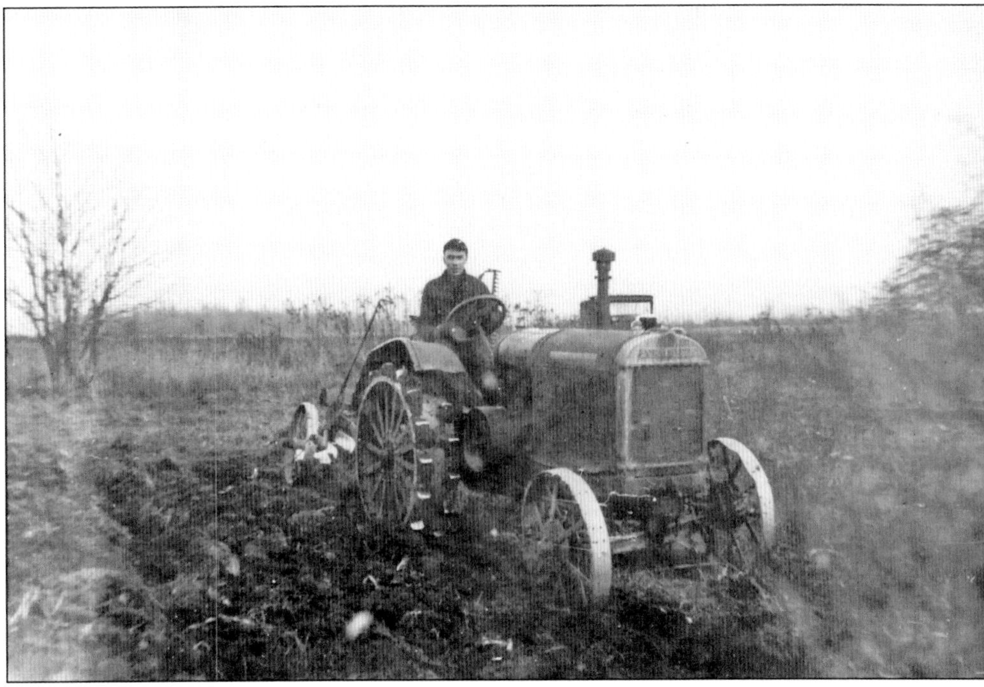

Ernest Eastman is plowing the land on his homestead farm with the first tractor that he owned. Heavy-duty tractors with lugs (spikes) were required to pull the plow through deep soil. The photograph was taken in December 1941, which indicates that farmwork had to be done throughout the entire year. (Courtesy of David Eastman.)

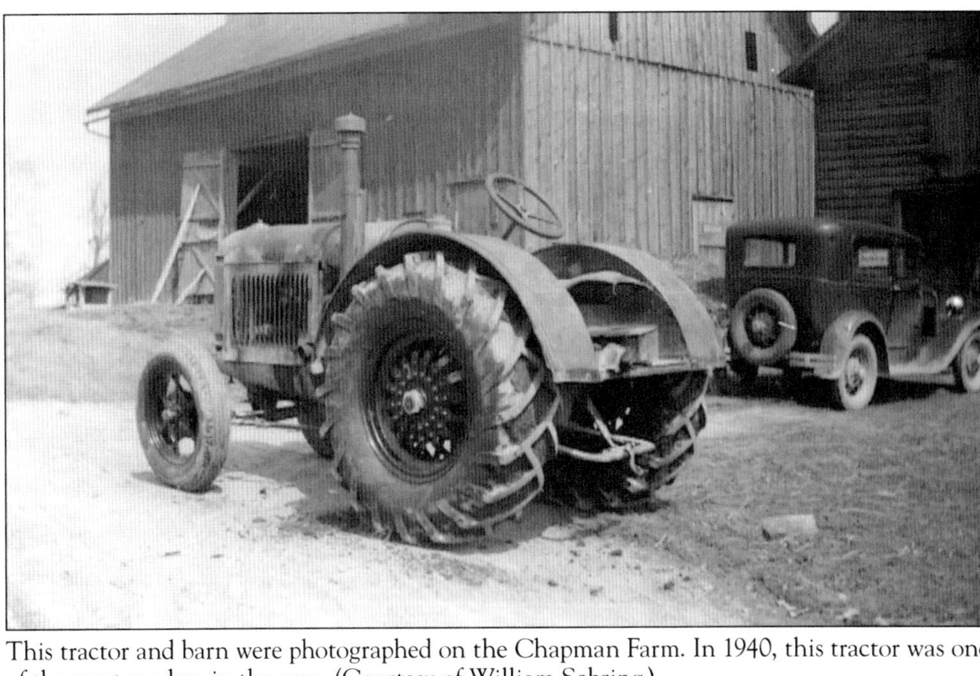

This tractor and barn were photographed on the Chapman Farm. In 1940, this tractor was one of the most modem in the area. (Courtesy of William Sebring.)

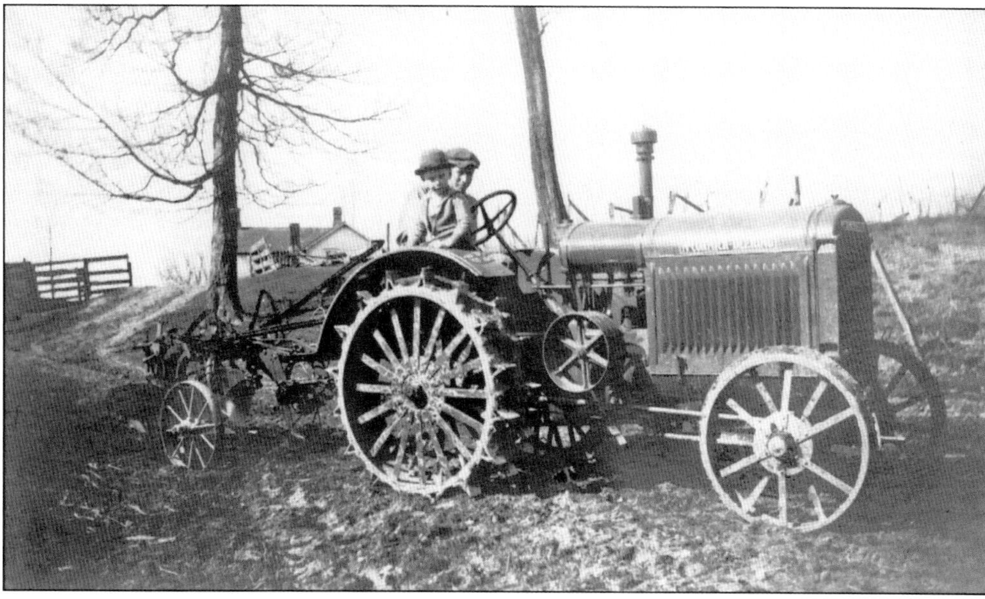

Burnham (driving) and his brother Clark Chapman are waiting to have their pictures taken on the new McCormick-Deering tractor purchased in March 1932. The new set of plows was delivered the following month, ready to begin preparing the land for planting.

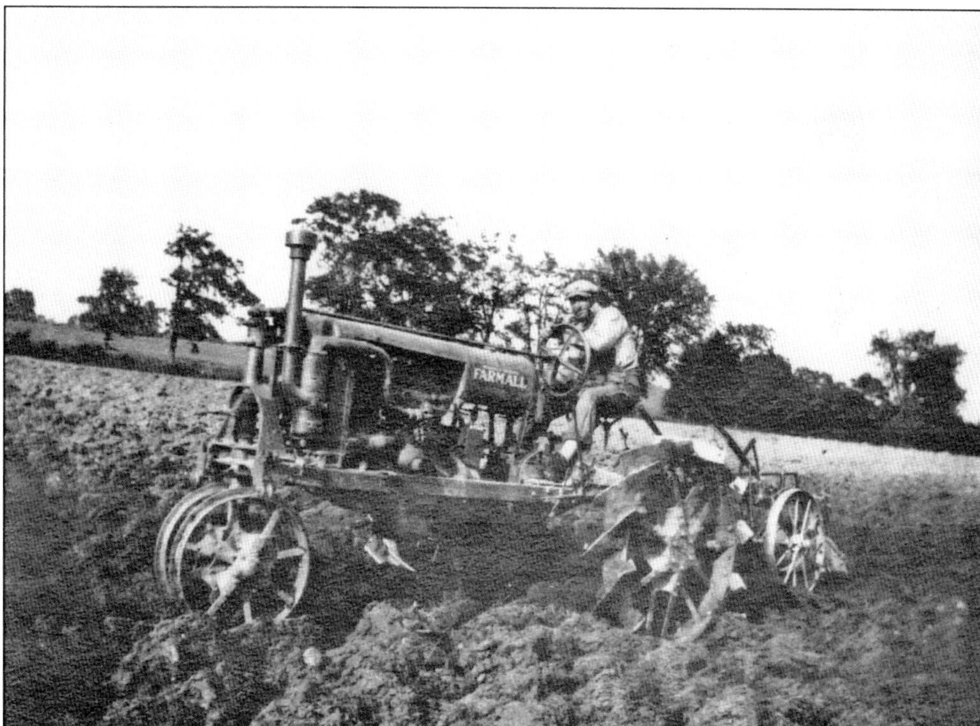

George Myer is driving his Farmall tractor on the Sheldrake farm in the early 1940s. Huge lugs on the wheels were needed to plow the heavy clay soil in the spring. Before the invention of tractors, farmers walked behind horse-drawn plows. Many family members, including women, were glad to release the horse reins and drive a tractor. (Courtesy of Naomi Brewer.)

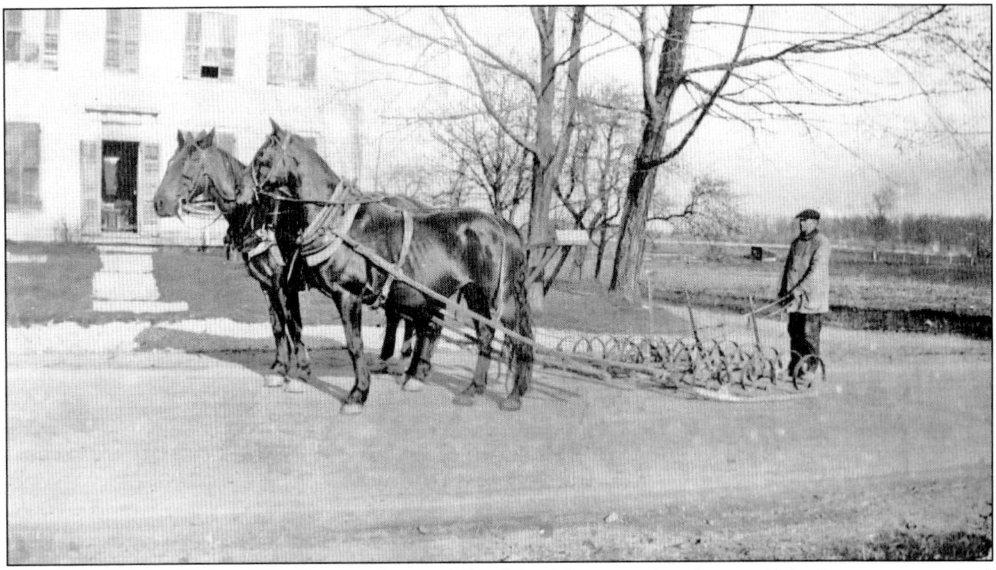

A team of workhorses is standing in front of the John Eastman farmhouse. The harness attached to the horse collar will pull the large drag harrow. John will walk behind this equipment while getting the field ready to plant the crops. (Courtesy of David Eastman.)

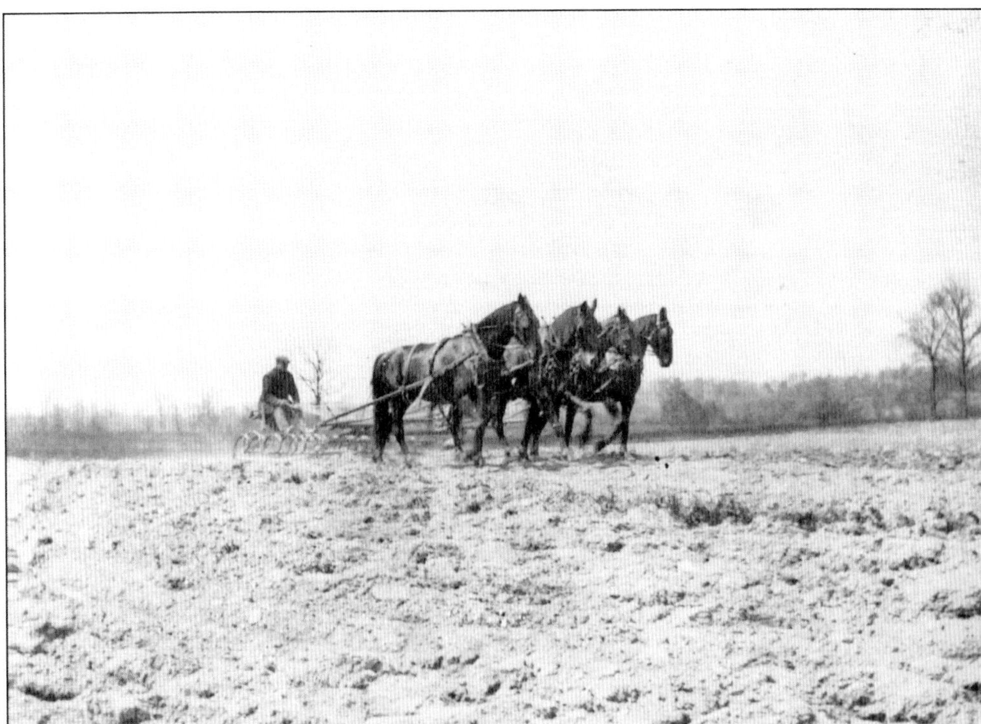

John Eastman is driving the four horses—Bird, Fritz, Jack, and Bess—on May 22, 1924. The farm is located halfway between Ovid and Lodi. It is now owned and operated by his grandson David Eastman, who is carrying on the family farming tradition. (Courtesy of David Eastman.)

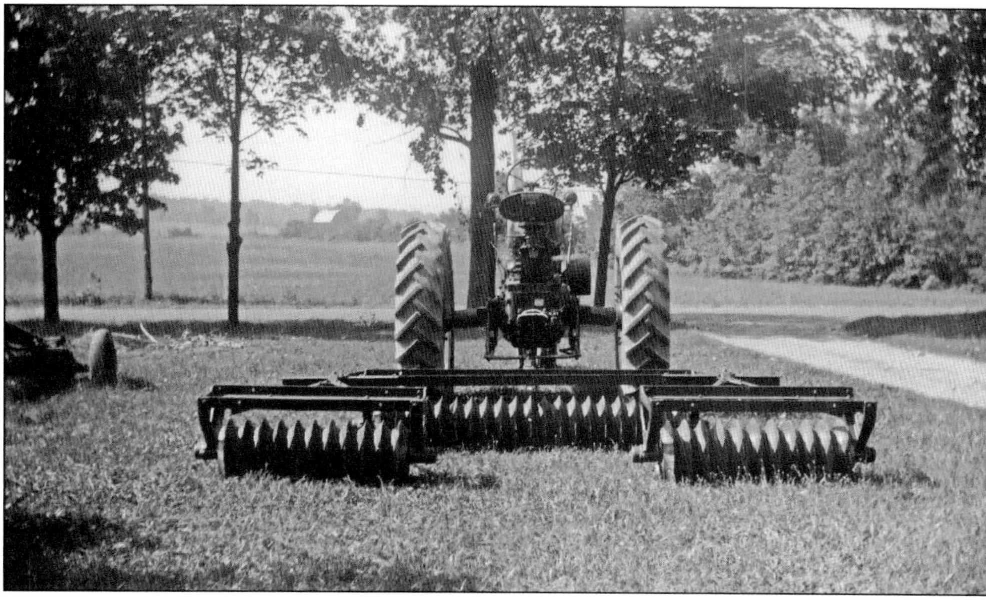

This three-section Dunham cultipacker was purchased in 1955. It smoothed and packed the soil after the plowing was completed. The work was done much faster due to the total width of 14 feet.

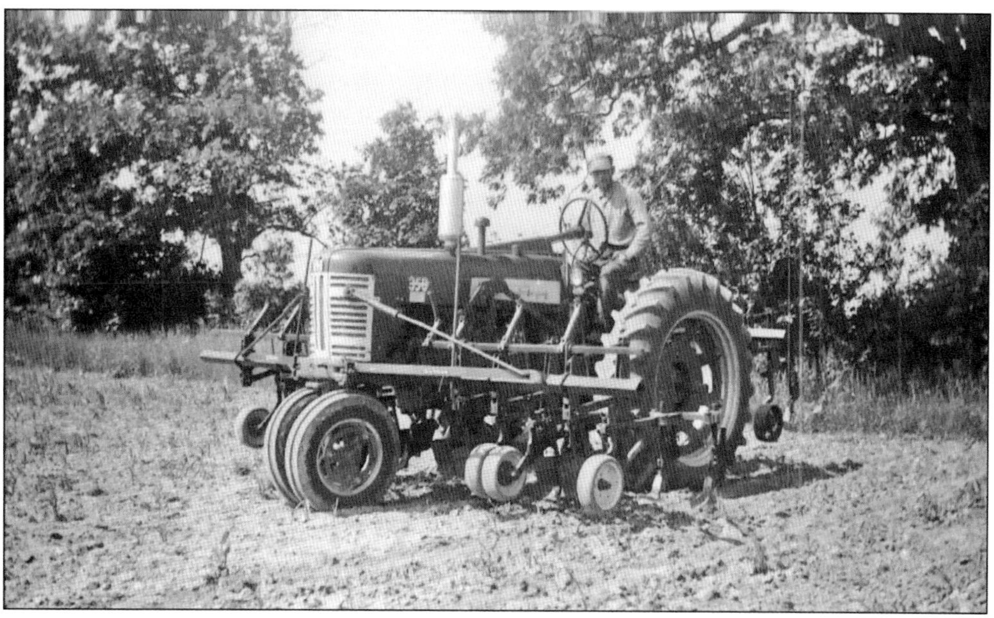

The 350 International Farmall tractor was purchased in May 1959 from Glanville and Werm for $394. Mounted on the tractor is a new cultivator obtained at the same time for $798. The picture was taken on the Boyce farm. The man is unidentified.

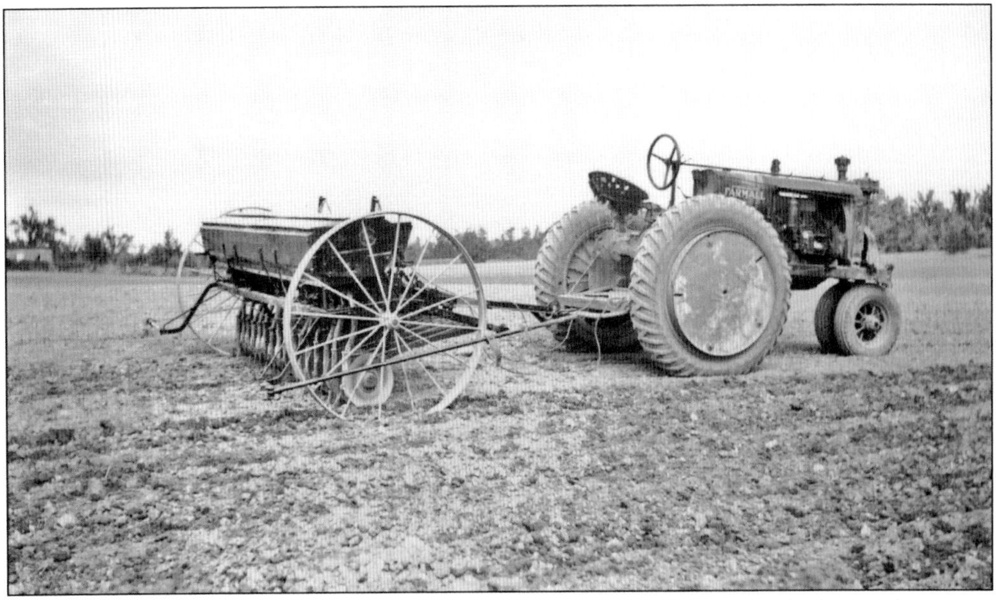

A 1937 steel grain drill planted the crops that were used to feed the animals during the winter months. Large wheels were needed to support the heavy box filled with seed.

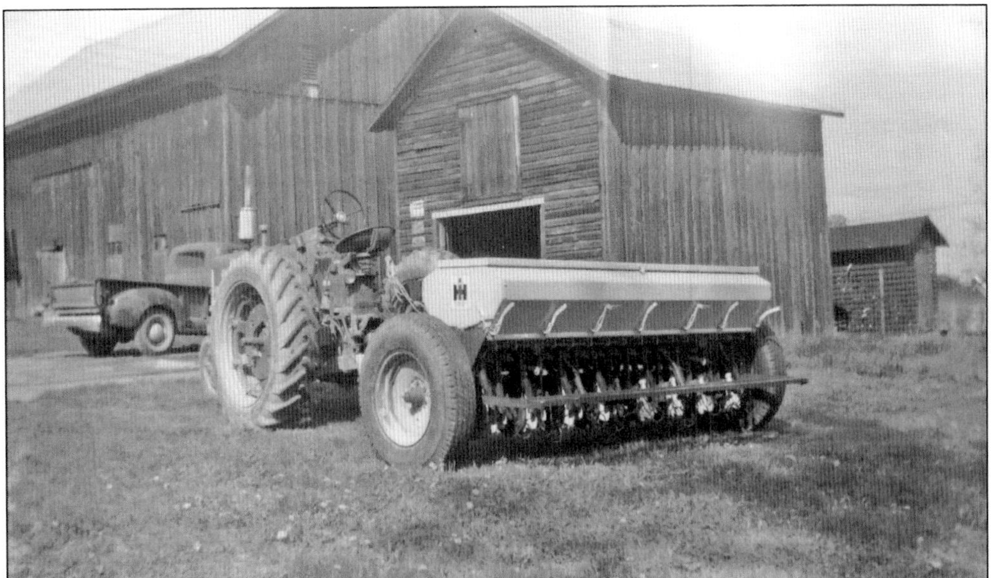

The International Harvester disk grain drill is updated equipment used for planting 16 rows at one time. Wheat, oats, and fertilizer are carried in the wide container on top. The 16 disks allow planting in narrow rows. Corn is planted in much wider rows so it can be cultivated.

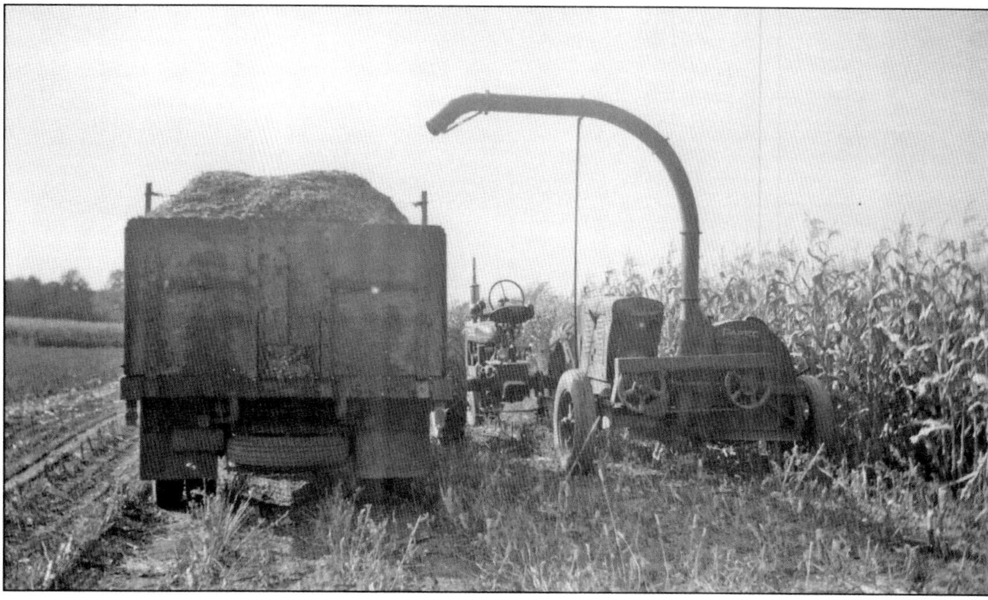

The field chopper is used to cut and grind the entire cornstalk. The corn is then transferred to the truck, taken to the barn, and blown into the silo. The silage is fed to dairy cows during the winter when they are unable to roam in the pastures.

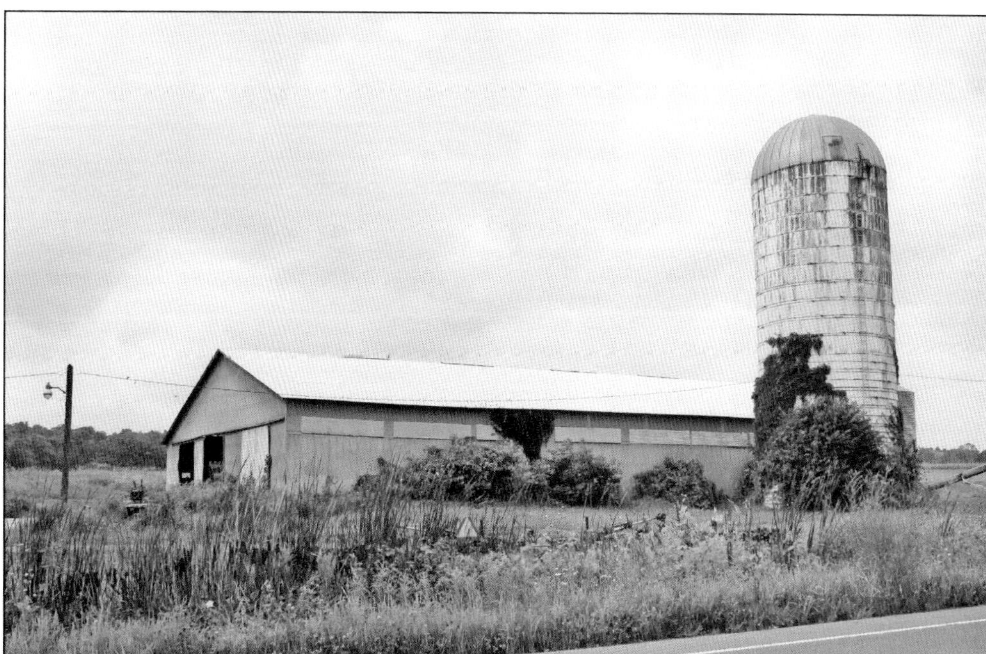

The tall, round silos are the portion of the dairy barn where corn is stored. The silage replaces the pasture grass in the cow's diet. Enough corn has to be raised to last the entire winter, as it is needed for the cows to produce milk. (Courtesy of LeConte and Ruth Myer.)

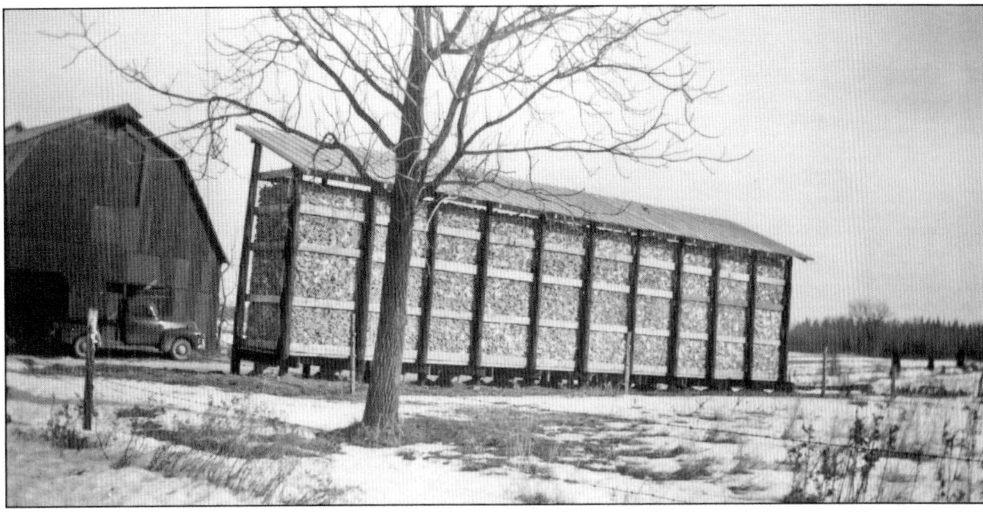

The contents of the huge corncrib could supply the farm animals during a long, cold winter. The pole barn construction ensures the necessary strength for the tons of corn that are stored. It also supports the aboveground floor, rather than allowing the corn to rest on the soil.

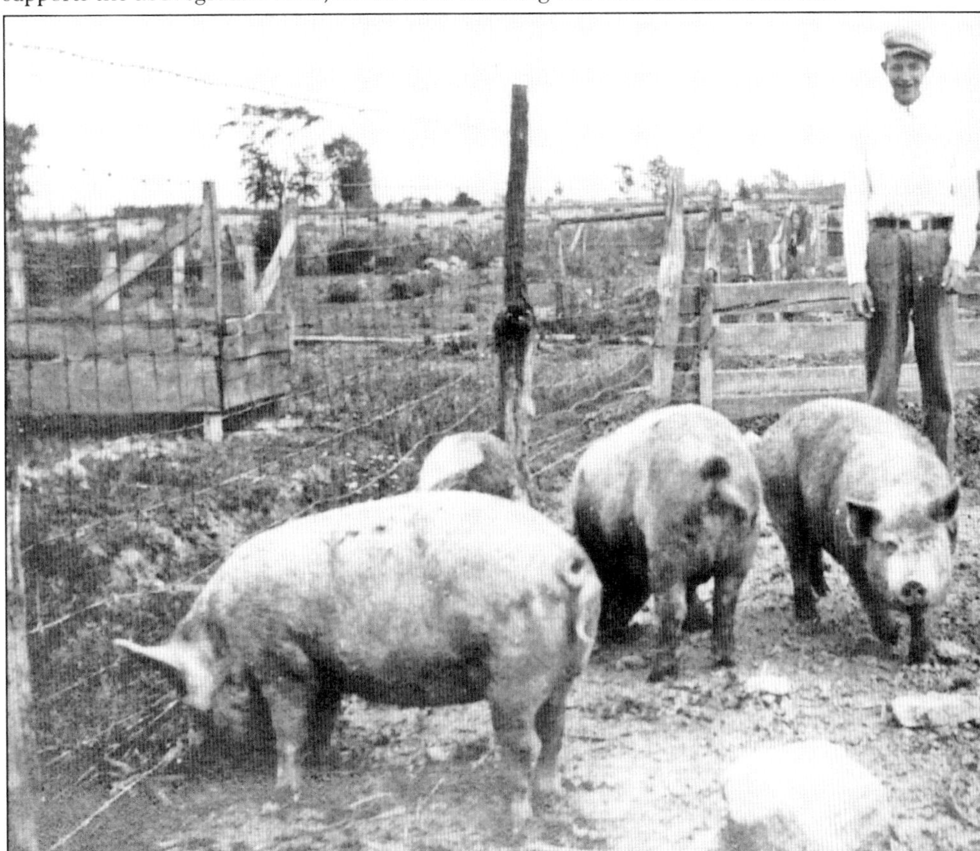

Hogs were a great addition to the animals raised on a farm. They were easily grown and provided the family with a variety of meat for meals. Bacon, ham, and pork chops were a nice diversion from chicken, turkey, and beef.

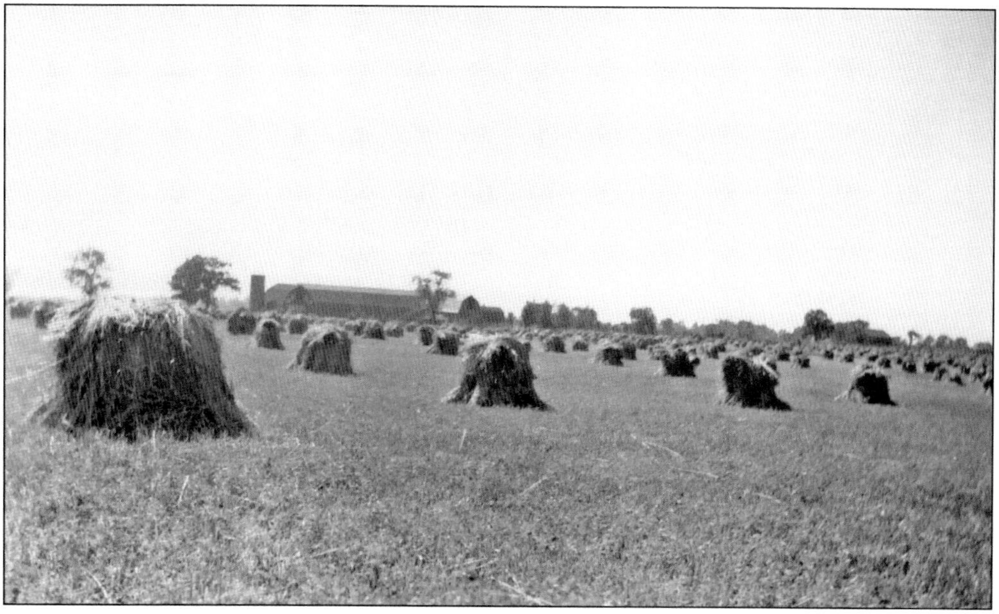

Four bundles of wheat are stacked to form the shocks, which are placed in rows. They are fashioned to allow time for the wheat and the straw to dry before being thrashed and stored in the barn. (Courtesy of William Sebring.)

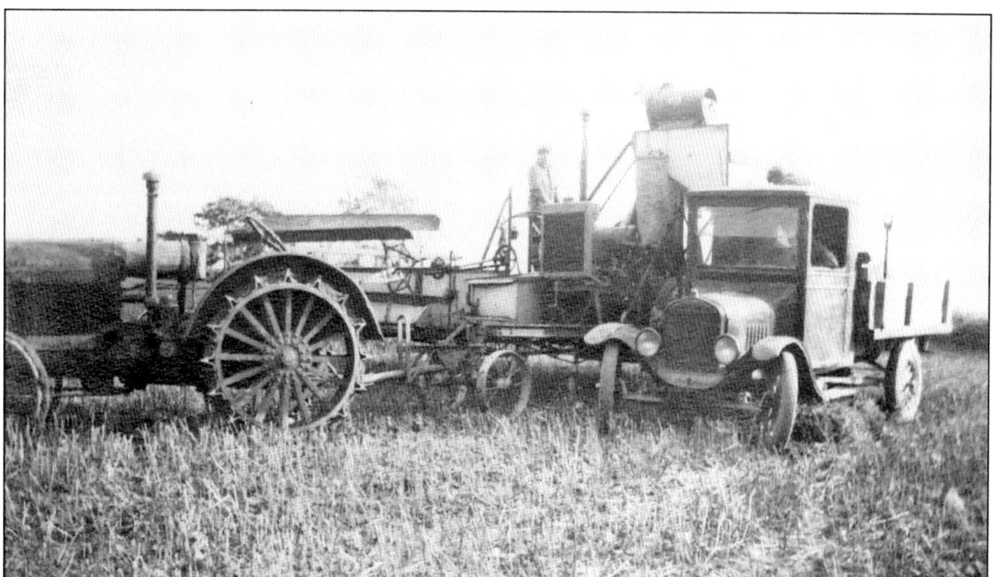

Leland Parish is combining buckwheat using the available equipment on October 13, 1934. Buckwheat was a hardy grain that was used at dairy farms in the area. (Courtesy of William Sebring.)

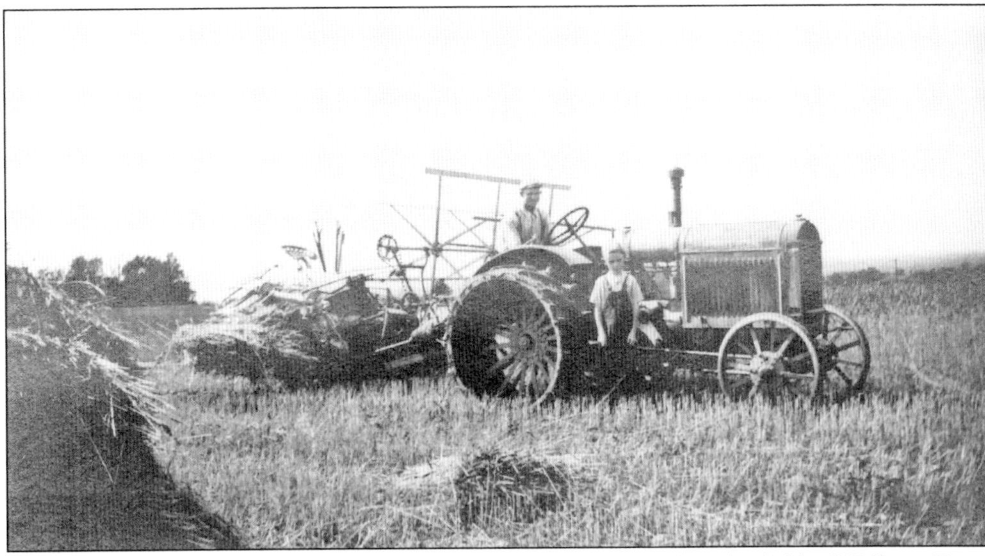

The new 10-foot wheat binder being pulled by a tractor was used in the field of William Terry. The photograph was made on the farm along Town Line Road on July 16, 1935. The people are unidentified.

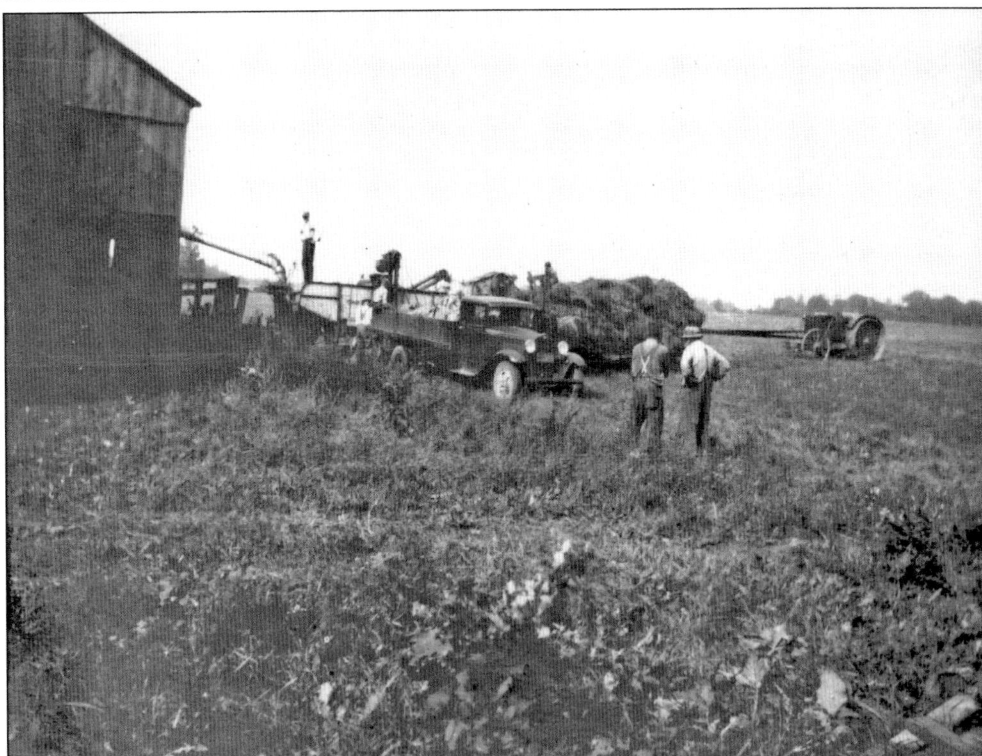

A thrashing machine was hired by Harry Blew at his farm in Sheldrake. The wheat shocks were pitched from the wagon to the bed of the thrashing machine. A tractor with a long belt provided the power for the thrasher. Bags of separated wheat were stacked on a truck to be transported to storage. (Courtesy of Naomi Brewer.)

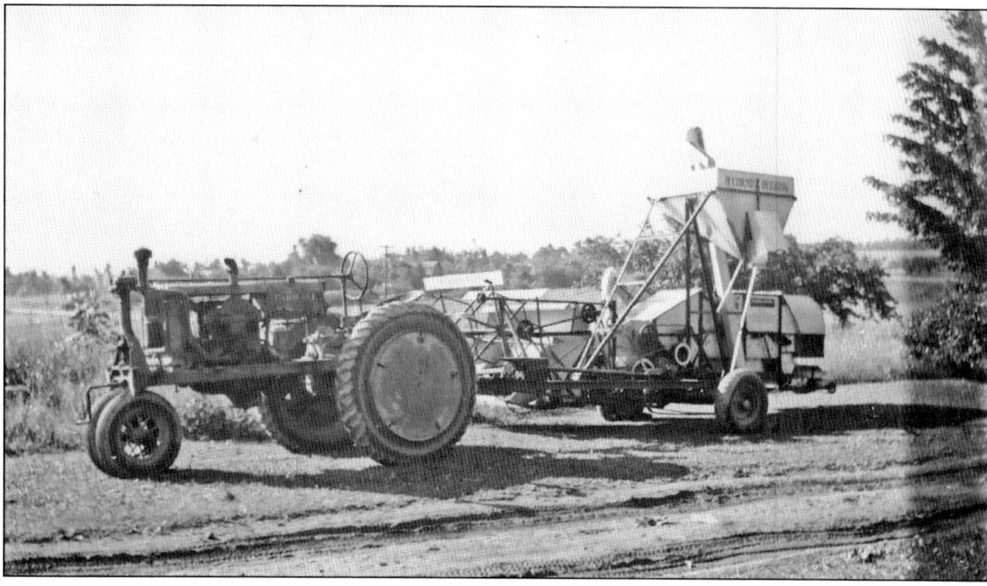

An early combine, a more modern version of the wheat binder, was used three years later in 1938. It separated the wheat from the straw in the field. The wheat was transported by wagon or truck, while the straw was raked into rows and gathered for farm bedding or sold.

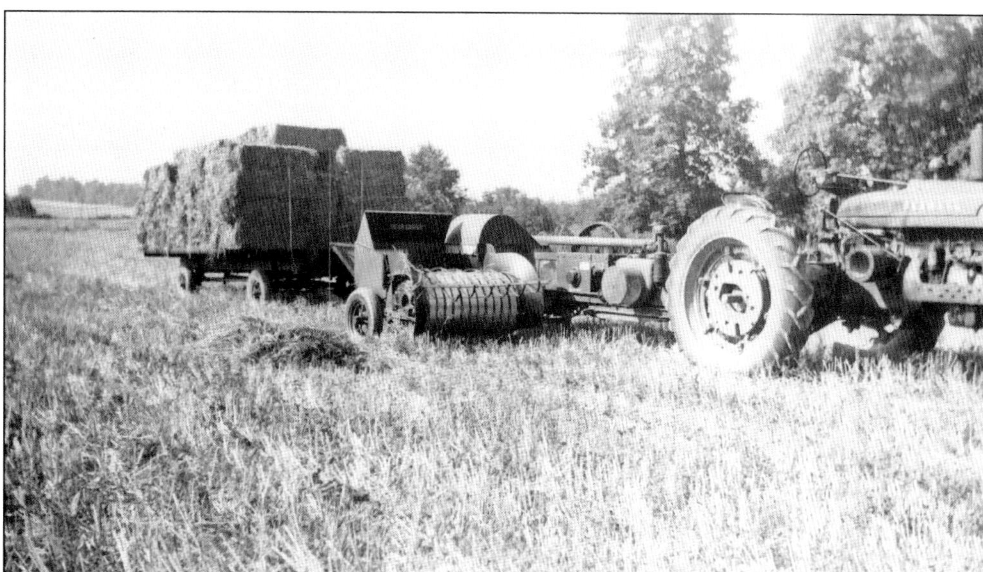

Hay was originally cut with a scythe and loaded on a wagon by pitchfork. The backbreaking process was slowly eliminated. By 1946, hay and straw balers made this load of 100 bales much easier to manage.

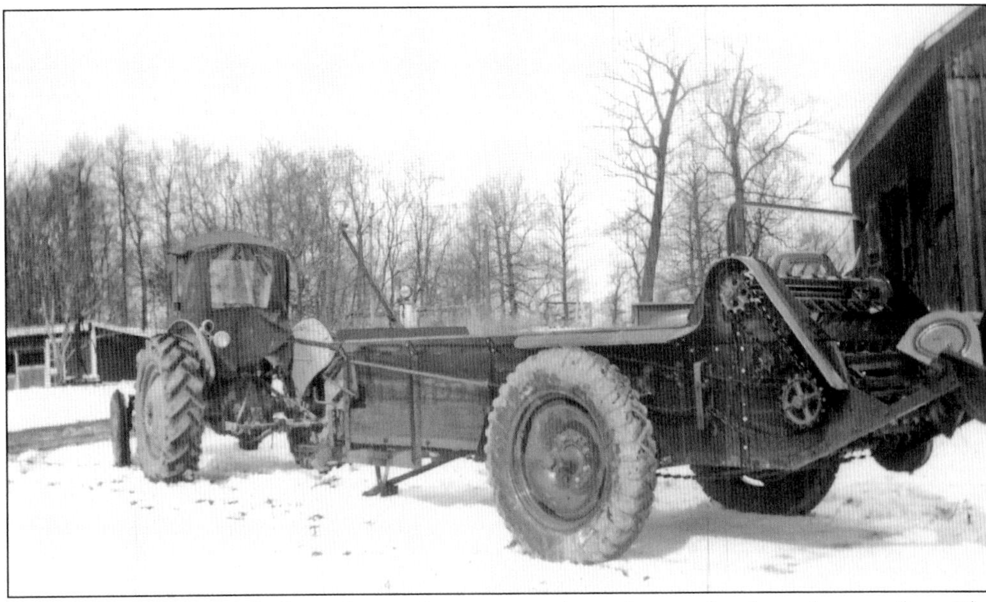

Many cows are kept in the barn during the winter, so barns have to be cleaned more often. The cab on the tractor makes the job of spreading the manure more comfortable. The spreader is a New Idea No. 2, more affectionately known as a honey wagon.

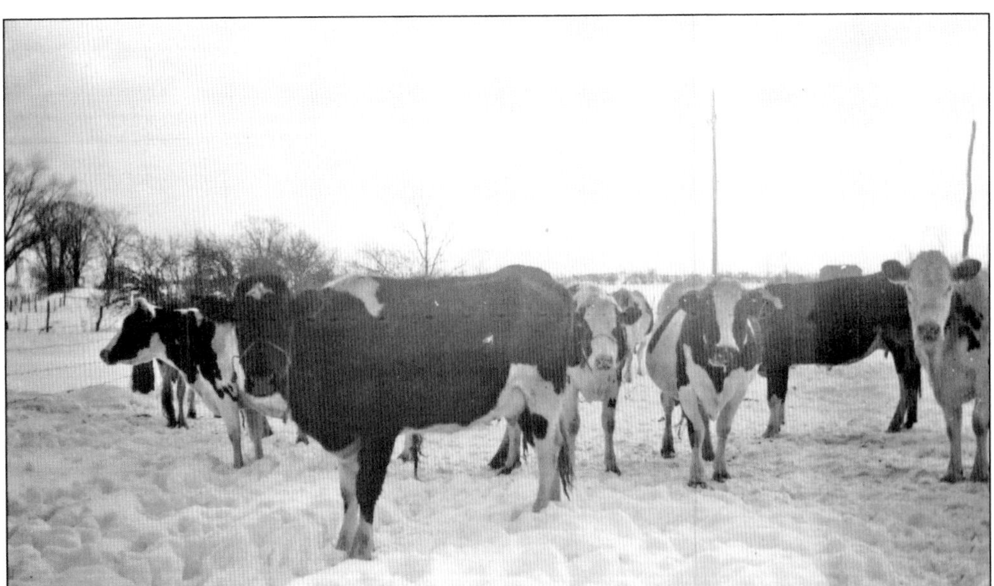

The cows are very patiently waiting for the barn to be cleaned. The snow is not deep, so they are enjoying the sunshine and fresh air for the short time that they are outside.

Four

Transportation

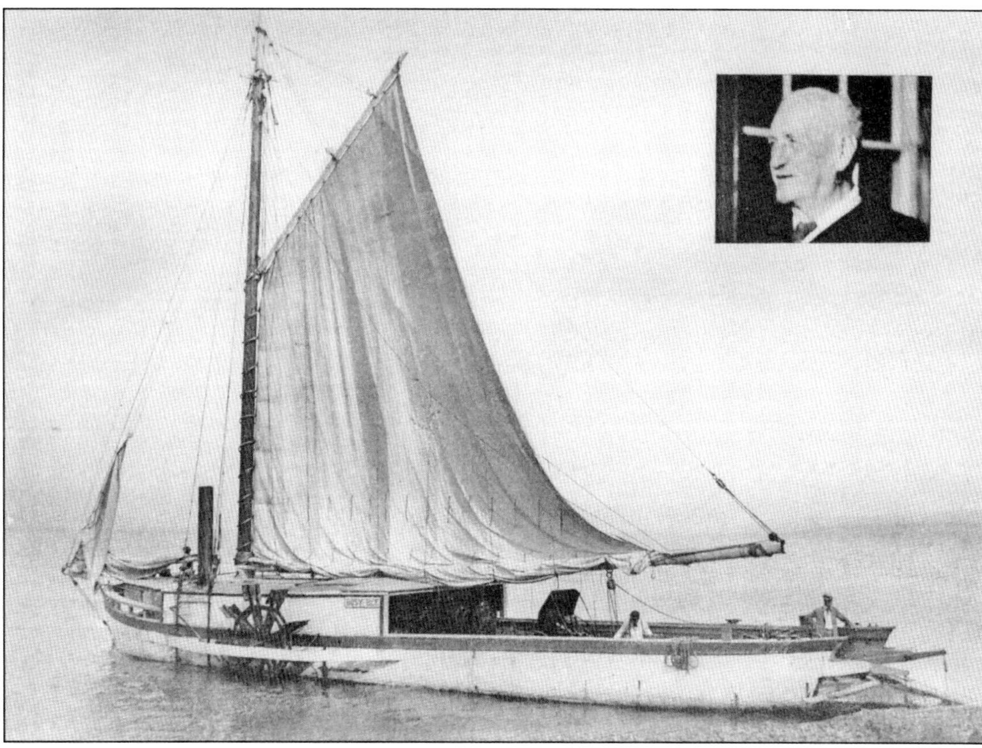

The *Busy Bee* ferryboat was built in 1884 by James Bennett of Sheldrake. The new owner was Capt. James Quick of Kidders (shown in the inset). It was a paddle-wheel boat that could be run by sail or steam. The ferry ran across Cayuga Lake from Kidders to King Ferry, where it met the train. Passengers and mail were transported back across the lake. In the fall of 1911, it needed repair, so it was sunk by the Kidders dock. The decaying hull could be viewed for many years.

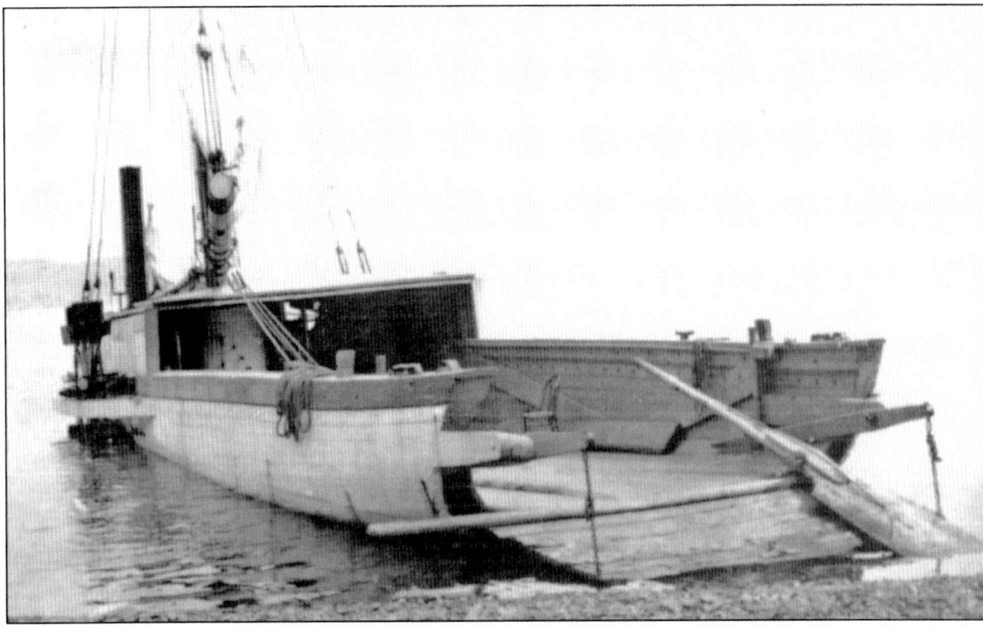

The *Busy Bee* is at the Kidders home port. The back of the boat is dropped to provide a bridge so people, horses, wagons, and carriages can come aboard. Captain Quick knew what his return run would carry by looking at the King Ferry board, which was black on one side and white on the other. White meant there were passengers waiting to come across.

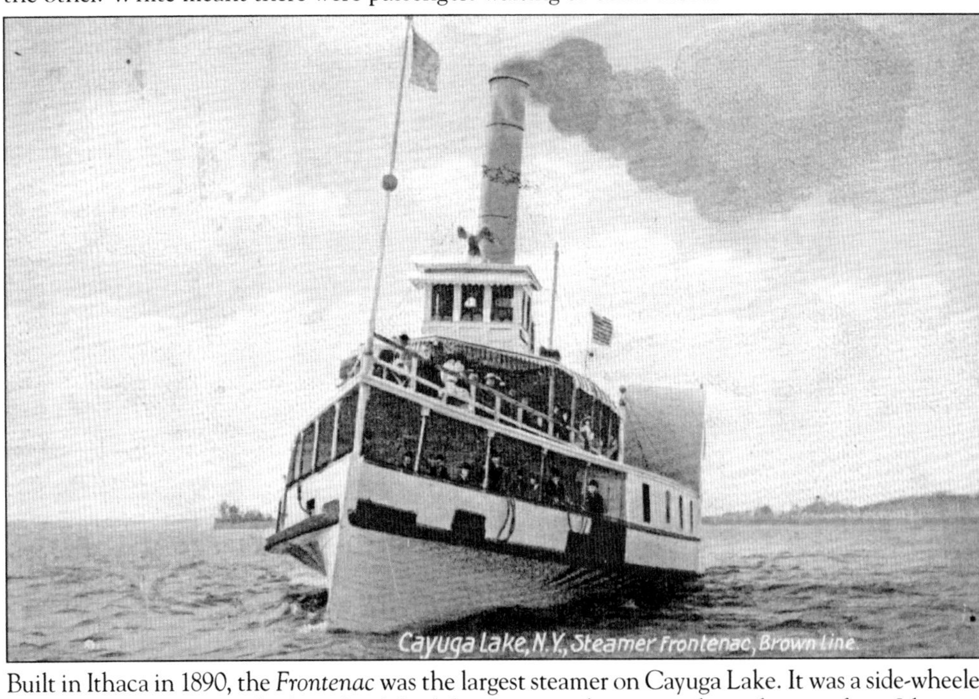

Built in Ithaca in 1890, the *Frontenac* was the largest steamer on Cayuga Lake. It was a side-wheeler that carried passengers the length of the lake. It stopped at ports along the way from Ithaca to Cayuga. On July 27, 1907, in rough water and gale winds, it caught fire near Farleys Point, on the east side of the lake. Eight passengers drowned. The wreck remained until it was salvaged for scrap iron during World War II.

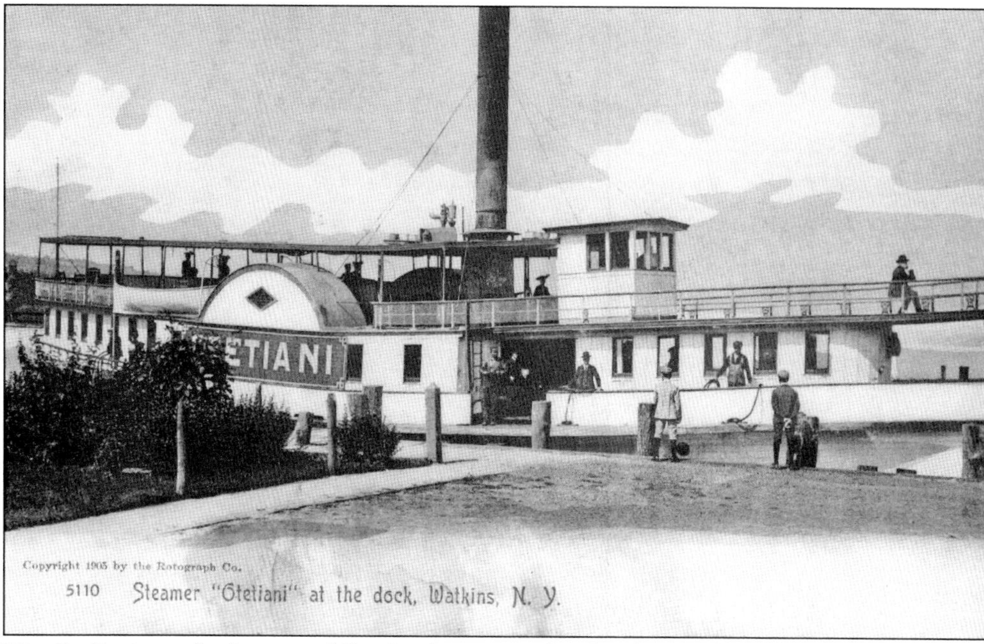

The *Oteliani* was the fastest paddle-wheel steamer of its kind. It made daily trips from Watkins to Geneva, on Seneca Lake, delivering passengers and cargo at stops including Ovid Landing. During one of the trips from Geneva, in 1899, Captain Herd allegedly hit the Seneca Lake "Sea Monster." This caused major damage, and the ship was dry-docked.

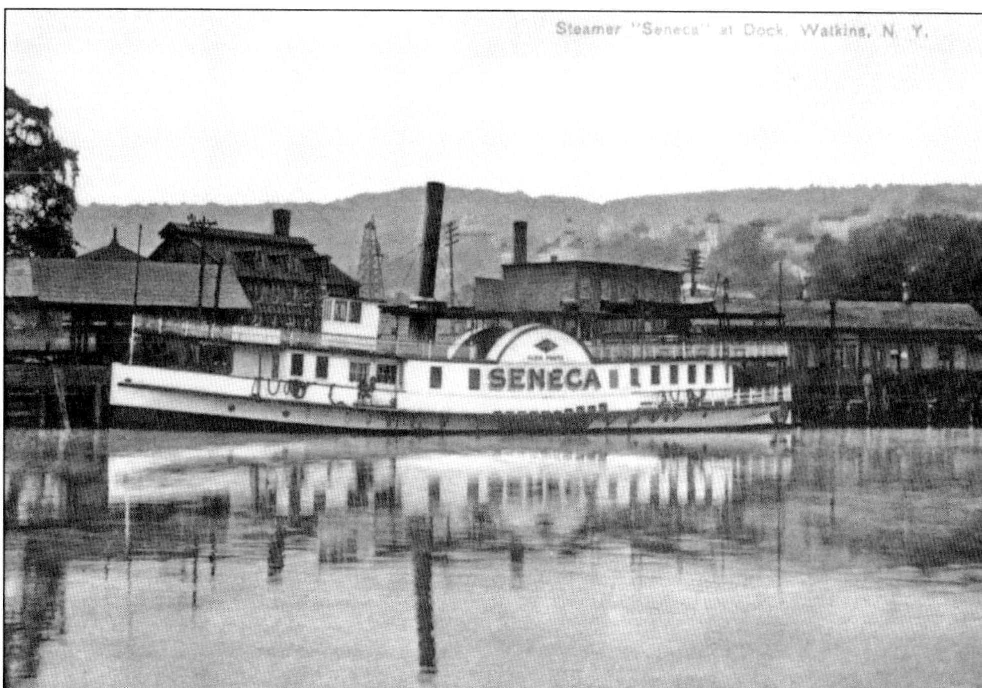

With repairs completed, the ship was rechristened *Seneca*. It was outfitted with a powerful electric searchlight and remained on the lake until it was forced out of business by the railroads.

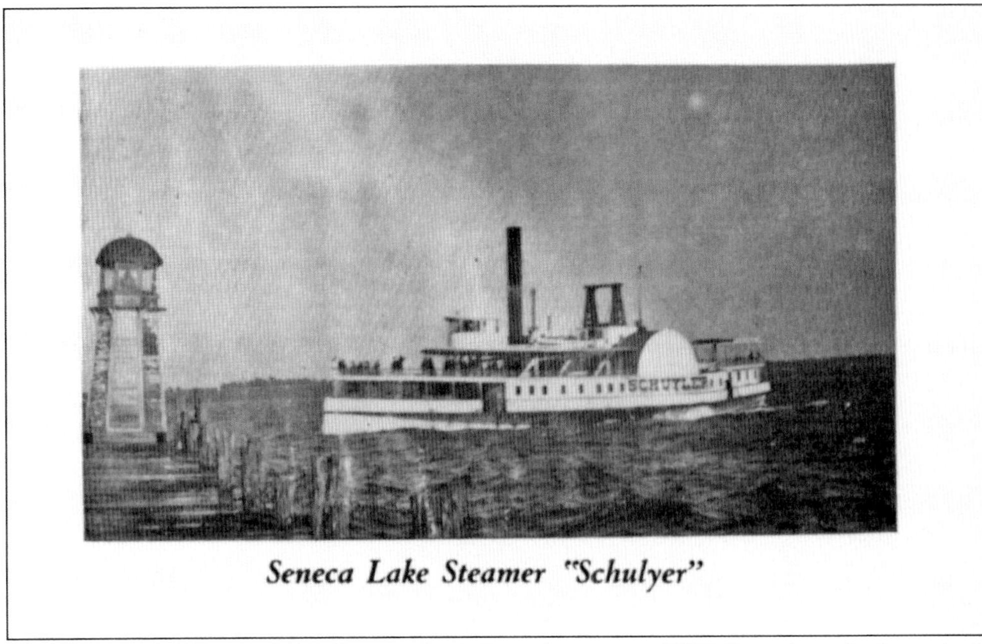

The Seneca Lake steamer *Schuyler* was rebuilt from the steamer *W.W. Rumgdon*, which was built in 1863. In 1871, fifteen feet were added to the keel of the *Schuyler*. This allowed for a much larger load to be handled. In 1893, the steamer was condemned and no longer used.

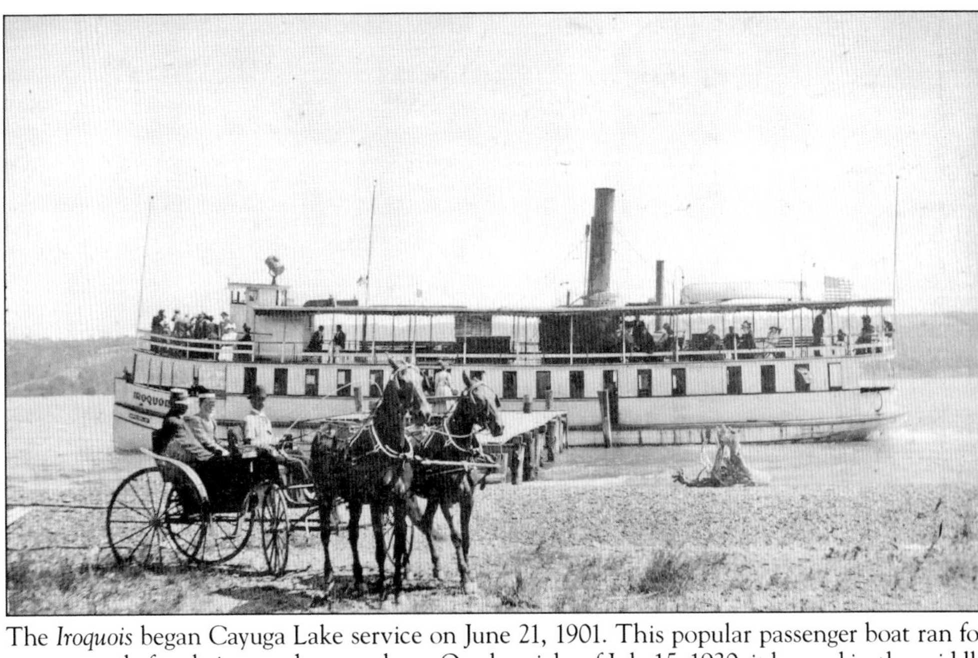

The *Iroquois* began Cayuga Lake service on June 21, 1901. This popular passenger boat ran for many years before being used as a tugboat. On the night of July 15, 1930, it burned in the middle of the lake. All those pictured are unidentified. (Courtesy of Kelly Fiske.)

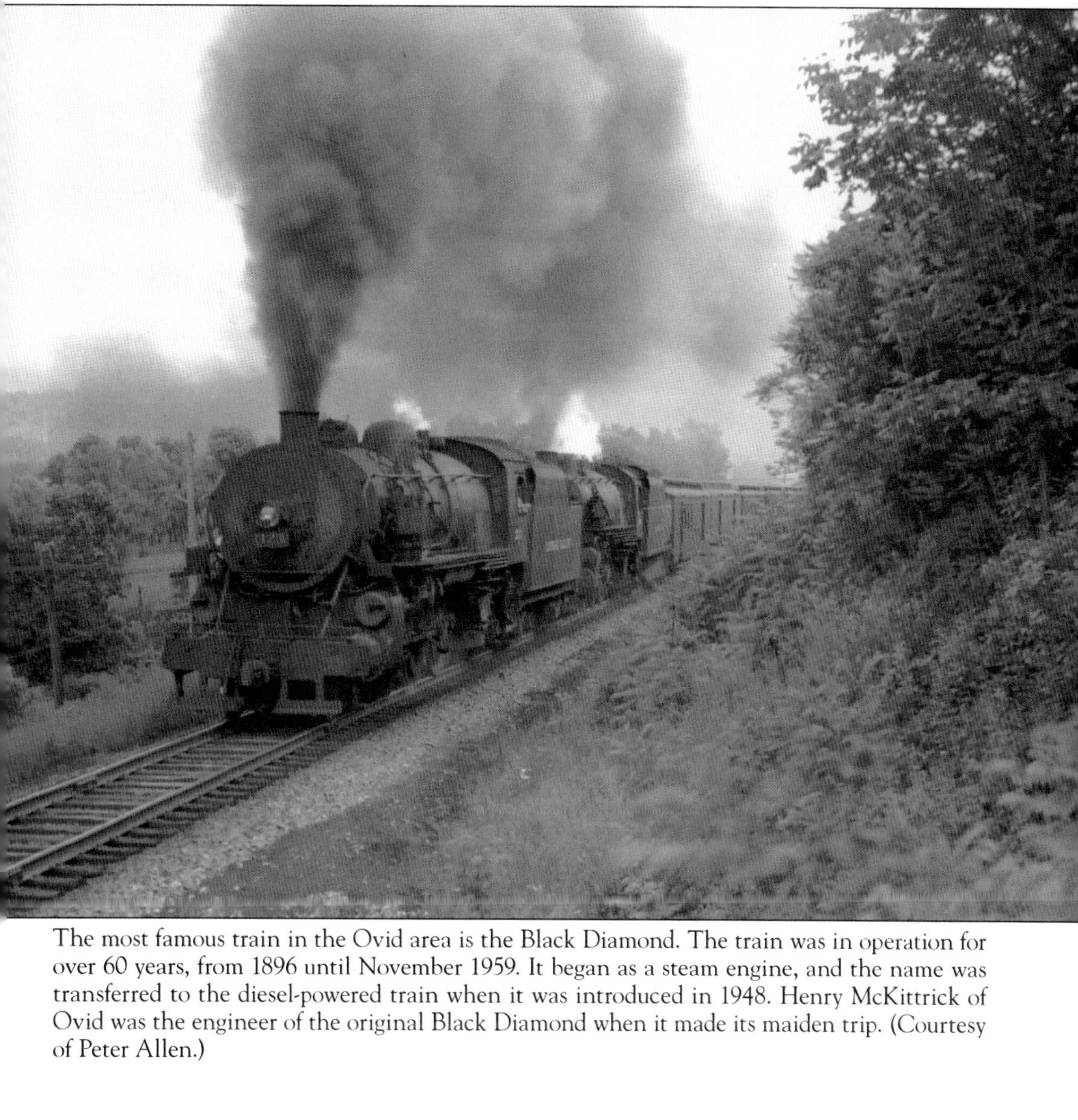

The most famous train in the Ovid area is the Black Diamond. The train was in operation for over 60 years, from 1896 until November 1959. It began as a steam engine, and the name was transferred to the diesel-powered train when it was introduced in 1948. Henry McKittrick of Ovid was the engineer of the original Black Diamond when it made its maiden trip. (Courtesy of Peter Allen.)

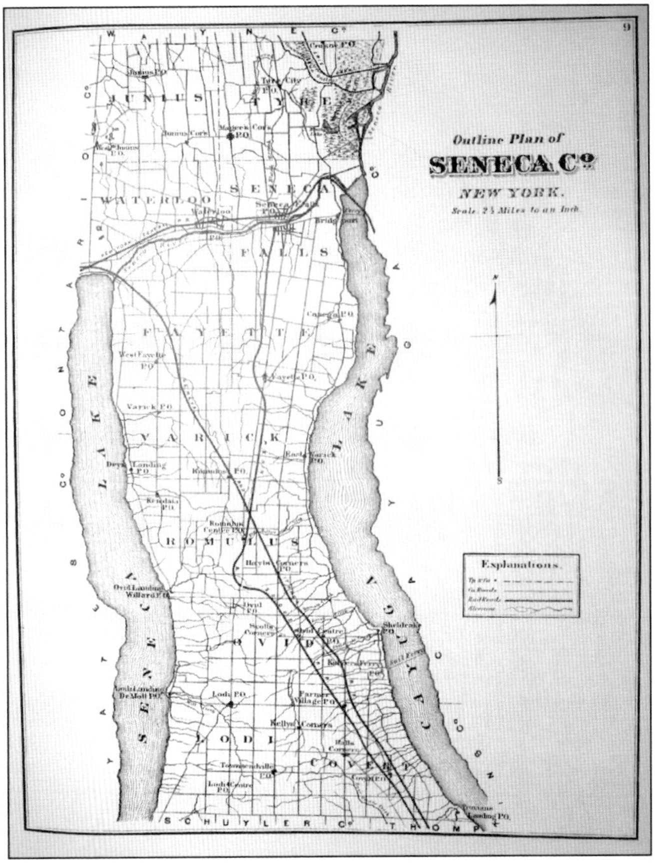

Seneca County had plans for two railroad lines crisscrossing its length. The only tracks that were ever built were the ones that ran from southeast to northwest. This was the Lehigh Valley Railroad that traveled through Ovid. The railroad that never passed the planning stage was the Penn & Sodus Bay Railroad.

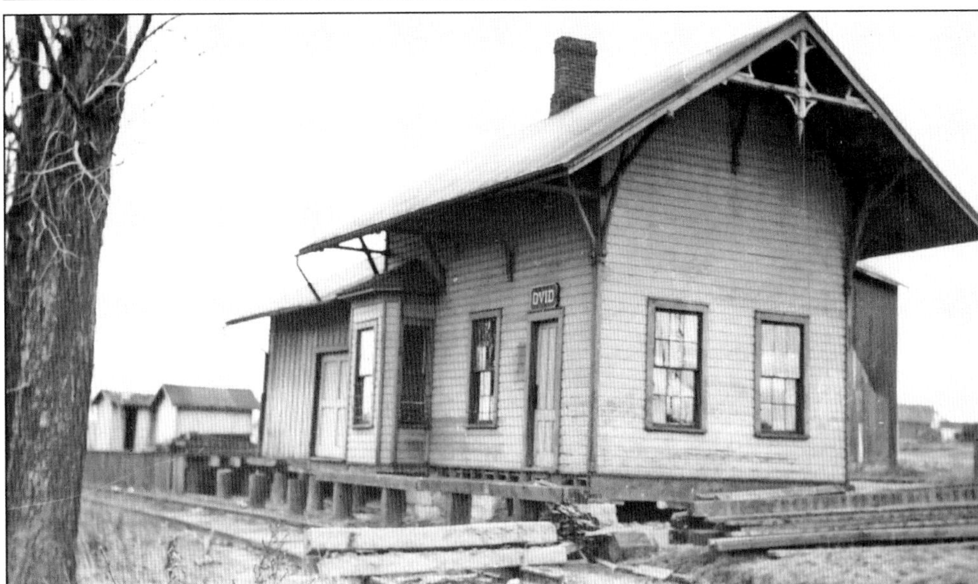

The Ovid Railroad Station was on the Hayes Corners, Ovid & Willard Railroad. It was north of the village of Ovid and was in business for many years. The Willard branch of the Lehigh Valley Railroad was used to deliver supplies to the Willard State Hospital.

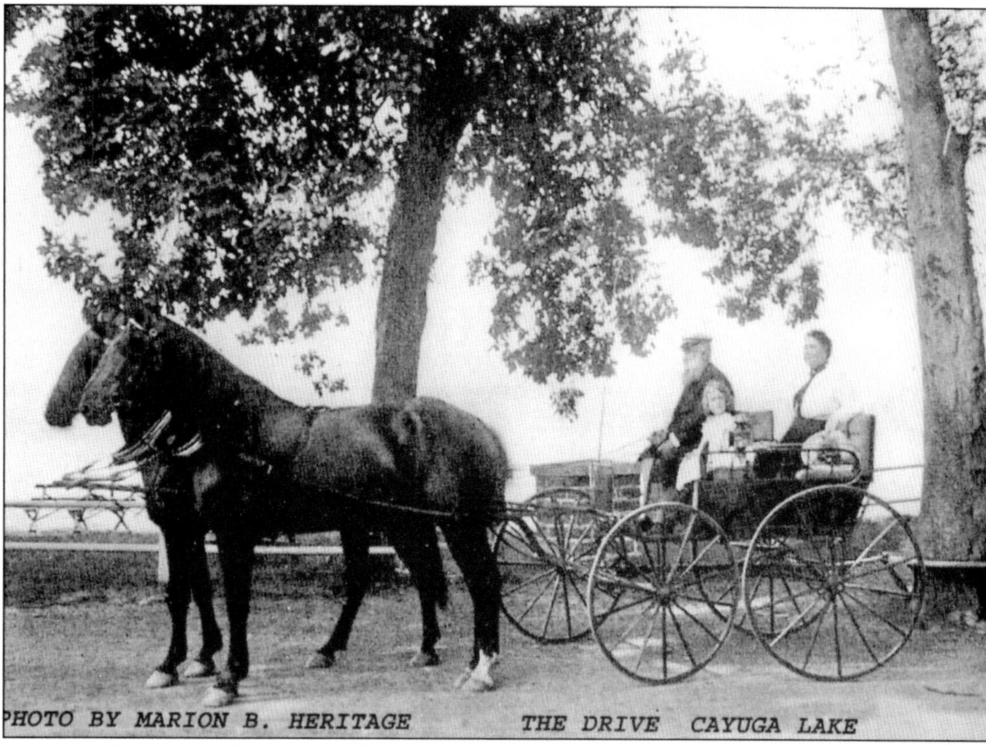

Area families enjoyed drives in their open carriages. Horses walked slowly, so the lake view could be thoroughly seen during their excursions. A picnic basket has been packed for a leisurely Sunday afternoon.

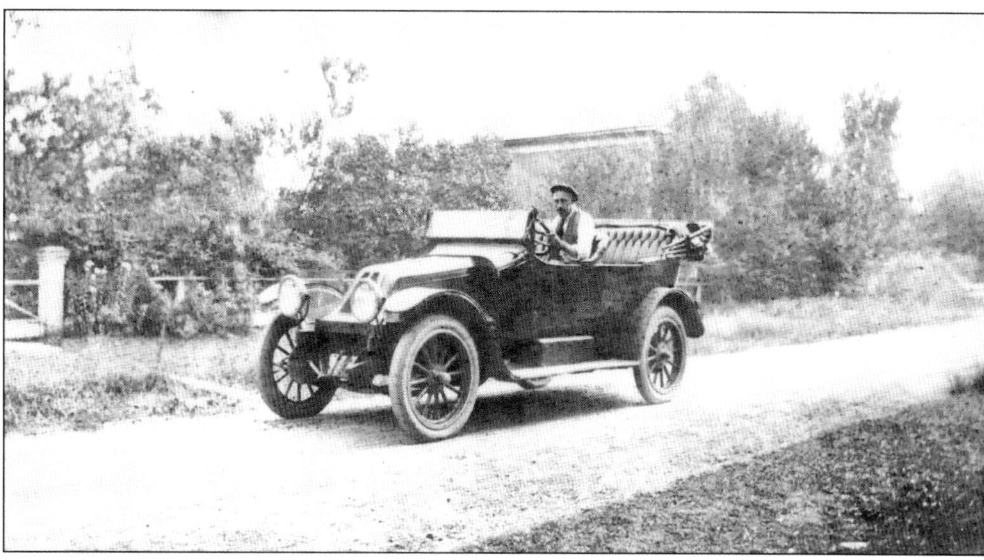

Jay Burlew is seen driving his touring car in 1930. Burlew lived with his parents on the former Mandeville farm and often visited his friends and relatives along Cayuga Lake. He was proud of his automobile and gave rides with the top down. (Courtesy of Naomi Brewer.)

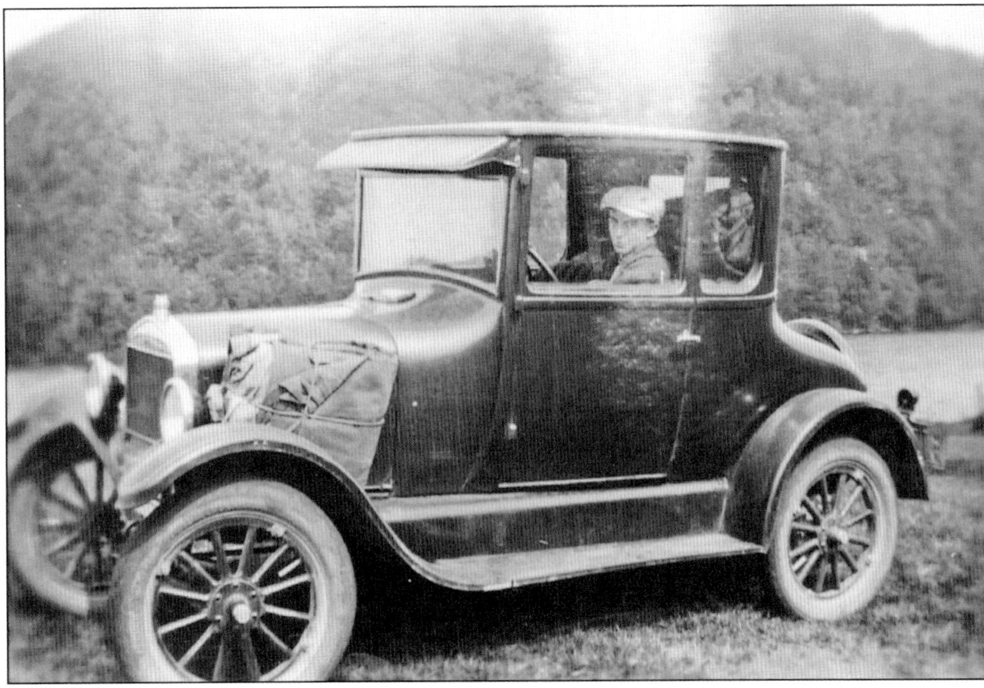

The Ford Roadster of the late 1920s is obviously a favorite vehicle of Daniel Powell. The package would likely indicate a trip is going to be taken. His father, Donald Powell, may not have approved, for Daniel appears to be too young to drive. It may have been legal, however, for at that time no one was required to have a driver's license.

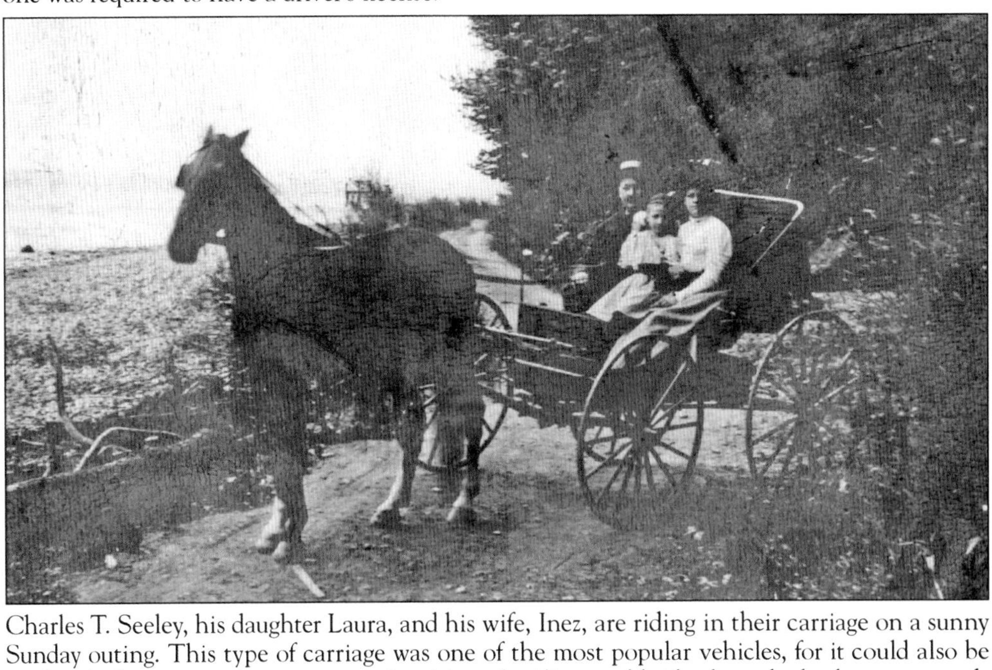

Charles T. Seeley, his daughter Laura, and his wife, Inez, are riding in their carriage on a sunny Sunday outing. This type of carriage was one of the most popular vehicles, for it could also be used with the top up when it was raining. Many families would ride along the backcountry roads to visit friends or just have a different view of scenery. This trip may have been to visit Seeley's relatives who were descendents of John Seeley, the pioneer of Ovid village.

Five

Businesses

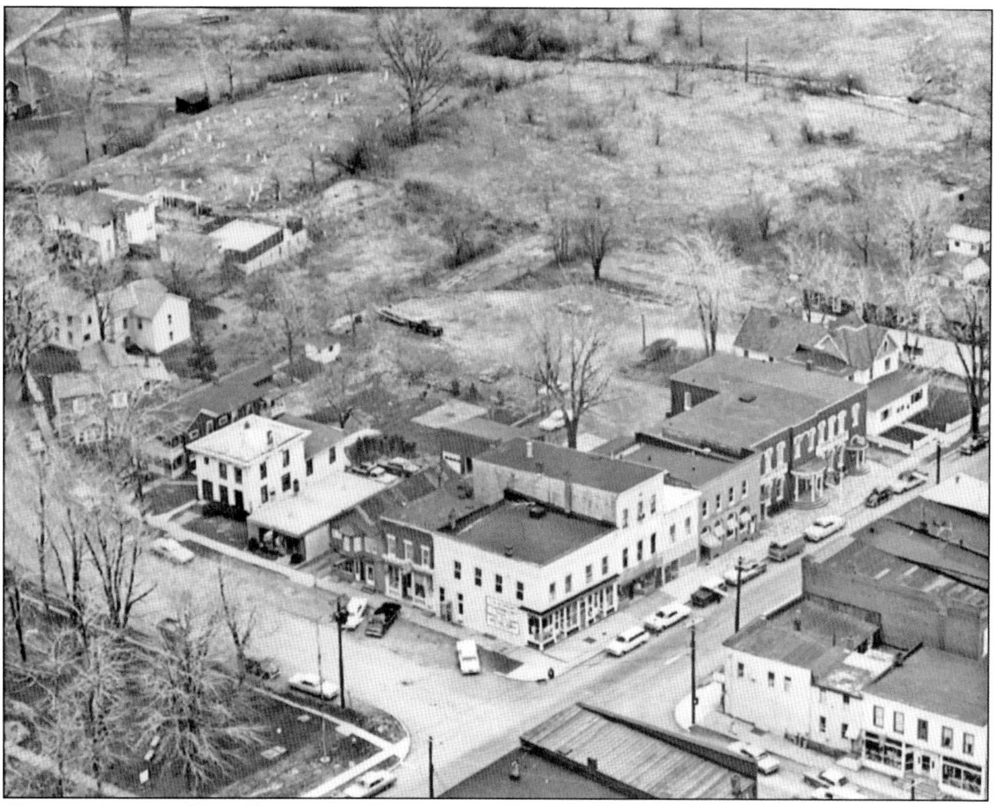

The aerial view of Ovid businesses shows the corner of South Main and East Seneca Streets. At the southeast corner of Main Street are the pharmacy, two stores, the bank, the Franklin Hotel, and the funeral home. On East Seneca Street, from the corner, are the pharmacy, meat market, a store that was later removed to make way for a bank drive-through, a liquor store, and the dentist office. The Old Ovid Cemetery may be seen in the upper left corner.

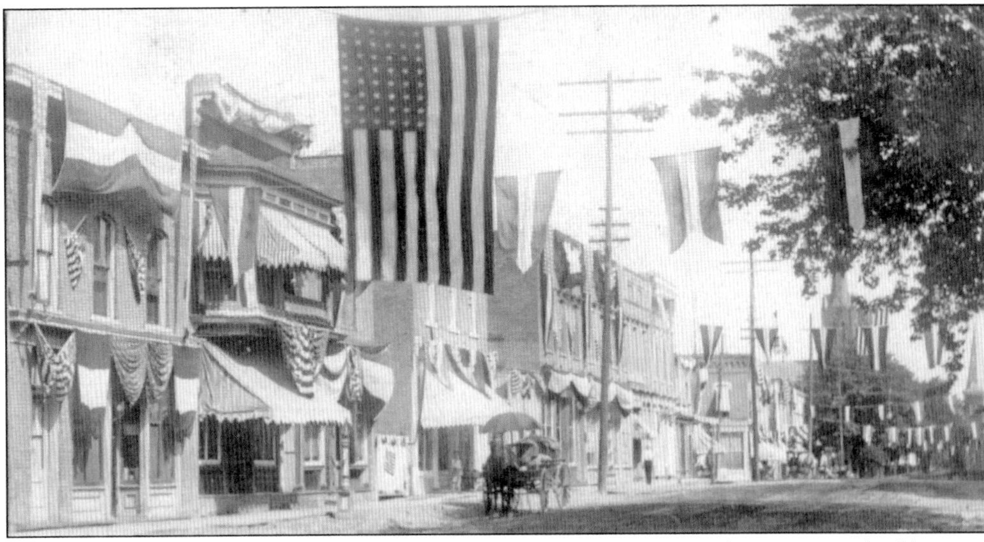

Old Home Week Celebration in Ovid was a very colorful event. Nearly every store had banners or flags displayed. Here, banners and a 48-star American flag are flying over the street. The shop awnings are opened to protect against what must have been a very warm day. Even the buggy has a raised umbrella to shade the horse.

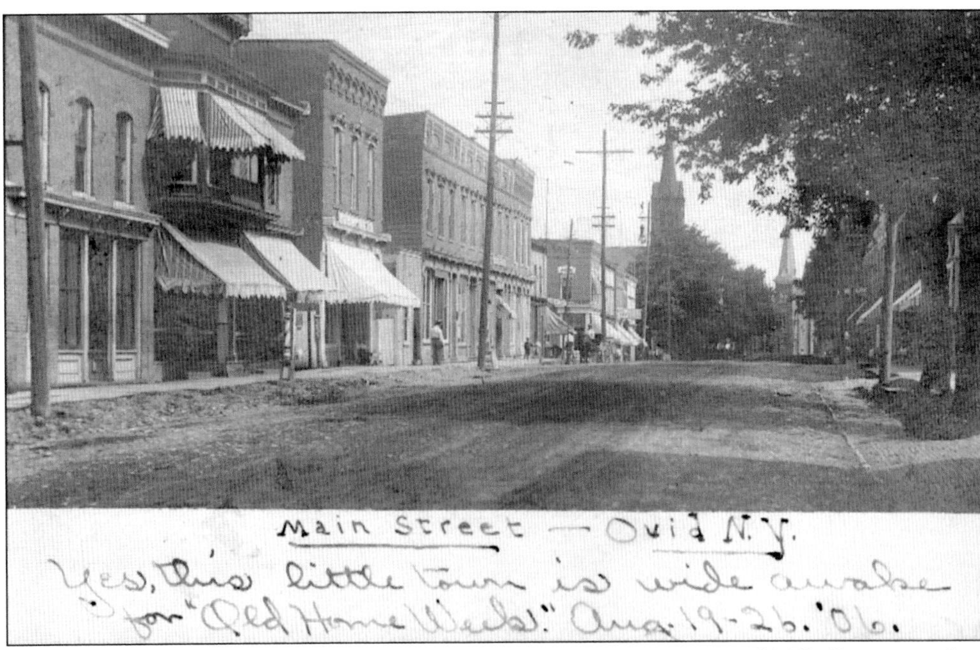

The hardware store, Market Basket grocery, George Depew garage, and N.R. Boyce gasoline station are on the west side of North Main Street. These buildings were made of brick after the wooden structures were lost. There were five devastating fires that destroyed all of the buildings on both sides of North and South Main Streets.

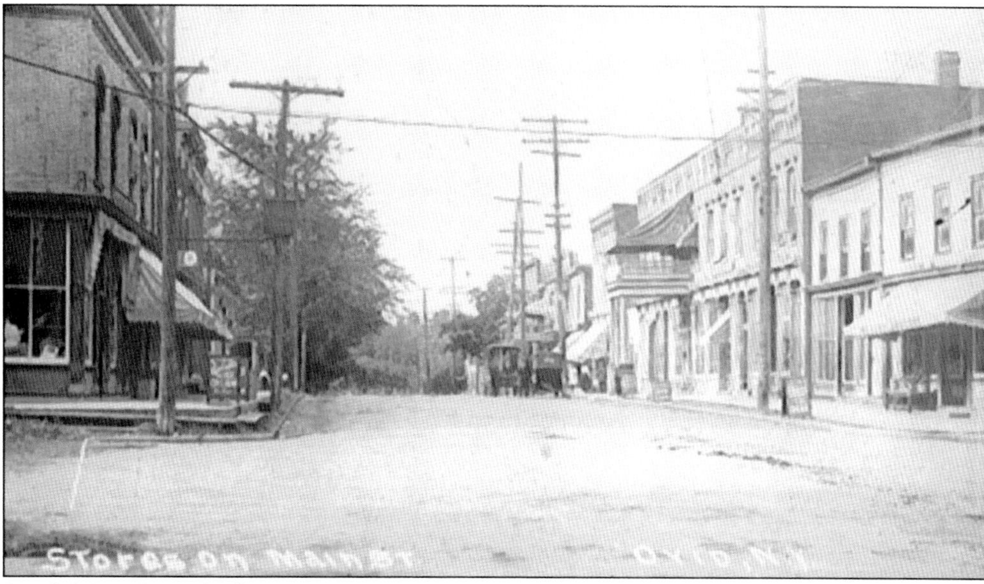

South Main Street had several stores that had porches or balconies over the sidewalk. The only balcony porch remaining has been enclosed. It still provides a front-row seat for anyone viewing a parade. The expensive upkeep of porches and shutters has prompted their removal. This has marred the handsome looks of the stores on Main Street.

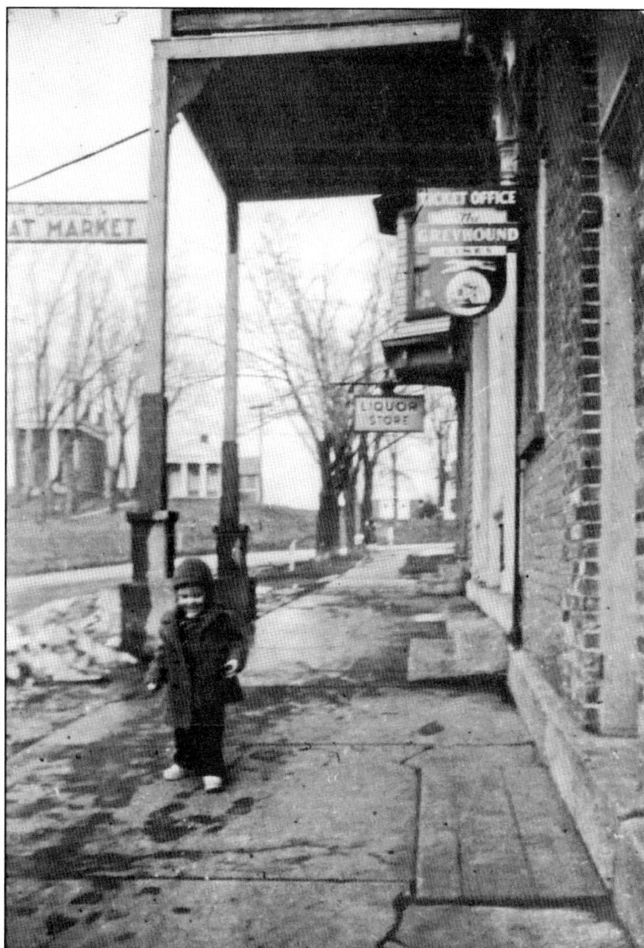

Greyhound bus tickets were purchased at the Depew Pharmacy on the comer of South Main and East Seneca Streets. Riders waited at the side door for the bus to stop. The stores next door were the Hughes Meat Market and a liquor store. The liquor store was later moved farther down the street to make way for a driveway from the bank.

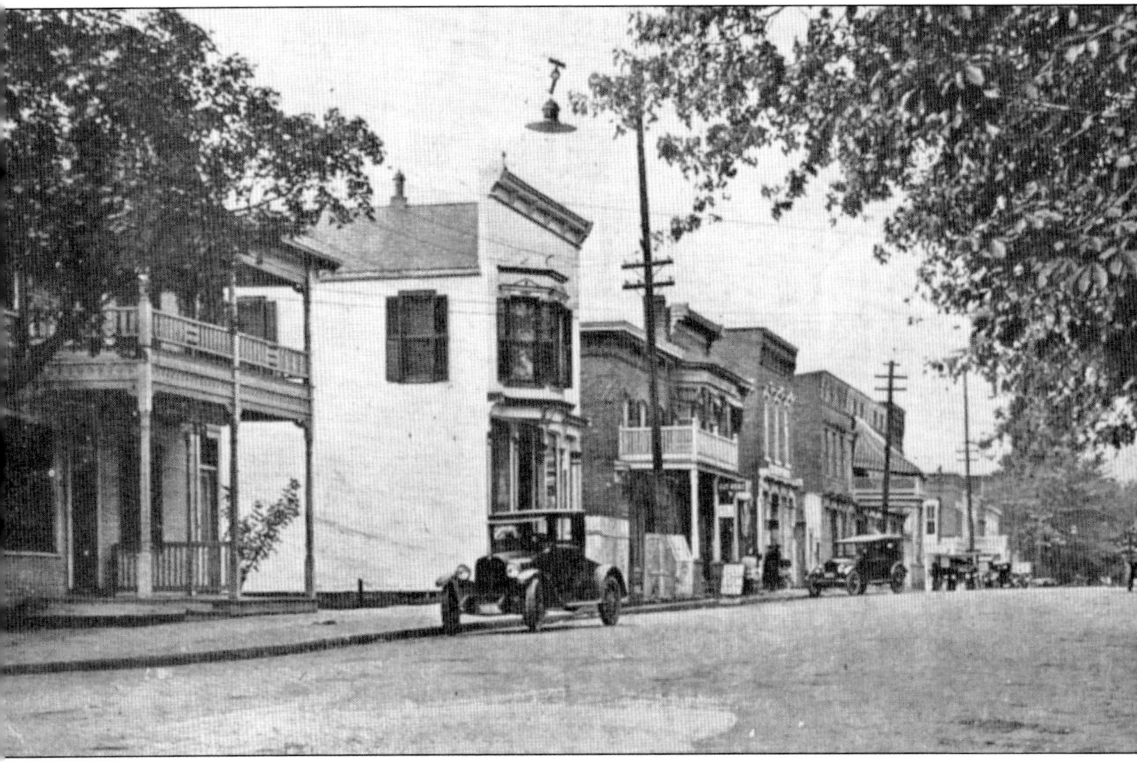

Unpaved South Main Street gave the appearance of being wider than when the concrete highway was installed. The 1820s founding fathers should be praised for establishing the large width of the main street. There was no crowding when the future double-lane highway was made.

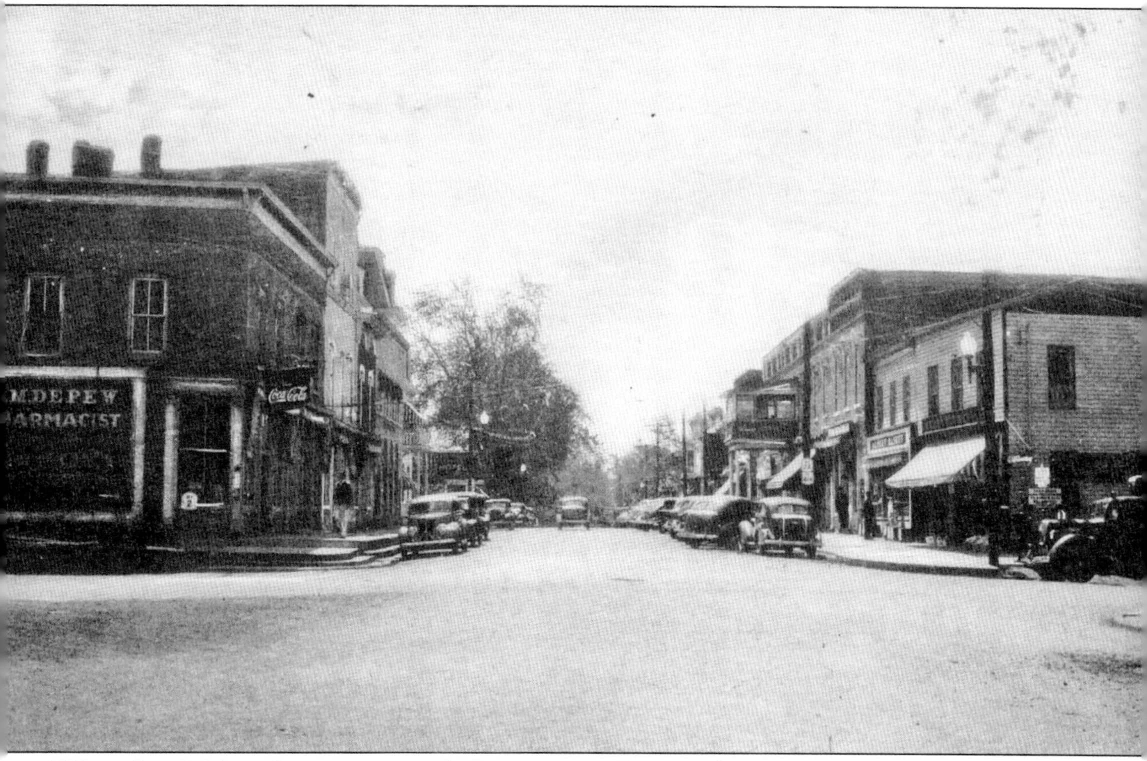

When South Main Street was paved, there was ample room for cars to parallel park on the east side of the street and park diagonally on the west side. This did not interfere with the cars traveling through Ovid. Here, the C.M. Depew Pharmacy sign occupies a large amount of space on the brick wall on the left.

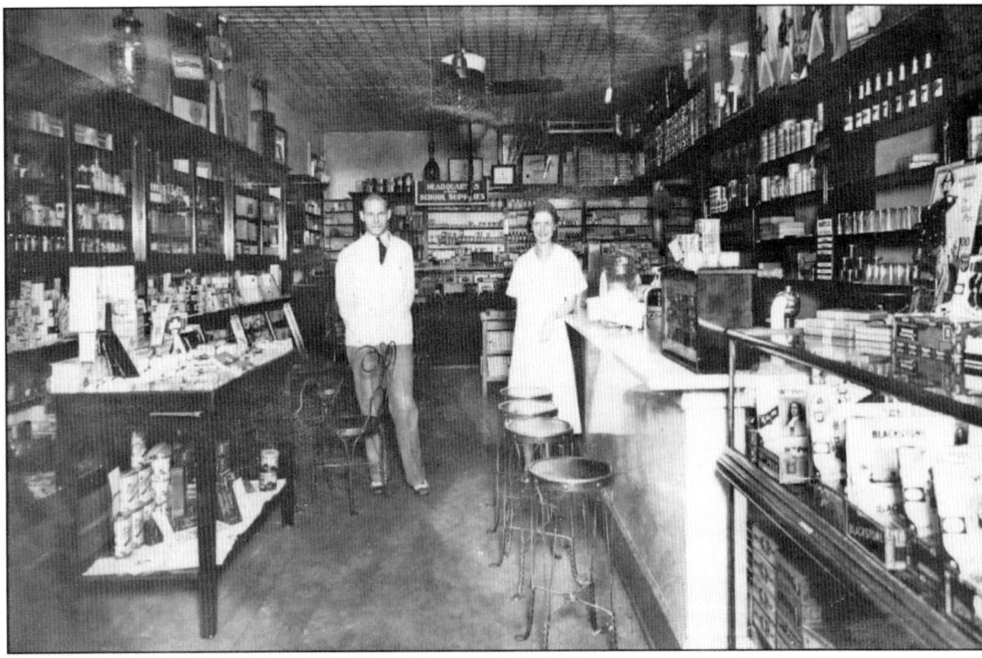

Pictured are Chauncey Depew (left) and an unidentified woman in the Depew Pharmacy on the corner of Main and East Seneca Streets. Seymour Horton owned the building and store from 1894 until he retired in 1931. Chauncey, who worked for Horton, bought the business that year. He retired in 1969 and sold the business and building to John Kavis. (Courtesy of Peter Depew.)

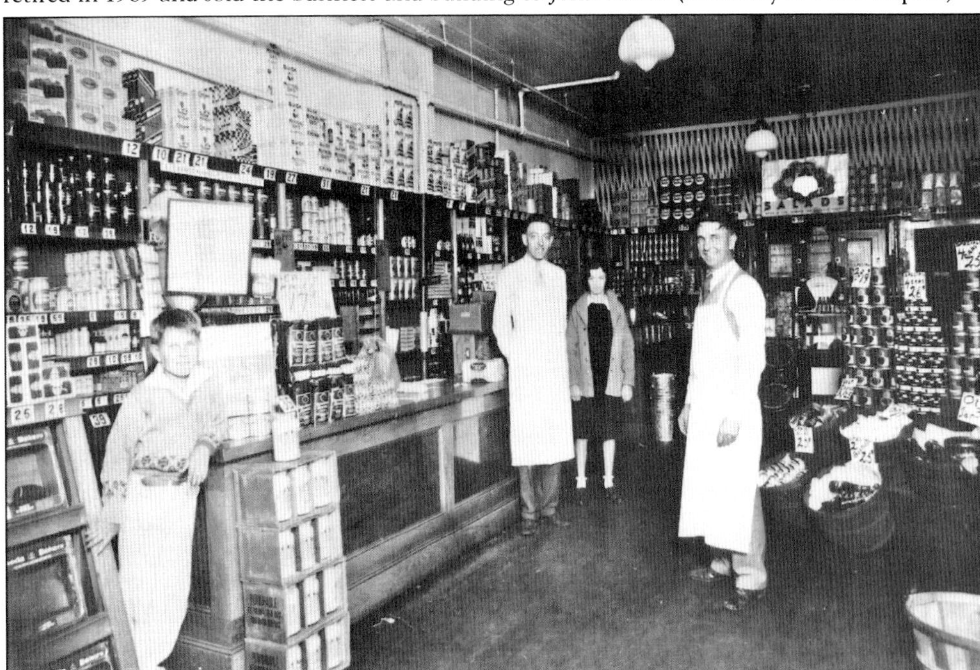

The Great Atlantic & Pacific Tea Co. grocery store was on the west side of South Main Street. Taken in the 1940s, this picture shows, from left to right, Robert Murphy (on roller skates), Arthur Hall, Eileen McGough, and store manager Clarence Murphy.

George Lynd bought the hardware store in 1941 from Percy W. Bristol. George was an expert tinsmith, store clerk, and hardware dealer. His wife, Ann, was the bookkeeper. Every morning, the front sidewalk was washed and the awning was lowered. Seasonal equipment and the flag were on the sidewalk on sunny days. They were returned every evening at 4:55. If one mentioned Ovid, New York, when traveling around the country, the question was often asked "Do you know George Lynd?" When he retired in 1971, employees Thomas and Virginia Martin took over the business.

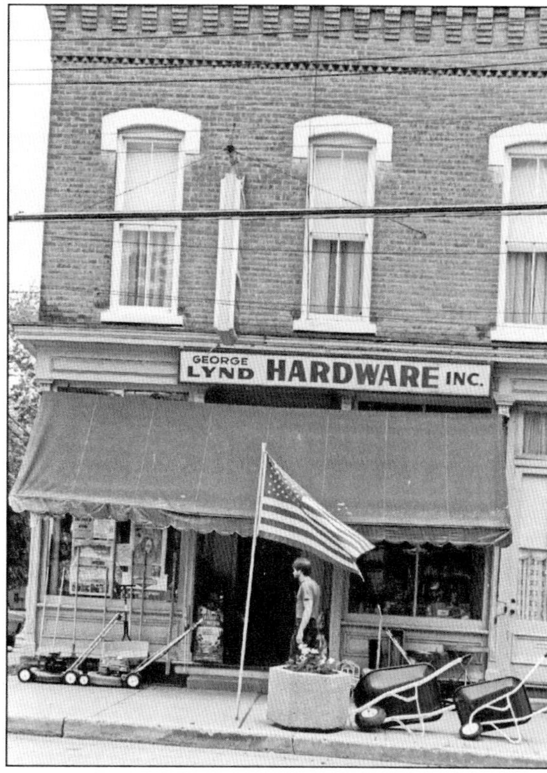

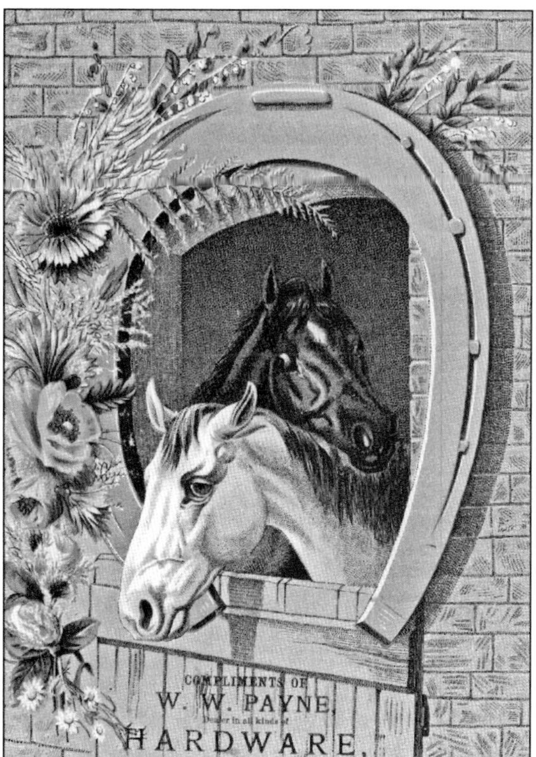

The W.W. Payne Hardware store was the first building north of the old Presbyterian church on North Main Street. He sold hardware, handmade tinware, tools, stoves, groceries, gasoline, and Pratt's Astrol oil. Payne also did general jobbing and repairing. The complimentary advertising cards were quite attractive and were distributed by many of the businesses in the area.

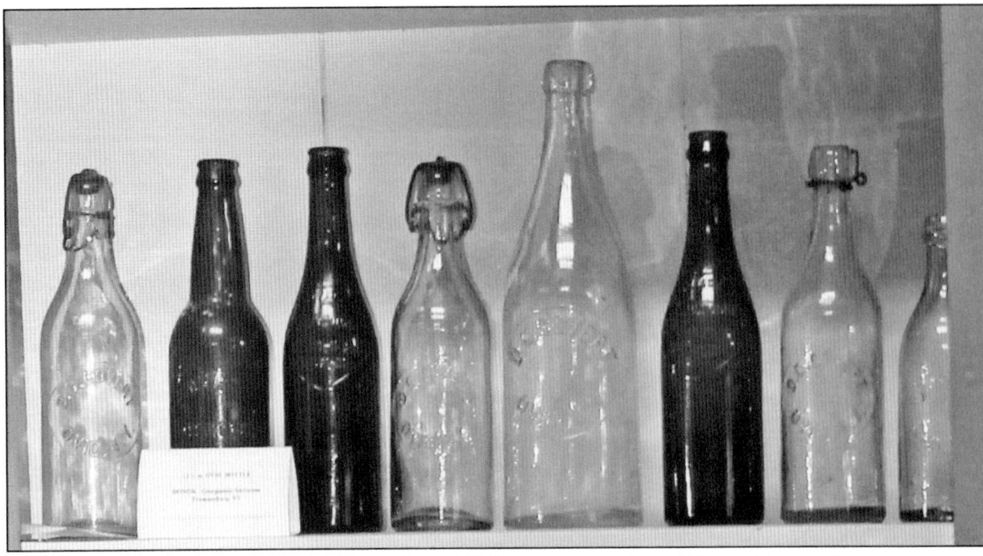

The Ovid Bottling Works, established in 1900, was located on Water Street. It was operated by Donald G. Covert, who bought the property in 1896. Pop and beer were bottled, but only sarsaparilla, orange soda, and root beer were made on the premises. The pop sold for 5¢ a bottle, and six bottles of beer were 25¢. No photographs of the building have been found, but a collection of the bottles can be found in the Ovid Historical Society Museum.

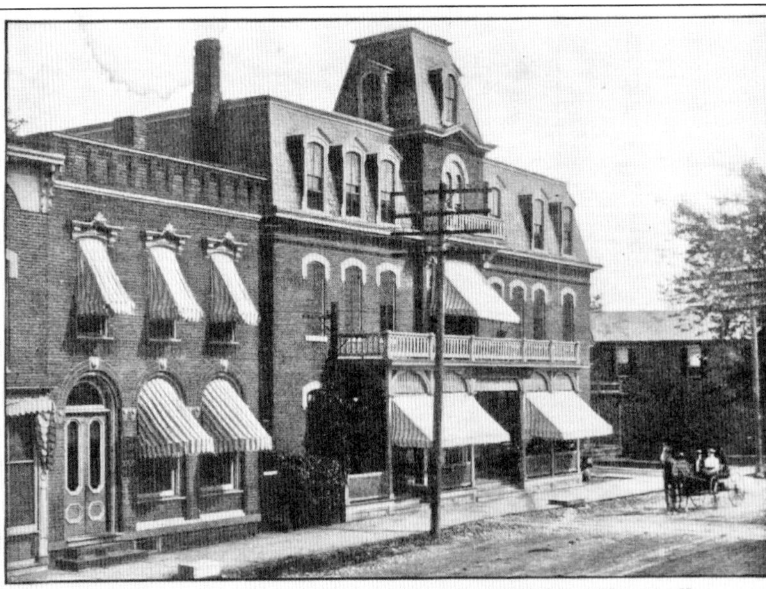

FRANKLIN HOUSE AND FIRST NATIONAL BANK, OVID, N. Y.

The Franklin Hotel was built in 1841 on the east side of South Main Street. The hotel burned in the 1874 village fire but was restored. It had several owners and survived another fire in 1953, when the third floor was removed. It was always a popular gathering place for food, drink, and entertainment. In 1972, the hotel closed and was torn down. The Community Bank addition, parking lot, and driveway now occupy the area.

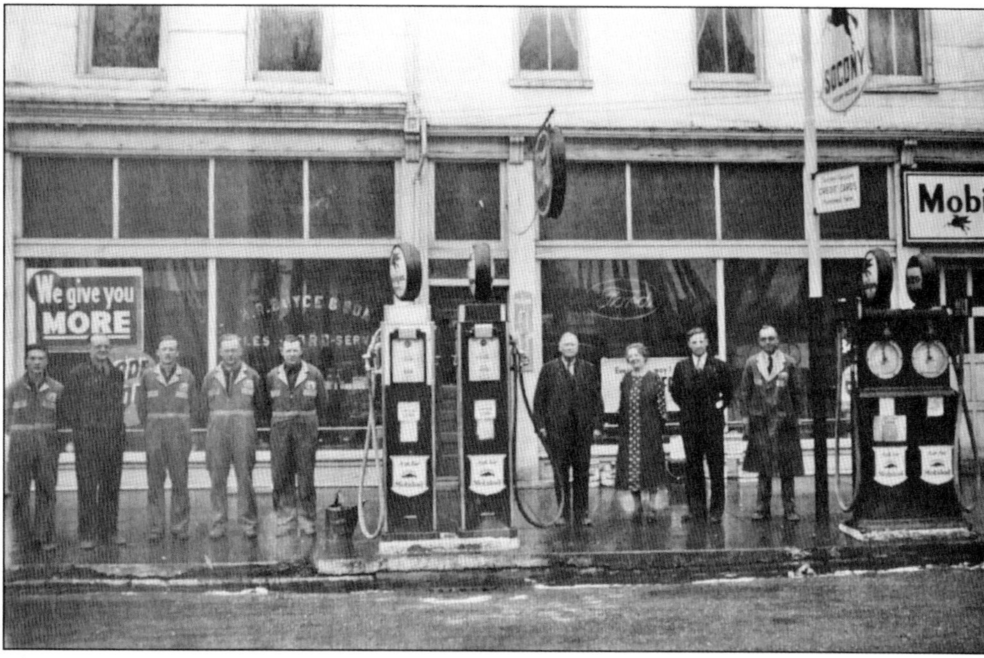

The Norman R. Boyce garage was established in 1913 on the west-side business block of North Main Street. The gasoline was Mobil, as seen in the signs. . The N.R. Boyce Company continues to be operated by the family. Proudly standing in front of the large garage are, from left to right, Stanley Brodnecki, Grant Newkirk, Adrian Steen, Lester Conkling, Edwin Lynch, Norman, Ida French, Marion, and Nealy Brewer.

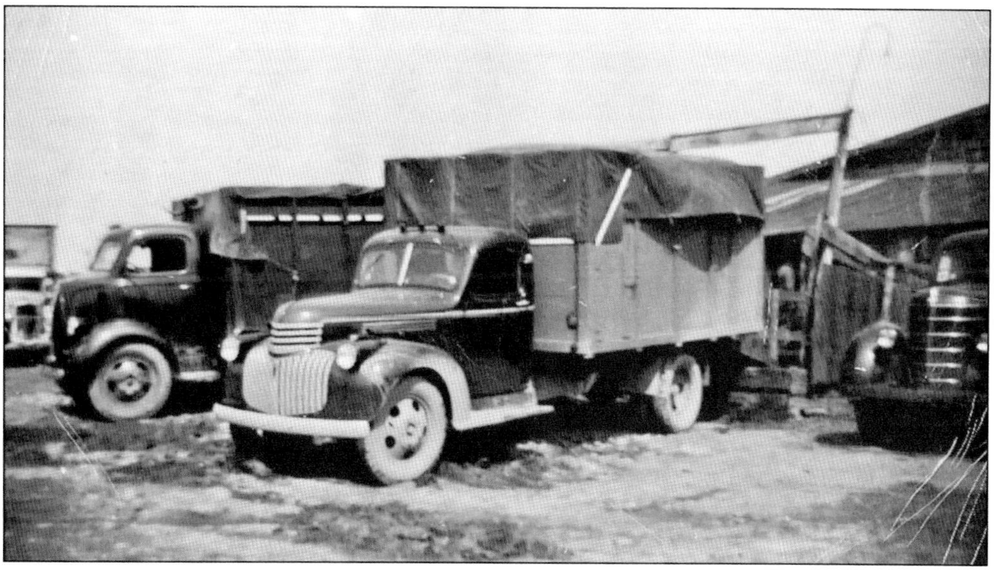

The Wickham Auction House was started by Leon C. Wickham in the 1930s. It began as a family-run business buying and selling livestock. Wickham bought horses in Nebraska and brought them to Ovid by train, and local farmers brought their livestock to be sold. Son Keith and his wife, Frances, helped at the auction house, which grew to include selling entire households, farms, and businesses. The auction complex closed in the 1970s and burned down in November 1983. (Courtesy of Frances Wickham.)

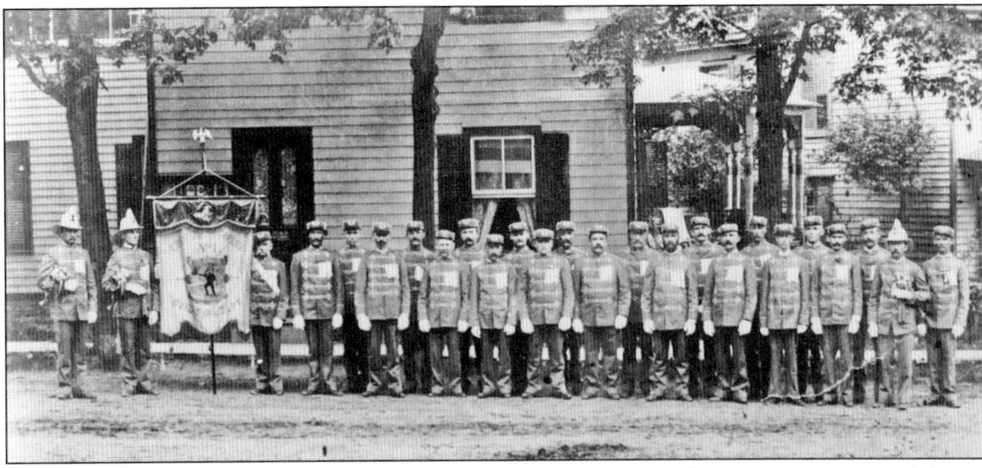

The Ovid fire department is officially named Croton Engine & Hose Company No. 1. It was organized on August 23, 1889, after Ovid residents had fought five huge fires. Pictured are, from left to right, Fred Crans, L.C. Pitcher, Clemenson Gorton, Owen Lochren, M.J. Finton, Joseph Morgan, Charles Griffin, D.P. Seeley, William Arden, John F. Covert, James Mullaney, James French, Edward Krug, A.D. Marsh, Alfred Havens, F.C. Allen, Hugh Hanlon, Abram Finnegan, Wallace Raymond, C.E. Garnett, Daniel Horton, Thomas Rafferty, B.V. Covert, Fred Thomas, and Roy Brokaw.

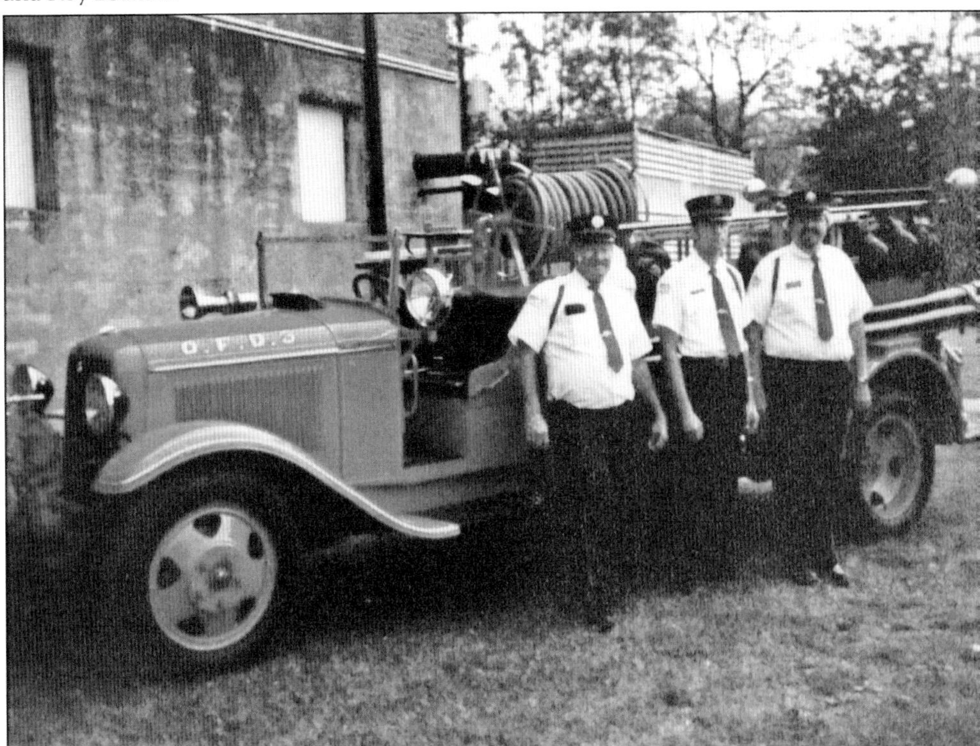

The 1932 Ford fire truck was purchased new by the Croton Engine & Hose Company, which is better known as the Ovid Fire Department. The pumper helped to put out fires until about 1951. Since that time, it has been in parades as an example of equipment used in days gone by. Pictured are, from left to right, firemen Herburt Reich, Richard Nixon, and William Braunig.

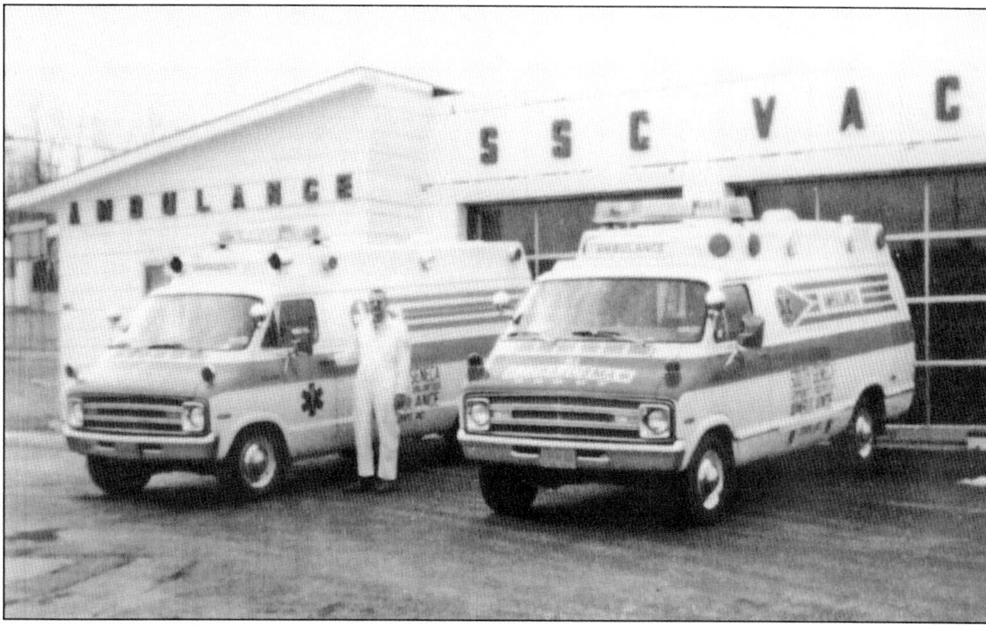

South Seneca Ambulance Corporation, Inc., began service in 1973. It started with one Cadillac ambulance and a lot of dedicated and well-trained volunteers. The headquarters were located on North Main Street, at the southwest comer of Route 96A and Route 414. The ambulance service later acquired more modem equipment as a result of many fundraising events. It is much needed and appreciated in Ovid and surrounding communities, because the hospitals are located 20 miles away. Joe Maleski is pictured standing between the two ambulances.

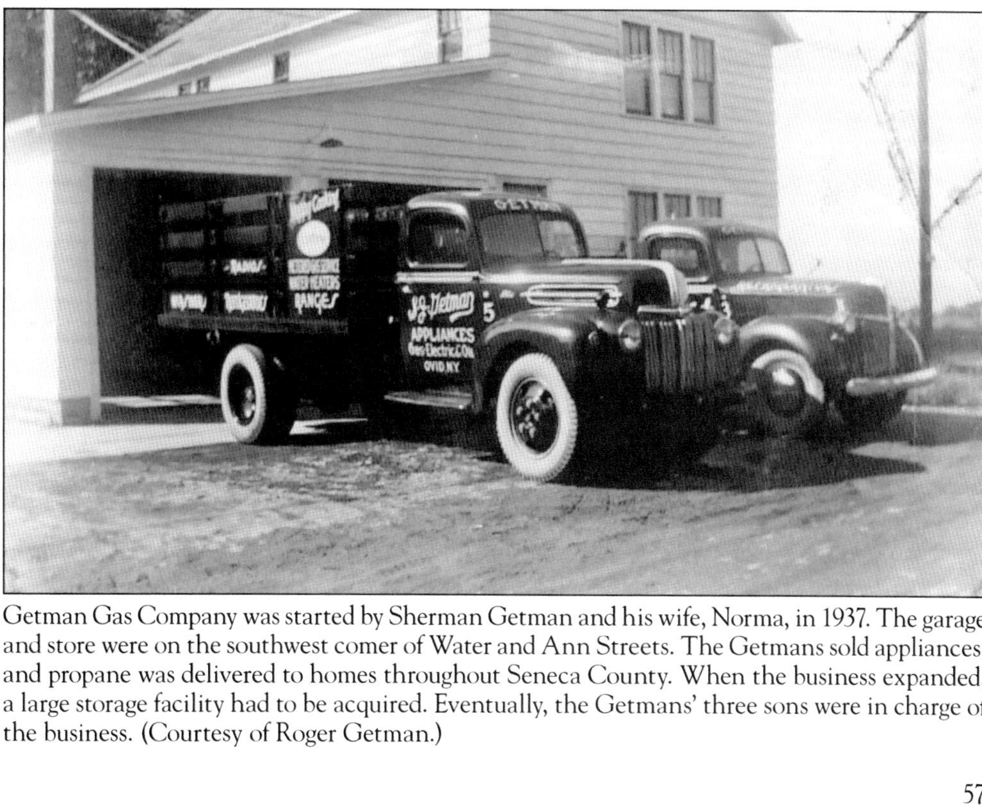

Getman Gas Company was started by Sherman Getman and his wife, Norma, in 1937. The garage and store were on the southwest comer of Water and Ann Streets. The Getmans sold appliances, and propane was delivered to homes throughout Seneca County. When the business expanded, a large storage facility had to be acquired. Eventually, the Getmans' three sons were in charge of the business. (Courtesy of Roger Getman.)

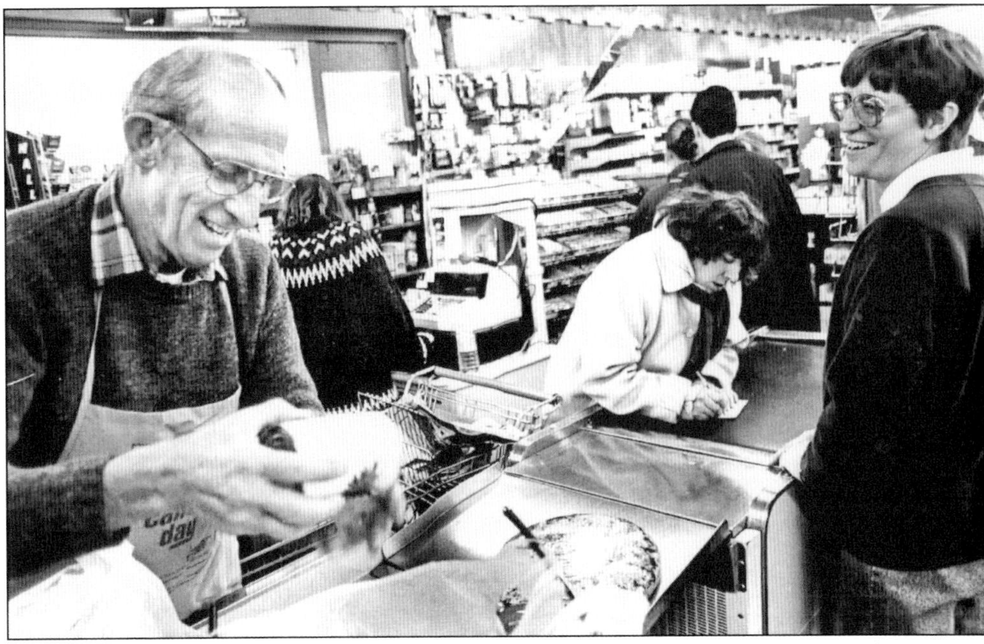

The Clover Farm Grocery was purchased by James and Eleanor McKee in 1970 from the owner of the IGA store. Later, the name was changed to Ovid Big M Supermarket. Mayor David Griffith (left) shares a laugh with cashier Mary Jane Rappleye as they and the Big M employees volunteer for the American Cancer Society Grocers Fight Cancer Day on December 21, 1994.

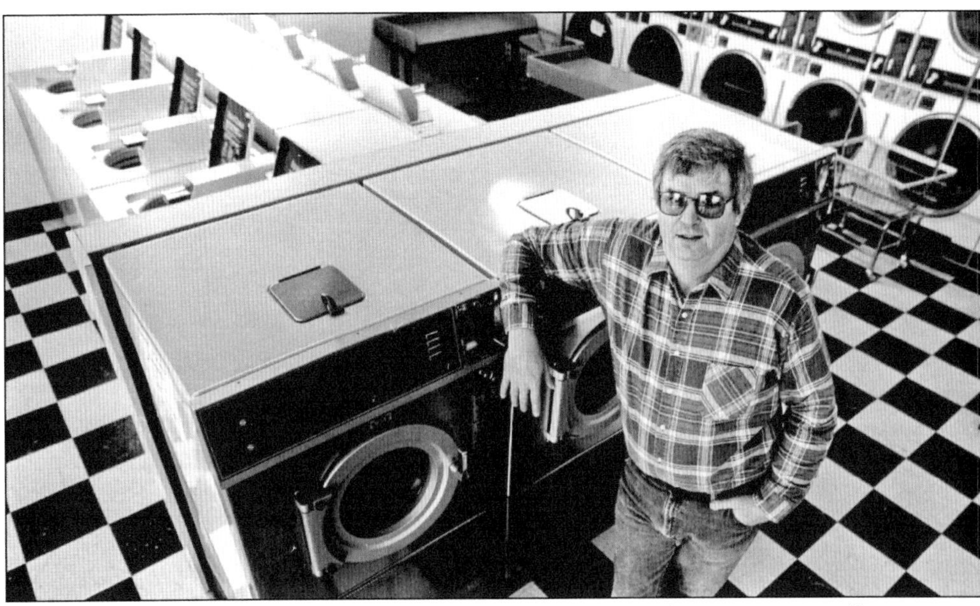

The Wet White and Blue Laundromat was owned by Leo Dougherty. It was a well-appreciated establishment on North Main Street. Many apartments did not have a washer and dryer. The water supply for some residents was not substantial enough for the cleaning of bulky items in addition to everyday use.

A carved wooden Indian greeted everyone who stopped at Jay's Soda Bar. It was located on the southern end of the retail stores at South Main Street and Water Street. There were many things to buy at this establishment, but the most popular pastime was sipping a soda while sitting at the bar.

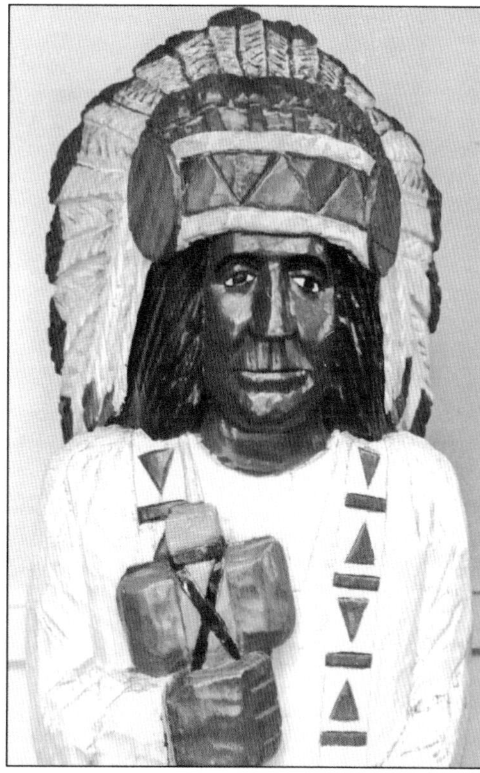

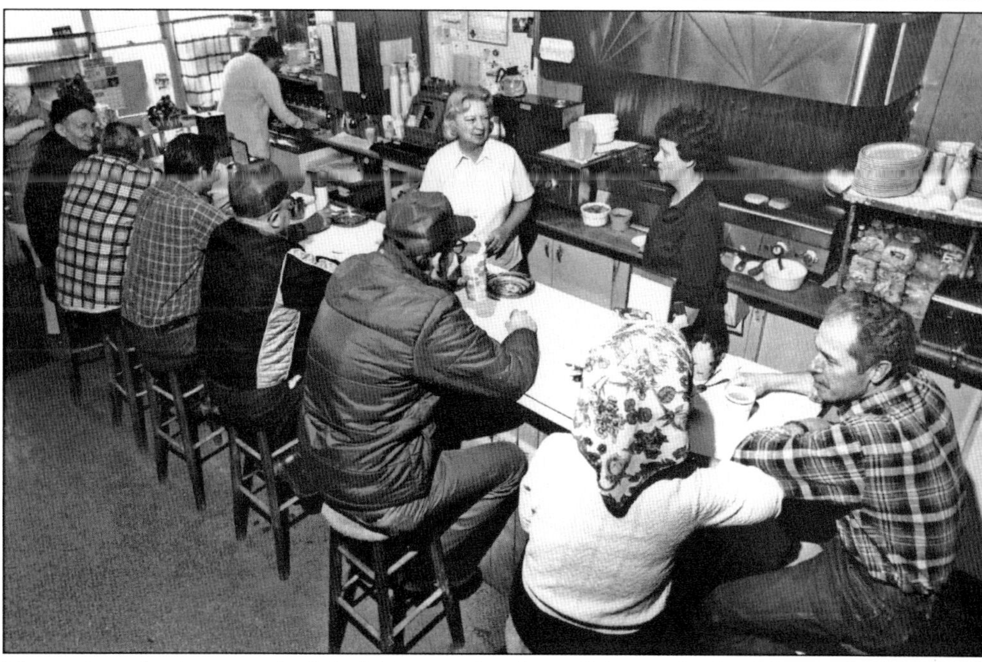

The cooks and waitresses at Jay's Soda Bar were kept busy all during the day. This can be determined by the number of patrons who filled every stool at the counter daily. Adults were served breakfast, lunch, and supper. When they were not there, the younger set stopped in after school and on the weekends to have a soda. The people pictured are unidentified.

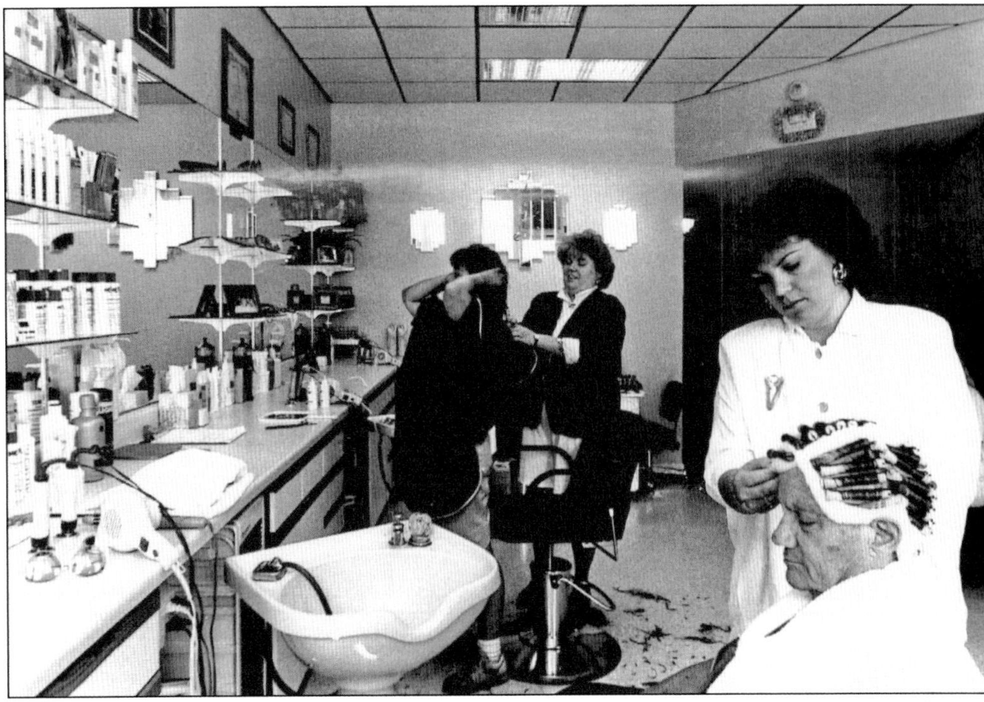

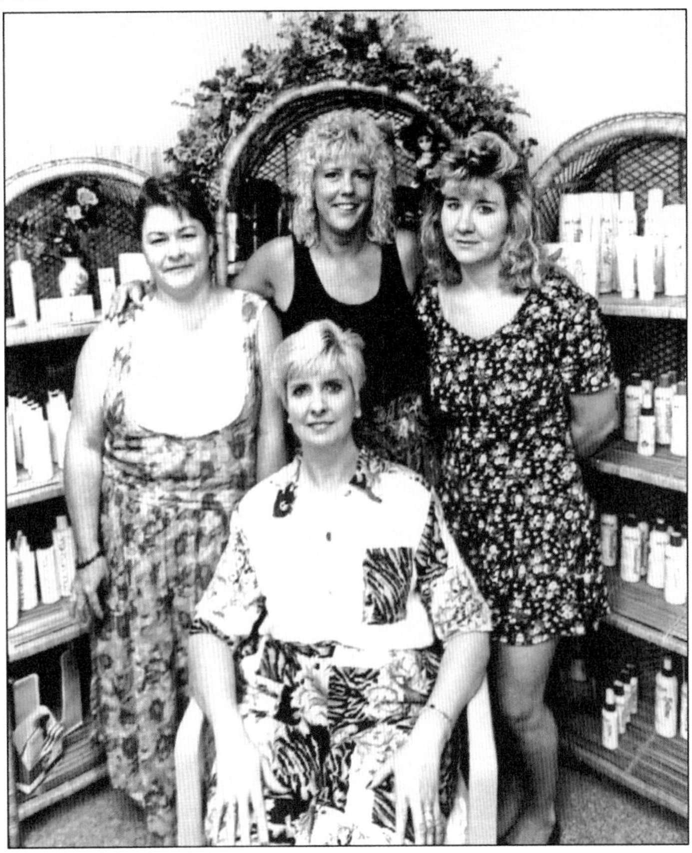

The Sally T hair salon was opened by Sally Tillinghast in 1991. It is in an original building on the west side of South Main Street. Women and men from Ovid and the surrounding area frequent her shop for haircuts, permanents, manicures, and more. Pictured are unidentified clients and hairdressers Missy Herman (left) and Sally Tillinghast.

Jackie Doran started as a hairdresser in 1970 under the instruction of Josephine Carlson. Later, Jackie acquired her own shop and opened a salon called Dynasty on Water Street. Pictured are (first row) Jackie Doran; (second row) from left to right, Edith McPike, Noelle Fabian, and Lisa Lynch.

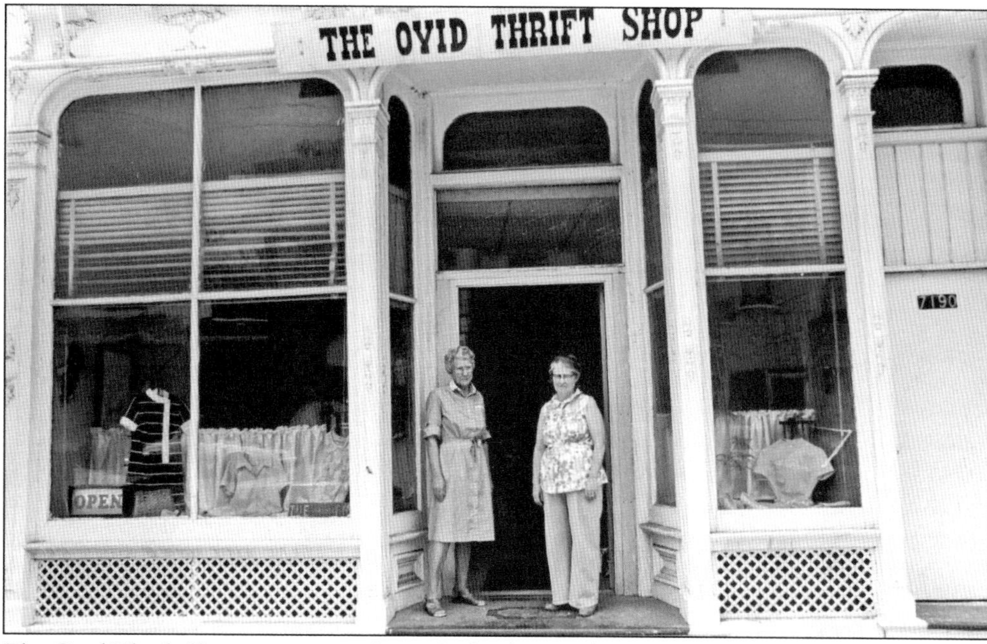

The Ovid Thrift Shop was initiated in 1972 by the Ovid Federated Church. It is a secondhand shop on the west side of South Main Street. Volunteers receive the donations and display the items as they would be found in a regular retail store. The proceeds go to community projects. Pictured are Sarah Dawley (left) and Esther Brown.

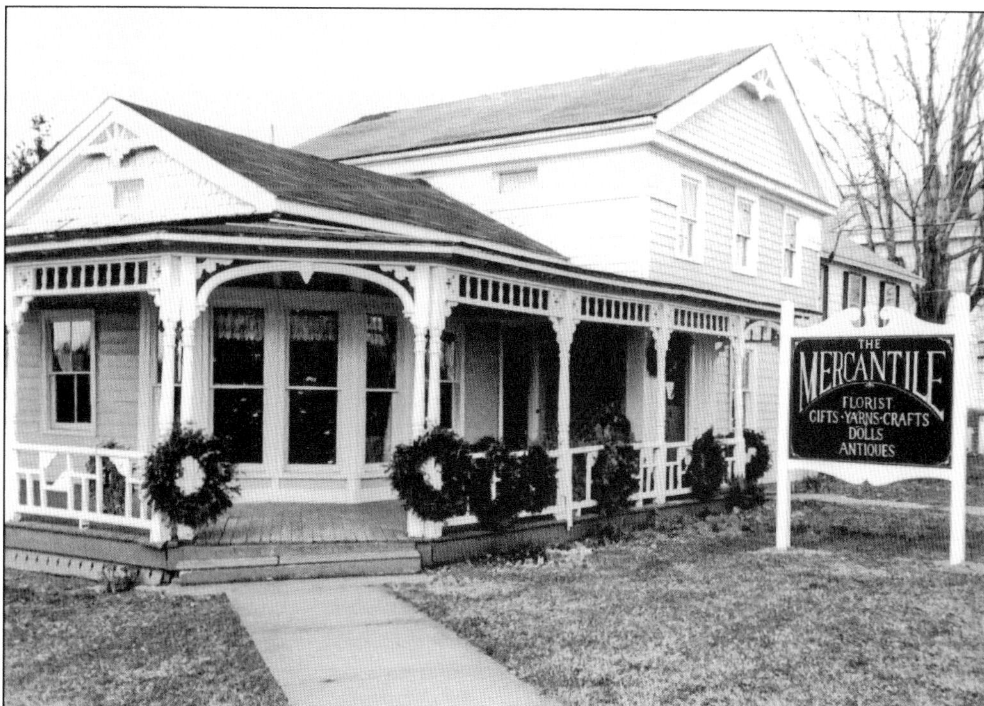

Dr. Amos B Smith had his office in his Greek Revival home on the west side of North Main Street in 1847. Patricia Guinan opened the Mercantile gift shop in 1986.

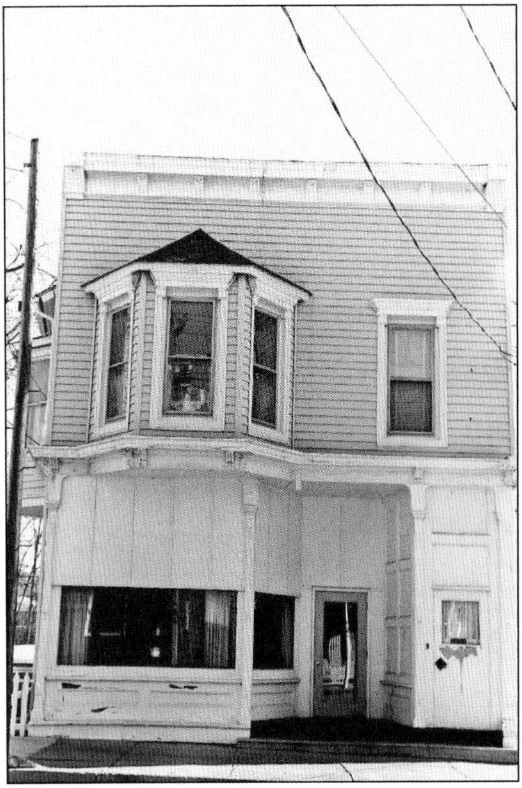

Charles Flynn was the undertaker in this building on the east side of South Main Street in 1855. Flynn also sold furniture, paints, and supplies at this location, known as the Paint Store. John Covert worked there in 1934 and bought the business in 1939. He continued the funeral business until his death on December 10, 1993.

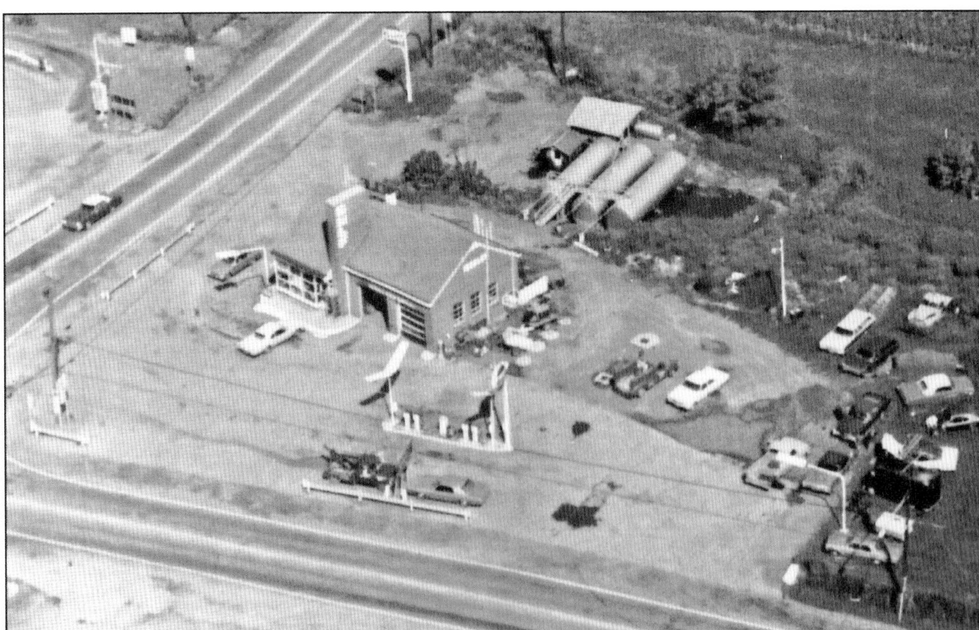

James and Lucille Slike acquired the Gulf gas station on the northeast corner of Route 96 and Route 414. It became a frequented business, being located at the crossroads of the north-south roads halfway between the ends of Seneca and Cayuga Lakes. The Slikes and their 10 children were active in the community. The gas station was sold after James died in 1978.

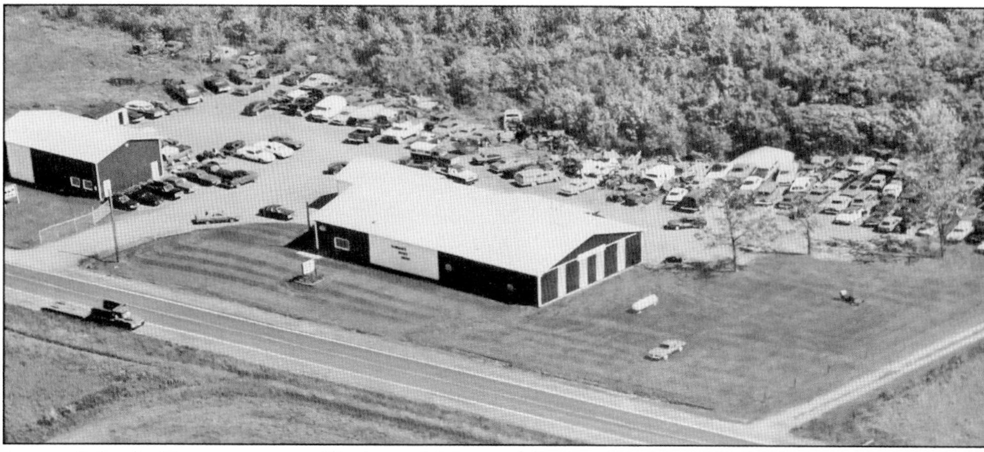

Ronnie's Body Shop was owned by Ronald Steve. The buildings were on the south side of Route 96, east of Ovid. In 1968, Ronald had a shop in a portion of the N.R. Boyce building where he did bodywork for customers. When the amount of work increased and more equipment was needed, he built his own business in 1980. The tow trucks required to bring vehicles to the shop were also used in his towing business.

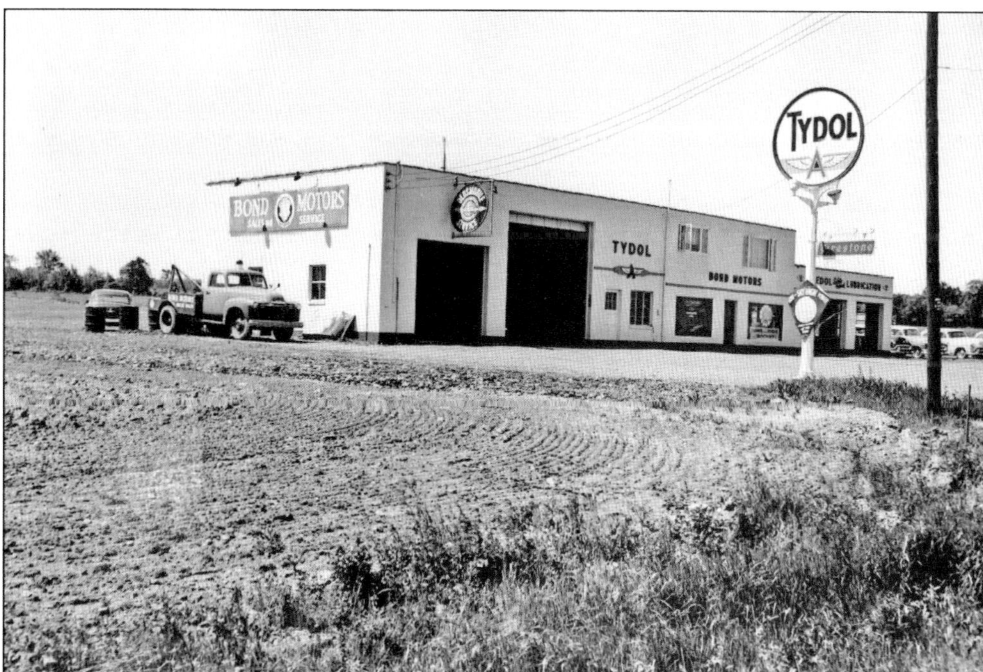

Miles J. Bond founded Bond Motors in September 1948. It was located on the south side of Route 96, between Ovid and Interlaken. He acquired the Oldsmobile franchise and did his own selling. When he added the Chevrolet franchise in 1958, full-time employees Thomas Rice, Harvey Brandt, and James Goodman were added. The part-time salesmen were Robert Shannon and Robert Covert.

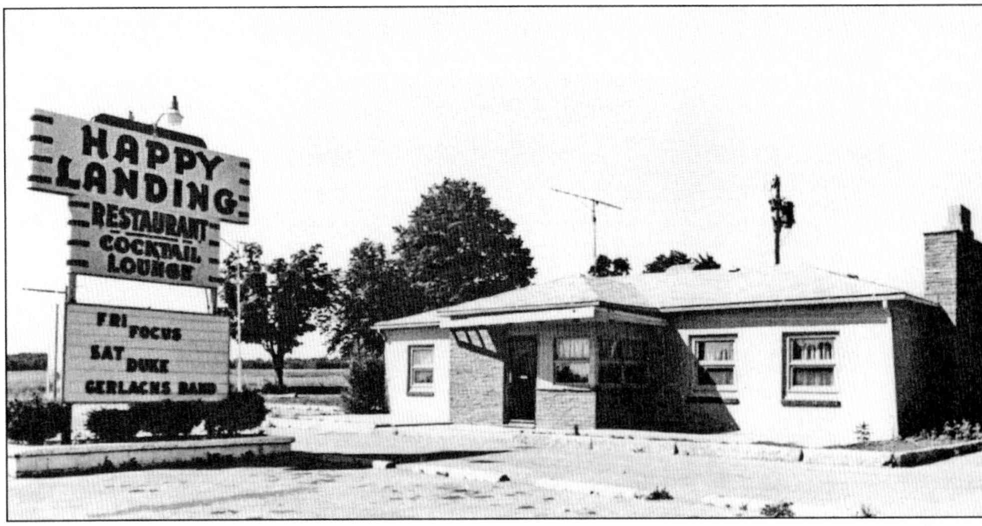

Happy Landing Restaurant, owned by Paul and Helen Smith, was at the southwest corner of Route 96 and County Road 139. In the 1950s, when the Seneca Army Depot and the Sampson Naval Base were nearby, it was a favorite place to eat. It was popular with local residents for many years but closed. In 1988, Robert and Phyllis Rainey reopened the restaurant, and it was frequented again for many years.

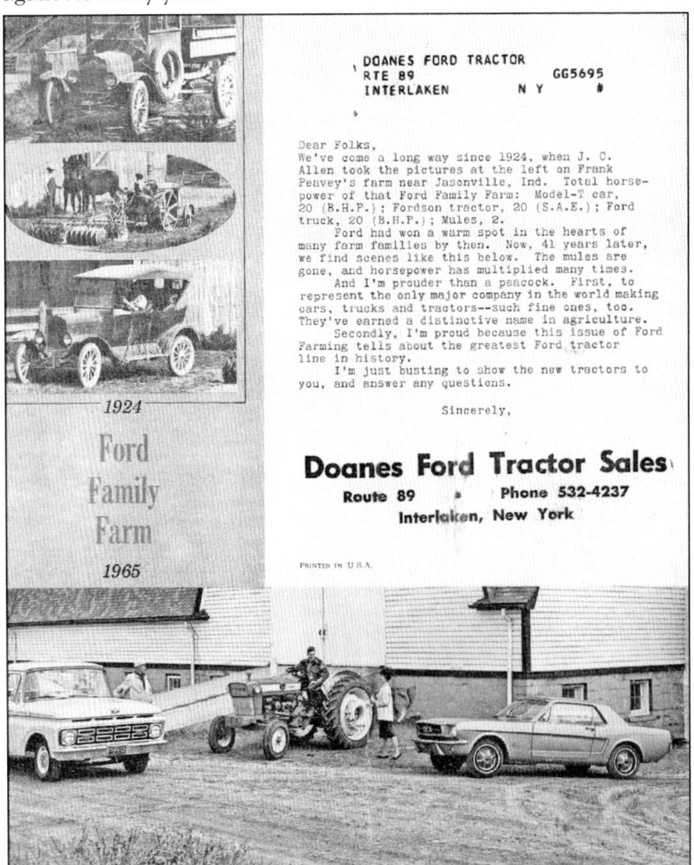

DOANES FORD TRACTOR
RTE 89 GG5695
INTERLAKEN N Y #

Dear Folks,
We've come a long way since 1924, when J. C. Allen took the pictures at the left on Frank Peavey's farm near Jasonville, Ind. Total horsepower of that Ford Family Farm: Model-T car, 20 (B.H.P.); Fordson tractor, 20 (S.A.E.); Ford truck, 20 (B.H.P.); Mules, 2.

Ford had won a warm spot in the hearts of many farm families by then. Now, 41 years later, we find scenes like this below. The mules are gone, and horsepower has multiplied many times.

And I'm prouder than a peacock. First, to represent the only major company in the world making cars, trucks and tractors--such fine ones, too. They've earned a distinctive name in agriculture.

Secondly, I'm proud because this issue of Ford Farming tells about the greatest Ford tractor line in history.

I'm just busting to show the new tractors to you, and answer any questions.

Sincerely,

Doanes Ford Tractor Sales
Route 89 Phone 532-4237
Interlaken, New York

PRINTED IN U.S.A.

1924
Ford
Family
Farm
1965

Robert Doane opened Doane's Ford Tractor Sales on Route 89 in 1965. He was quoted as saying "I'm prouder than a peacock" to represent the only major company in the world that makes cars, trucks, and tractors. "I'm just busting to show the new tractors to you, and answer any questions." He sold Ford tractors until Edwin Compton's business, Route 89 Auto, started in 1986. Compton repairs cars and trucks and is known for his wrecking and towing business. (Courtesy of Edwin Compton.)

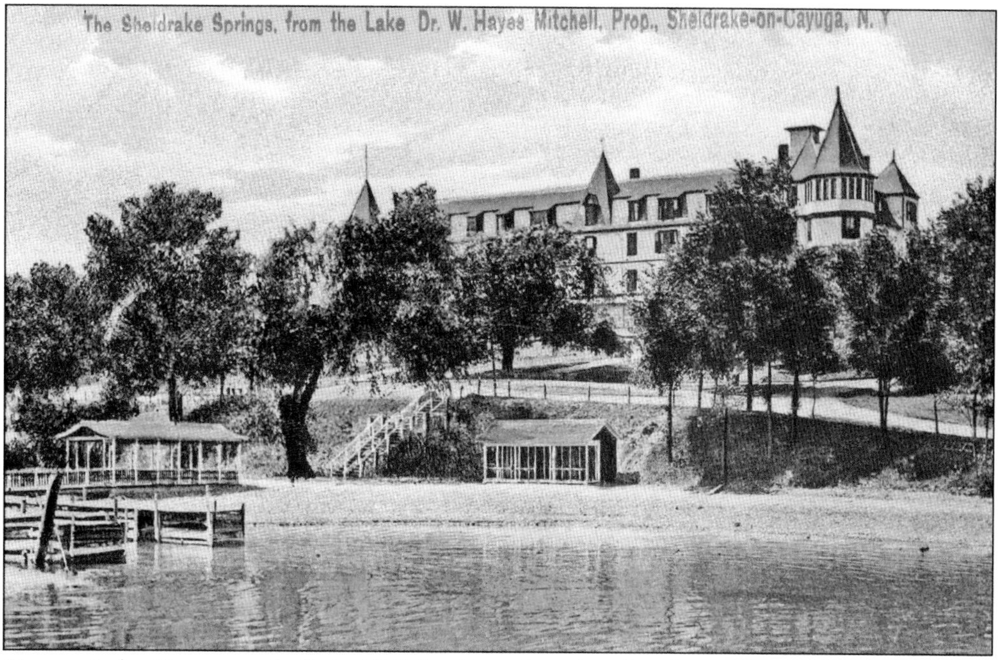

Cayuga Lake House was built in 1872 for Cornelius Rapalye, James Burroughs, and Charles Leverich. It was four stories tall and had a tower at each end and a long piazza that overlooked Cayuga Lake at Sheldrake. New York City families vacationed here, arriving on a steamboat and tally-ho coach to enjoy the golf course. On November 3, 1914, it burned to the ground.

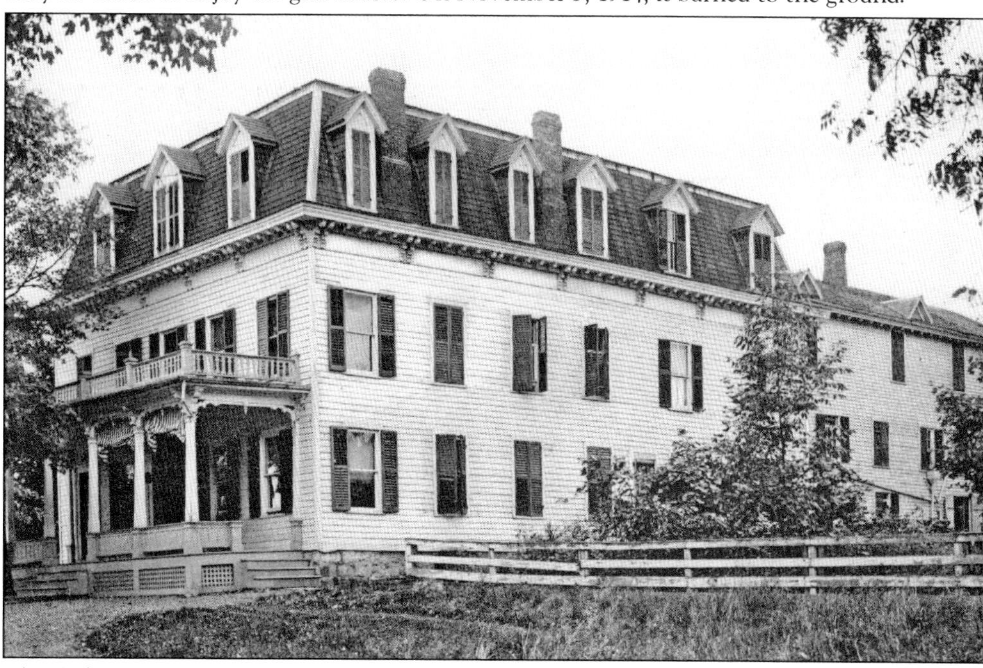

The Coleman Hotel was built at Kidders in 1852 by Horace Tracy. It was sold in 1867 to Myron Cole, previously the sheriff of Seneca County. He also owned the steamboat landing on Cayuga Lake across from the hotel. After Cole died in 1892, his niece Carrie Coleman and her son managed the establishment. It was sold in 1925 and burned down in 1972.

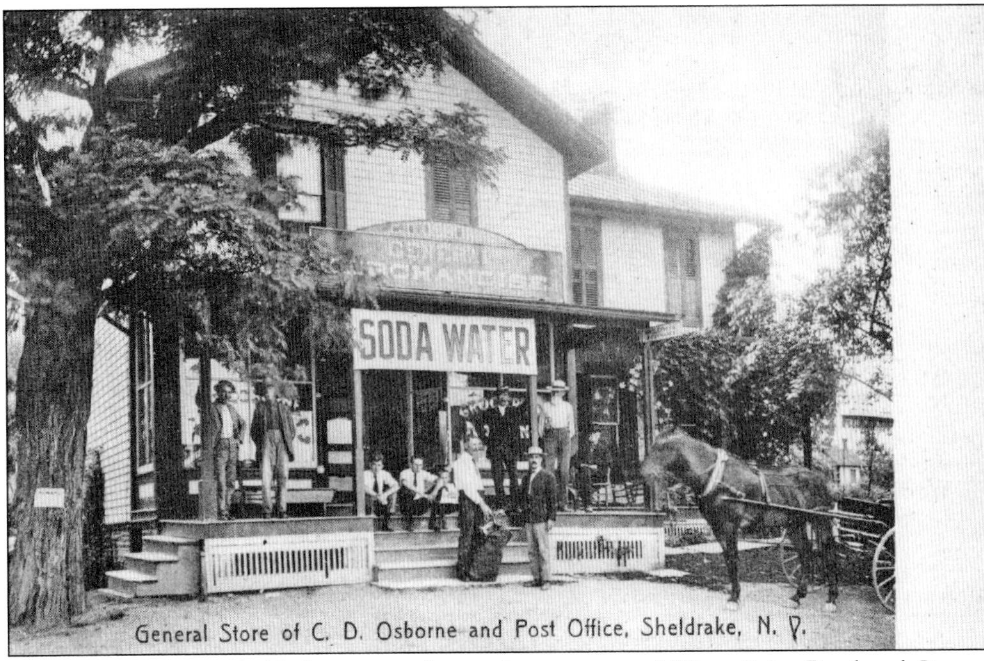

The general store in Sheldrake was on the northwest comer of Wyers Point Road and County Road 139. C.D. Osborne was the owner and the postmaster for Sheldrake. The sign "General Merchandise" aptly describes the items that were for sale. Groceries and many other items were available. The soda water must have been in great demand, judging by the size of the sign. Everyone pictured is unidentified, including the horse.

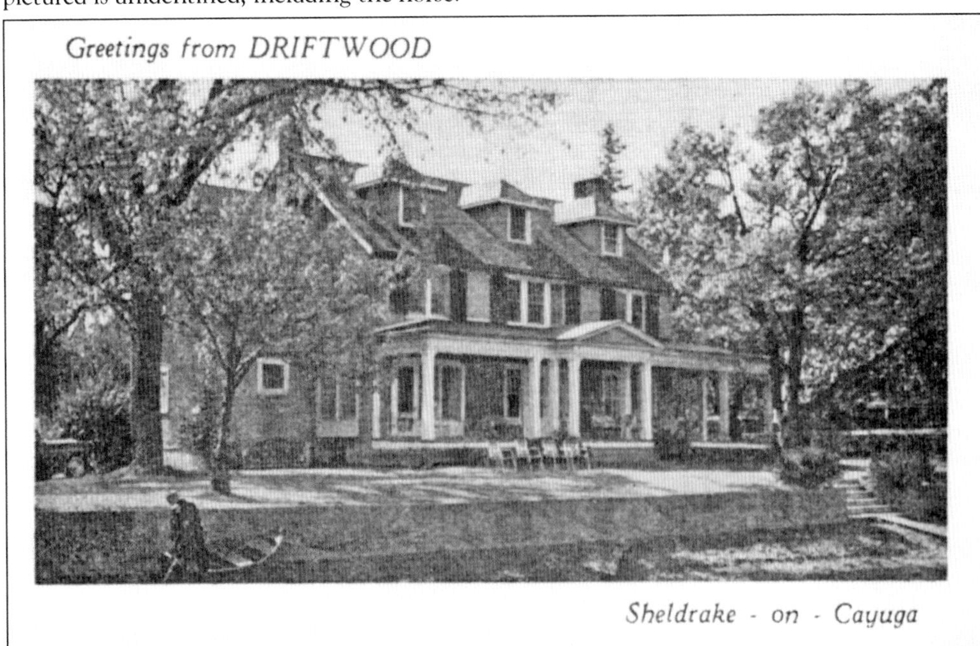

Driftwood Bed and Breakfast is on the shore of Cayuga Lake at Sheldrake. It is a stucco house built in 1913 by James and Elsie Robinson. First a family home, it has been a tourist haven for years. It has been operated by generations of the Robinson family.

Six

People

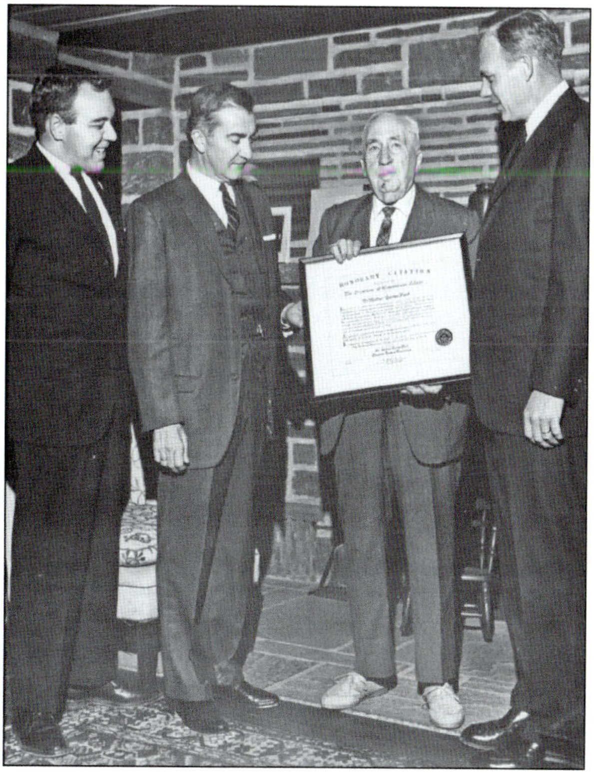

Dr. Walter Burton Ford received a certificate in recognition of his service as a charter trustee of Eisenhower College in nearby Seneca Falls, New York. Walter Ford was one of the most prominent mathematicians in the United States. He coauthored mathematics textbooks and taught mathematics at the University of Michigan for 35 years. He and his wife, Edith Banker Ford, a native of Ovid, built a stone house on Cayuga Lake in 1932. They lived there, where their two sons and families visited and where they retired in 1940. When Edith died in 1959, Dr. Ford donated money to build the Edith B. Ford Memorial Library in Ovid. He also donated the funds for the municipal building that held the fire department trucks, offices, and community rooms. Walter died in 1971 at the age of 97. He and his wife are buried in the Ovid Union Cemetery.

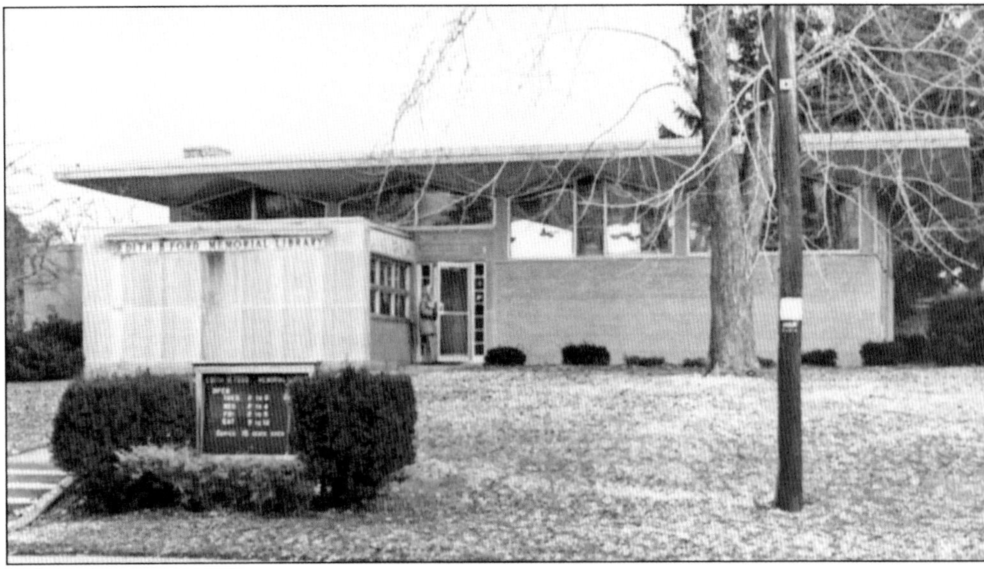

The Edith B. Ford Memorial Library was given by Walter B. Ford in memory of his wife. It is on the east side of North Main Street, where the original library was located in the home of James French. From 1905 until the move to the Ford Library in 1962, the library was in the county clerk's building, known as Mama Bear.

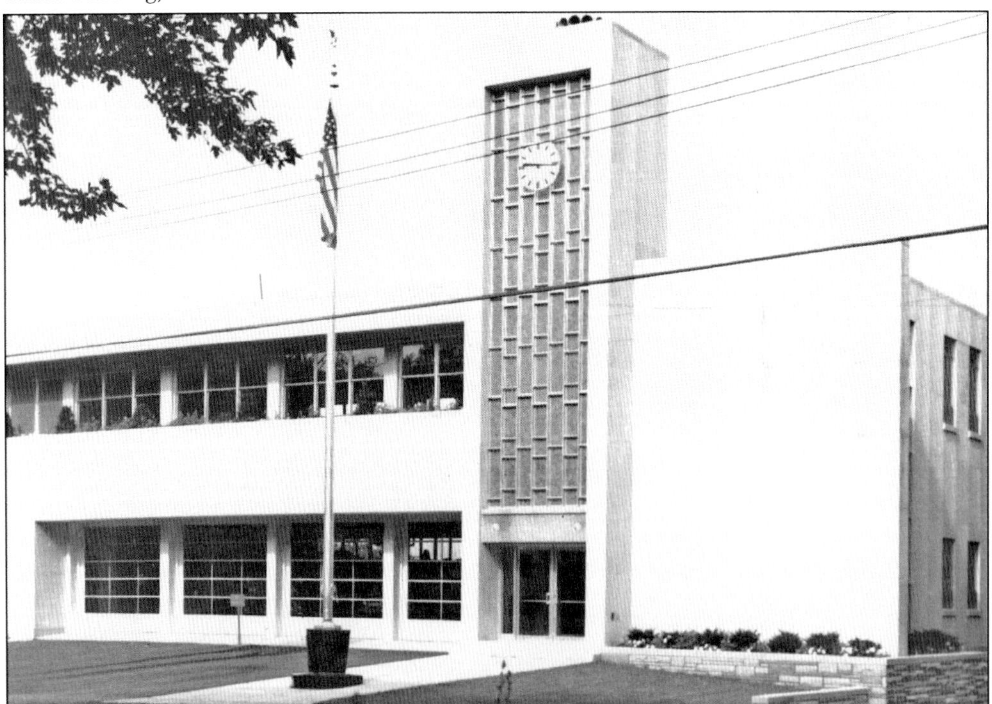

The Ovid Municipal Building was constructed in 1959, a gift to the village of Ovid from Dr. Walter B. and Edith B. Ford. The three stories were made of fireproof steel and concrete and faced with stone. The first floor became the home of the Ovid Fire Department and the department office. A large meeting room and kitchen occupied the second floor. The structure was a beautiful addition to the west side of North Main Street.

Dr. Claudius Coan was born in Massachusetts in 1794, the same year the town of Ovid was incorporated. He studied medicine in Canandaigua, New York, and opened a practice in 1816. The Coan family lived in the brick home of John McMath from 1835 until his death on February 28, 1878. This location, south of the village of Ovid, became known as Coan Corners.

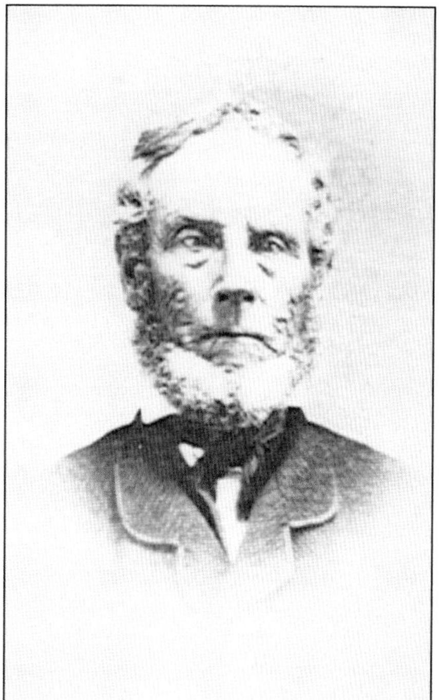

Dr. Claudius C. Coan

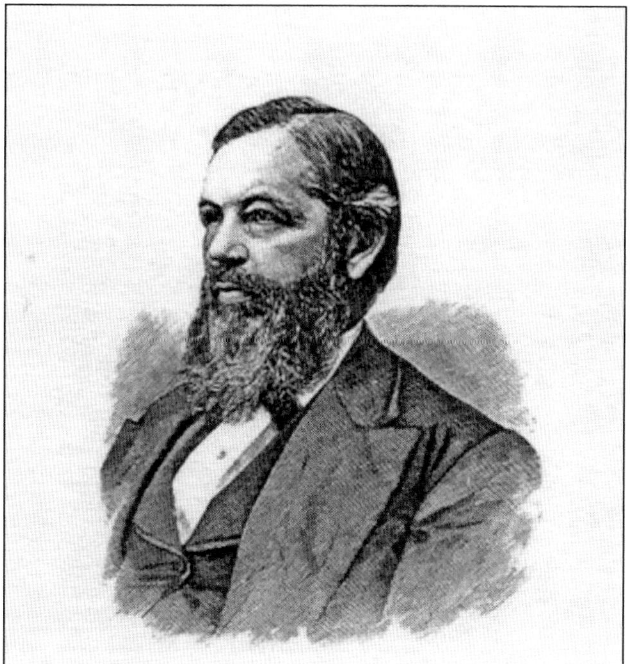

PROF. THOMAS R. LOUNSBURY.

Thomas Raynesford Lounsbury was born in Ovid on January 1, 1838. He graduated from Yale University in 1859 and became a well-known professor of English and literature at Yale. He also received degrees from Harvard and Princeton. His publications include *Life of James Fennimore Cooper* and *Standard Pronunciation of English*, which he wrote in 1904. He died in 1915 in New Haven, Connecticut.

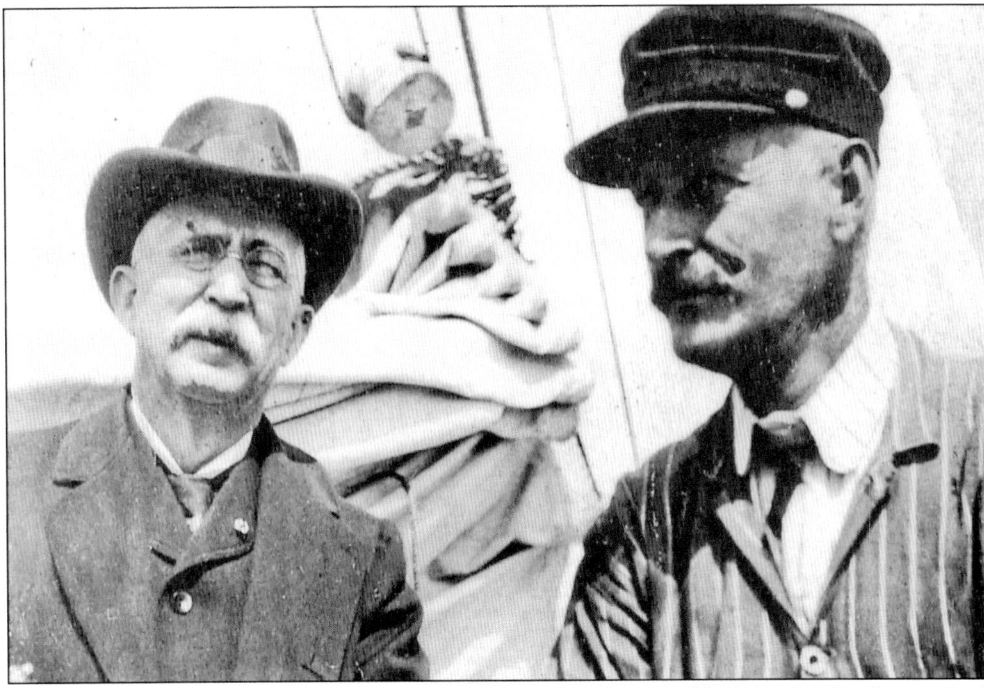

George Westinghouse (left) and Capt. James Quick are by the sails of the *Busy Bee* ferryboat, which brought Westinghouse across Cayuga Lake. He visited his brother Herman Westinghouse, who lived in a huge house that was acquired in 1899. The two brothers worked on many inventions in Herman's barn. George invented the air brake and founded the Westinghouse Electric Corporation. (Courtesy of Phyllis Betzler.)

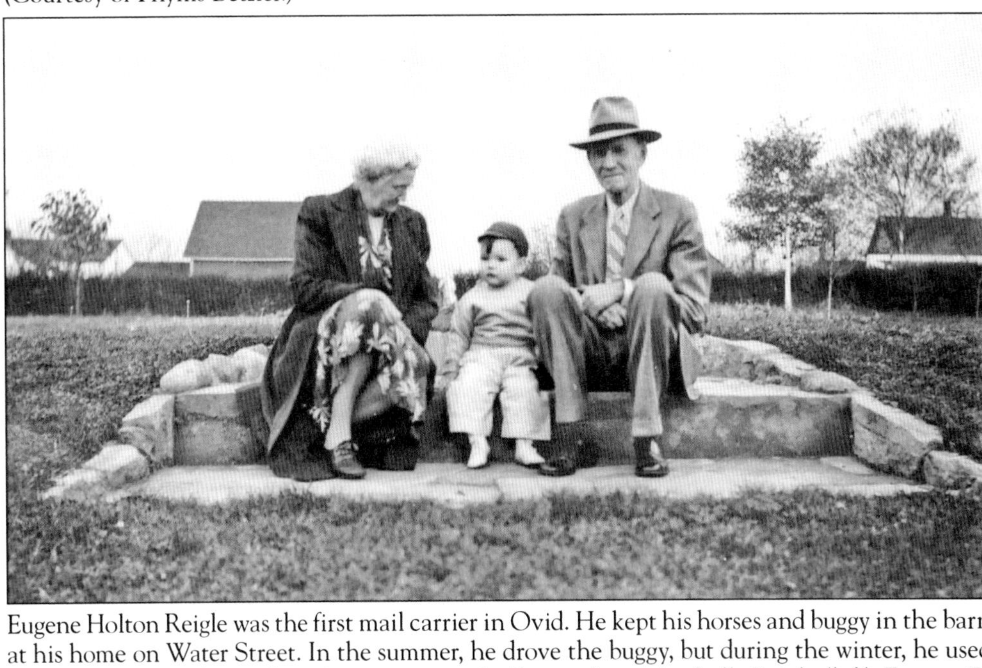

Eugene Holton Reigle was the first mail carrier in Ovid. He kept his horses and buggy in the barn at his home on Water Street. In the summer, he drove the buggy, but during the winter, he used a sleigh to deliver the mail on the country roads. Pictured are Marybelle Reigle (left), Eugene C. Reigle, and E.H. Reigle. (Courtesy of Eugene Clifford Reigle.)

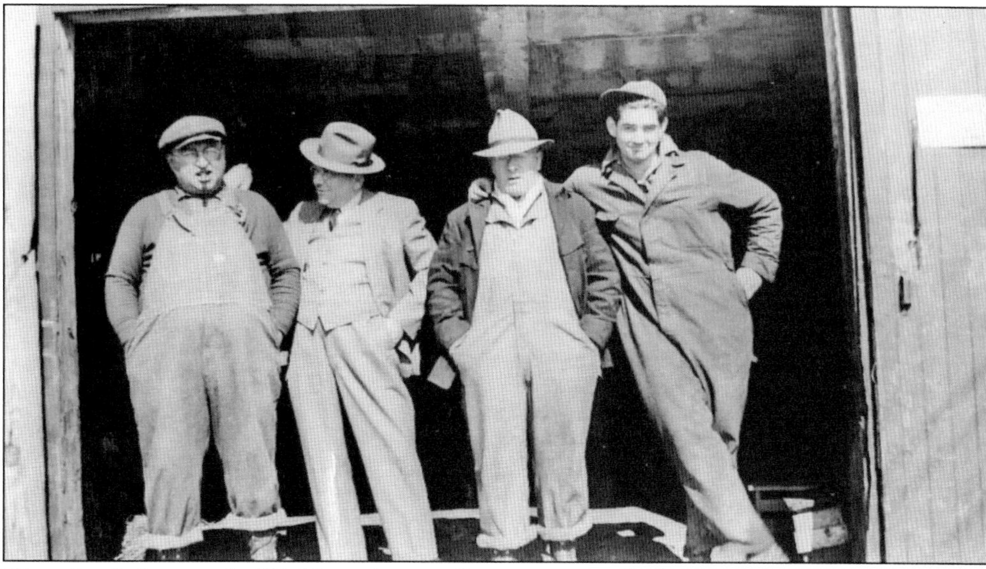

These four helpers at the Wickham Auction House appear to be having a great time working with one another. They may have had a successful day at the auction, with nothing out of the ordinary going wrong. They are, from left to right, Leon McCullriegh, Wesley Upham, Jack McArdle, and Keith Wickham. (Courtesy of Jack Wickham.)

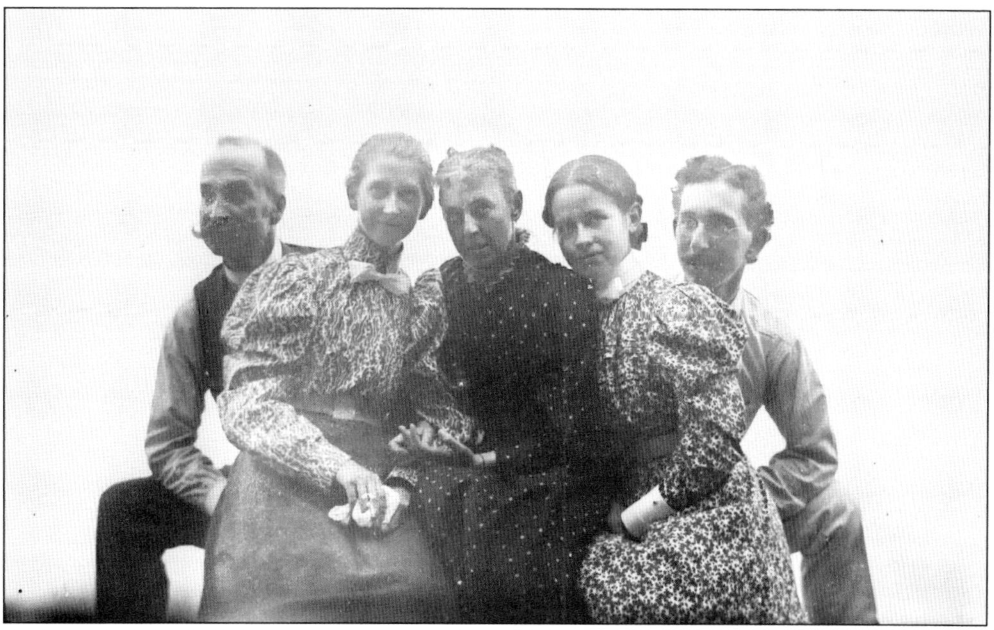

William W., Maude V., Florence S., Pauline H., and an unidentified man are seen here. They are best known for the hardware store that they co-owned in Ovid. William sold many handmade tinwares, tools, stoves, groceries, and gasoline. He also did general jobbing and repairing. The family also worked alongside him.

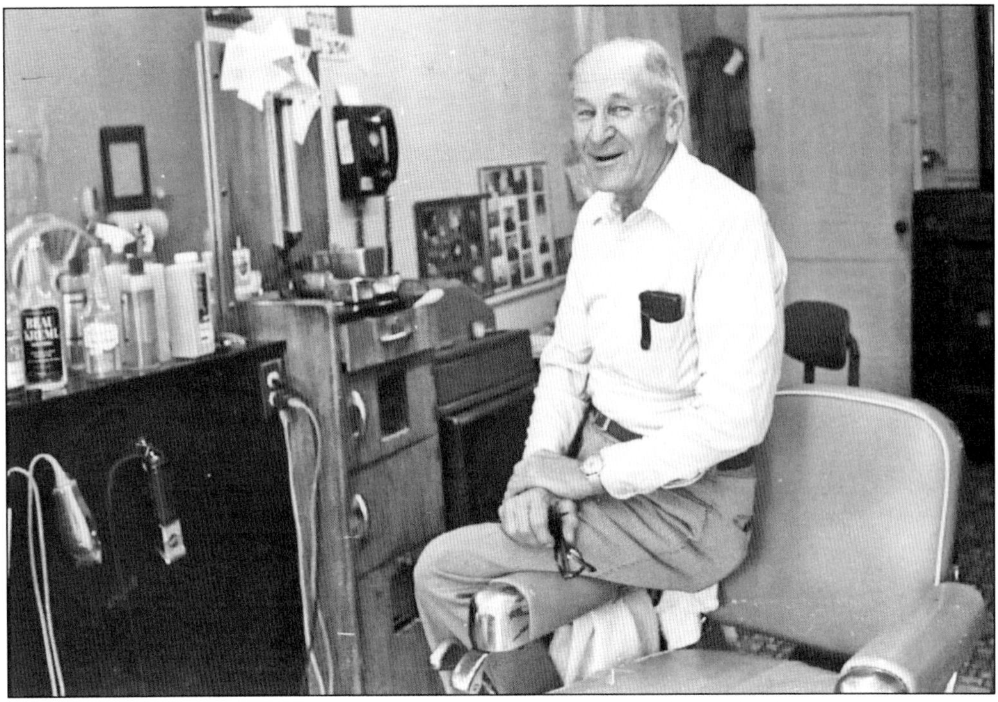

Stanley Gorski is amused by something as his picture is being taken in his barbershop on South Main Street. Gorski cut hair from the mid-1940s until he sold the business in 1989. The tiny building that held the barbershop can still be found on Main Street.

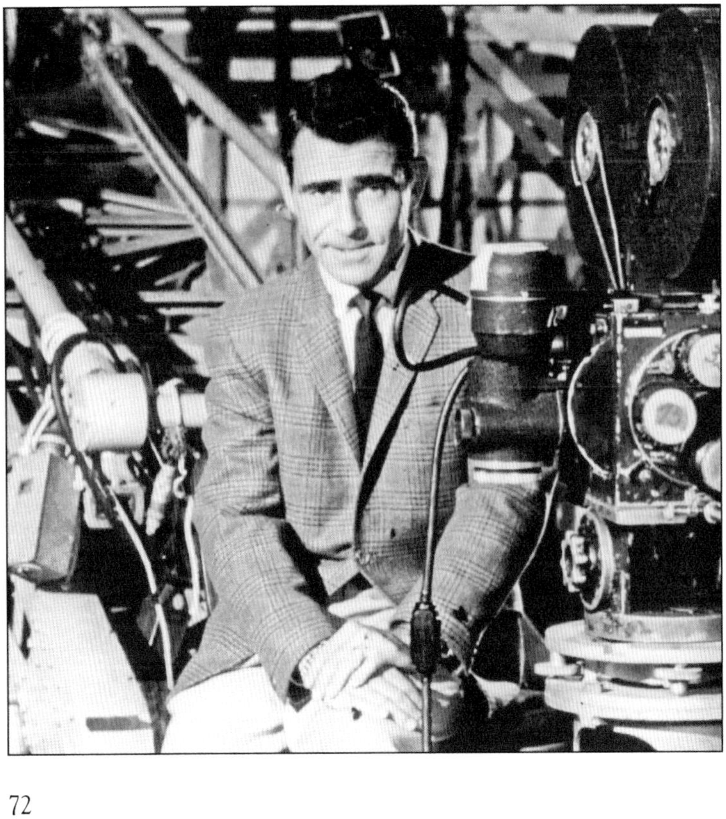

Rodman Edward "Rod" Serling was born on Christmas Day 1924, in Syracuse, New York. He met his future wife, Carol Kramer, at Antioch College in Ohio. She lived with her grandparents and summered in their home at Kidders, Wahuta. Rod was a prolific writer here and in California, where he created the TV program *Twilight Zone*. He had a heart attack at the Cayuga Lake cottage and died in Rochester, New York, in June 1975. (Courtesy of Carol Serling.)

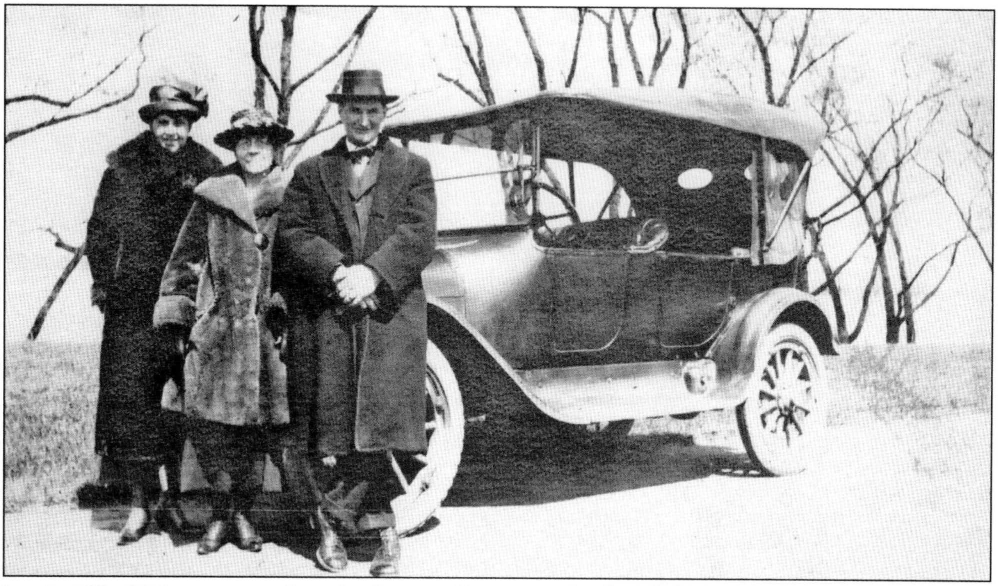

Lewis Alfred Morgan served as the Seneca County undersheriff from 1927 to 1931. He, his wife, Luella, and their youngest son, 14-year-old Lewis Jr., lived in the sheriff's quarters on the second floor of the courthouse. Lewis owned and operated a farm on Morgan Road. He was active in the Farm Bureau and was a dealer in Ayrshire dairy cattle.

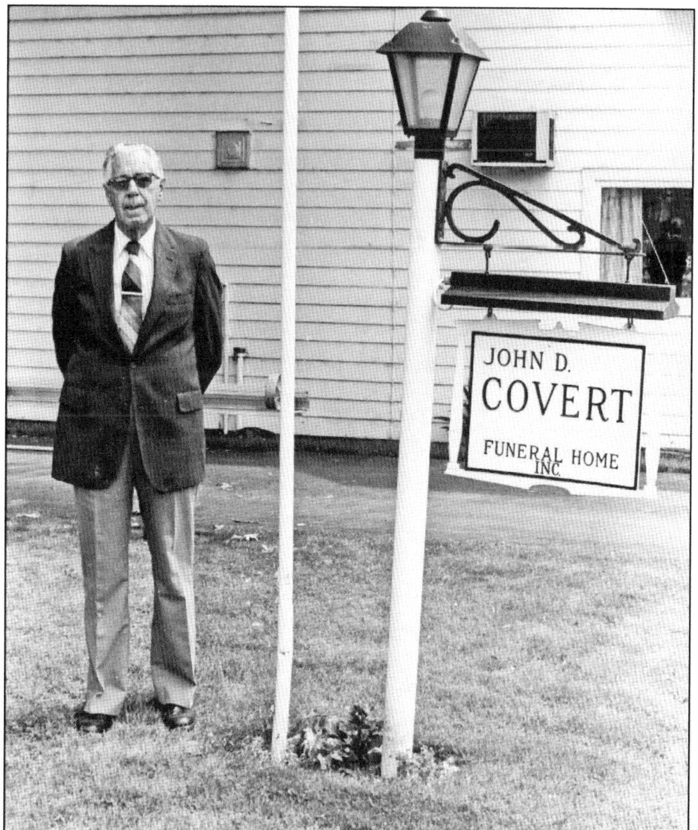

John D. Covert was a funeral director in Ovid for many years. He is shown standing by the funeral home sign on the east side of South Main Street. He began working for undertaker Lee Early in 1934. Covert was employed by Early until 1939, when the business was put up for sale. Covert purchased the funeral home, and it was incorporated in 1969. The funeral home was family operated until his death on December 10, 1993.

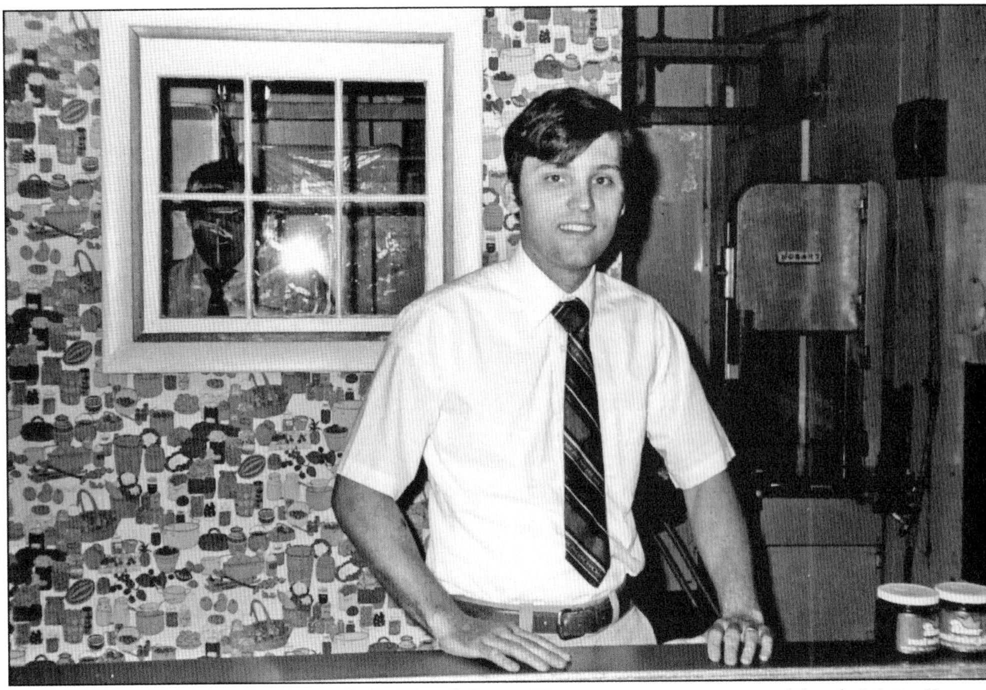

David Chalker was the owner of the Ovid Super-Duper grocery store on North Main Street. There have been numerous grocery stores in Ovid, his being the only one on the east side of the street. It shared a driveway with the new post office, so there were many races to find a parking place during the peak hours.

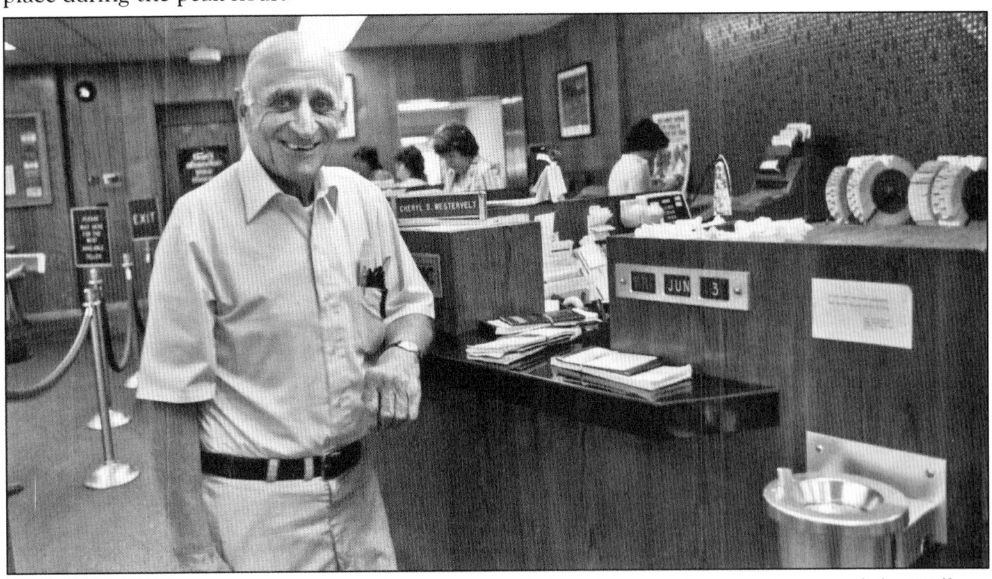

Lawrence Wilkins was the supervisor for the Town of Ovid for over 20 years. He owned the Wilkins farm south of Ovid. Working on the farm did not keep him from being totally involved in the duties of his office. Jay's Soda Bar was frequented to find the political wishes of the residents. He also enjoyed various activities in Ovid. One of his favorites was assisting in hanging the village Christmas streetlights. His tractor and lift were used to attach the old-fashioned lanterns to every pole on Main Street.

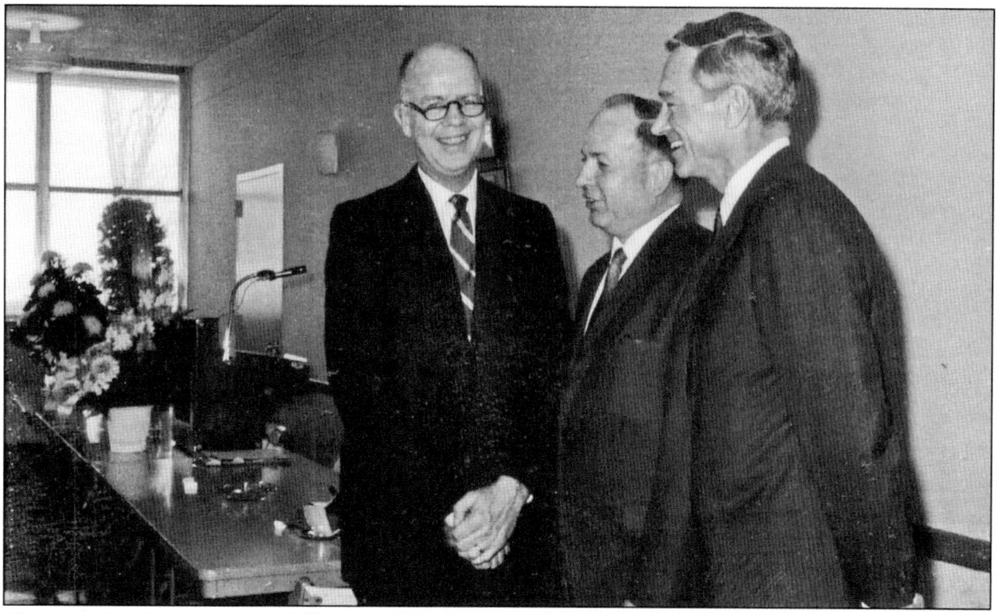

The new brick Ovid Post Office, on North Main Street, was dedicated on January 21, 1970. Previously, the post office had been located in a building on South Main Street. There was very little parking available at that location, so a property with good parking space was selected. Postmaster William Fritz (left) is being congratulated by Post Office Department officer Dean Fleming (center) and Congressman Samuel Stratton (right).

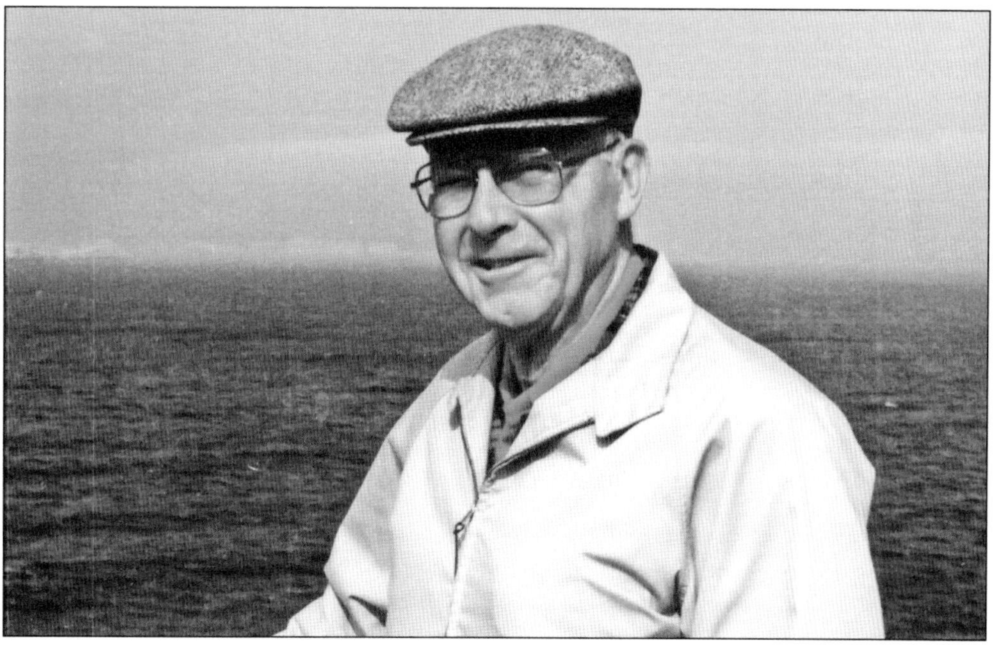

Benjamin Franklin was the fourth generation of his family to practice law in Ovid. In 1854, his great-grandfather George W. Franklin was the first lawyer in the Franklin family. His grandfather Benjamin Franklin became a lawyer in 1887. George T. Franklin, his father, was a lawyer in 1920. Benjamin was admitted to the bar in 1953 and was still in his law office in 1994. (Courtesy of Carol Franklin.)

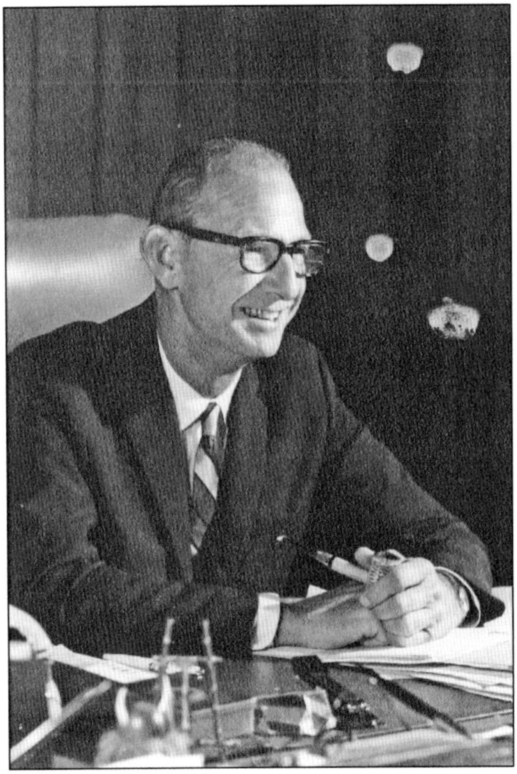

Theodore Day was born in New York City in 1917. He was a dairy farmer in this area when he became the owner of the farm of his great-grandfather Charles Duncan Leverich. From 1966 until 1972, Day was a member of the US Senate. Later, he was appointed assistant New York State commissioner of agriculture and markets.

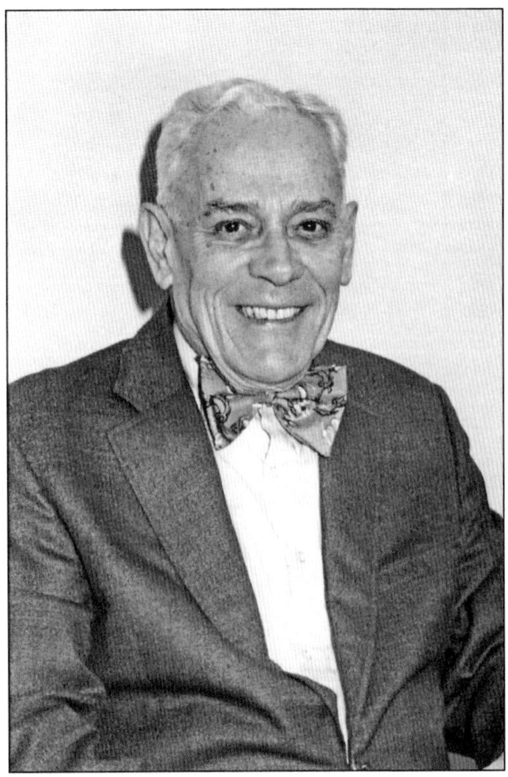

John McCauley retired from the Willard Psychiatric Center as the business officer. He started a second career as a highly qualified tax preparer. He ran his tax preparation business for about 15 years. Donalie Kelly worked as a tax preparer with John during the last four years of the practice. She began her own tax business when he retired the second time.

Harriet Coryell and her husband, Ralph Coryell, were the owners of the Coryell Funeral Home on South Main Street. She was very civic-minded in all community activities and played in the Senior Citizens Kitchen Band. She was most active in connection with the community plays that were produced every summer. Following the final night of each play, everyone connected with the production was invited to her home for refreshments and a viewing of the play that had been recorded.

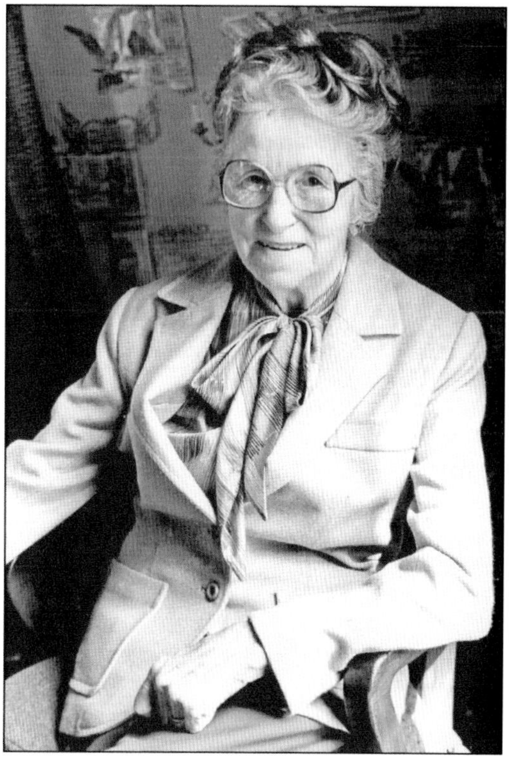

Dr. Willis Allen began his medical practice in 1952. He had an office on North Main Street but made house calls if they were requested. He was the school physician at the nearby Ovid Central School but also delivered babies in hospitals up to 15 to 20 miles away. Upon retiring, Allen was quoted as saying, "I experienced the golden age of medicine from 'the practice of' to the 'business of medicine.'"

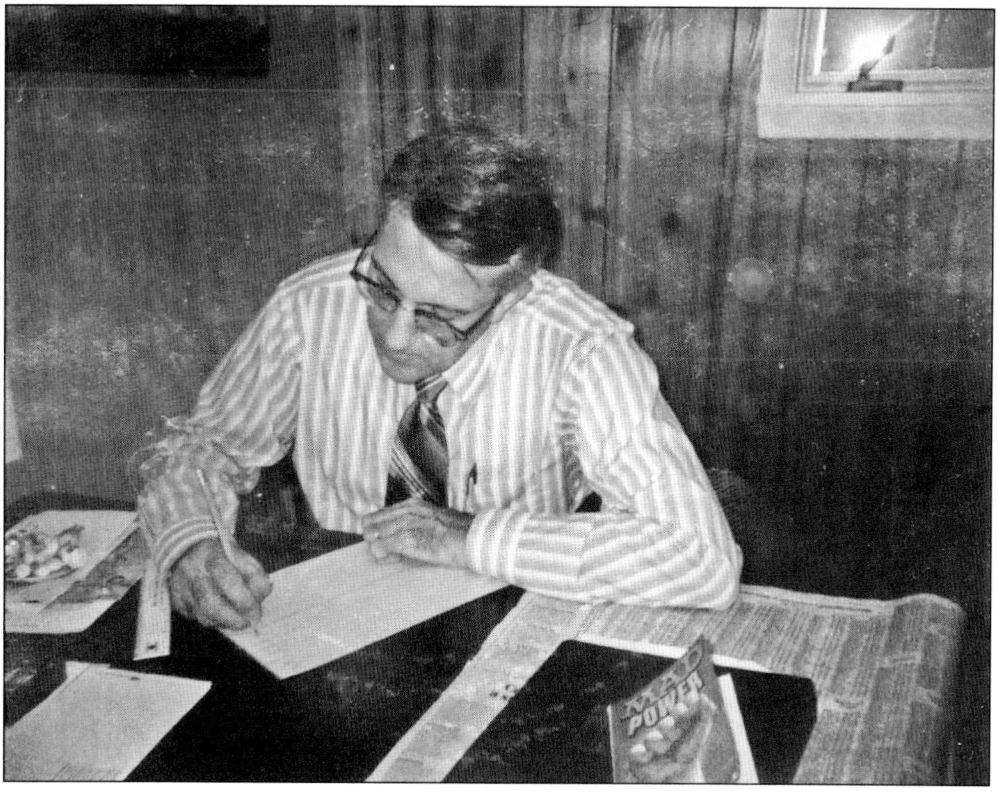

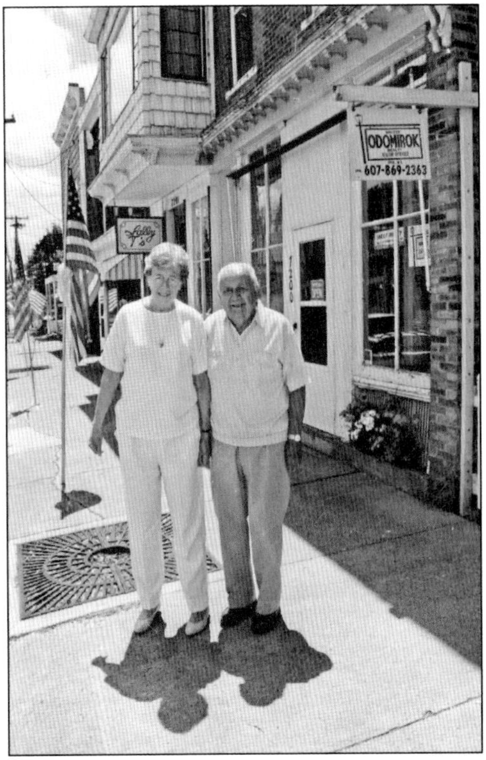

Walter Odomirok came to the Finger Lakes area when he was stationed at the Sampson military base. He met and married his wife, Shirley, and remained here for the rest of his life. They managed the Odomirok Real Estate business from their office on South Main Street, where this photograph was taken.

Robert Harman is a native of Ovid, where he lived with his parents as a child. He moved to California and became an art teacher, illustrator, and stage actor. Harman became great friends with many famous movie stars and drew caricatures of his fellow performers. He retired in Ovid but continued sending hand-drawn Christmas cards to those he knew in Hollywood. Harman (foreground) is shown in 1971 with, from left to right, Mertie Bloomer; his mother, Lottie Lee Harman; and Laura Chapman.

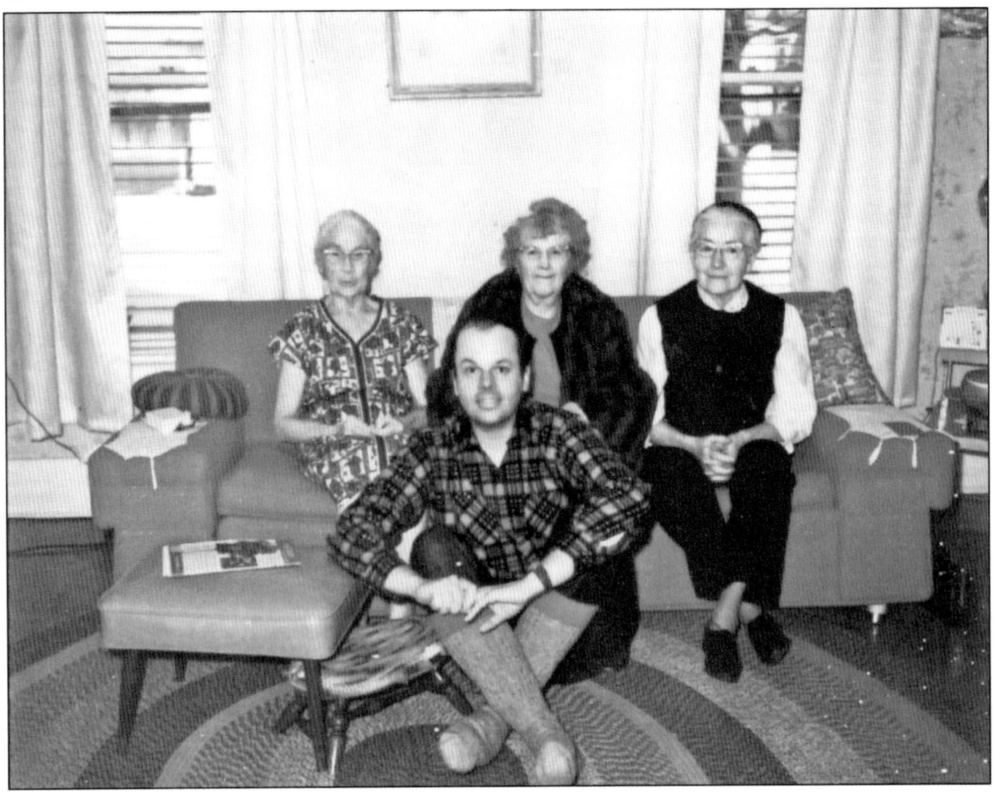

Wayne E. Morrison Sr. was a publisher and printer. He and his wife, Patricia, are standing on the porch entrance of their shop in their Greek Revival home. They purchased the business from Stephen McKeel in 1971. Wayne has written history books on the towns of Ovid, Covert, Lodi Romulus, Varick, and Fayette. He obtained the right to reprint the *Old History of Seneca County* and several other counties in New York State.

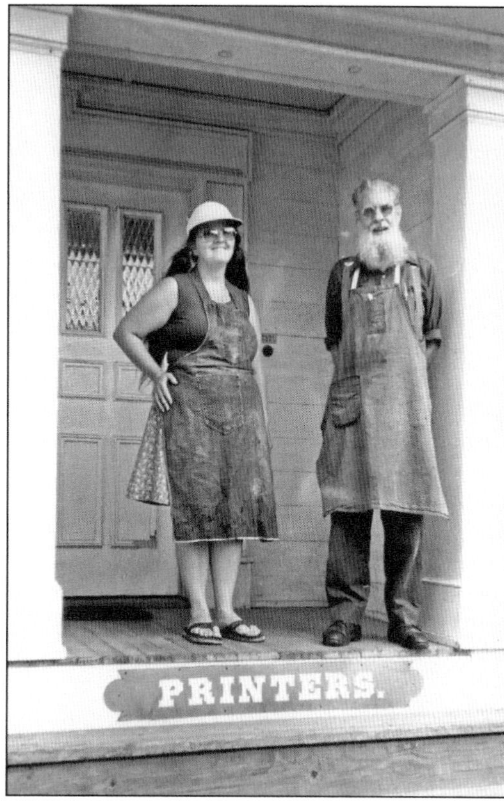

The Morrisons are using the old printing machines in their shop. Patricia is printing on the job press, which is used to make cards, envelopes, tickets, and postcards. Wayne is using another type of letter press called a Heidelberg printing press. It is used to produce larger items such as the Roxin Printers calendars and the calendars that were given each Christmas. The usual projects, which are done each year, are the writing and printing of history-related books and pamphlets.

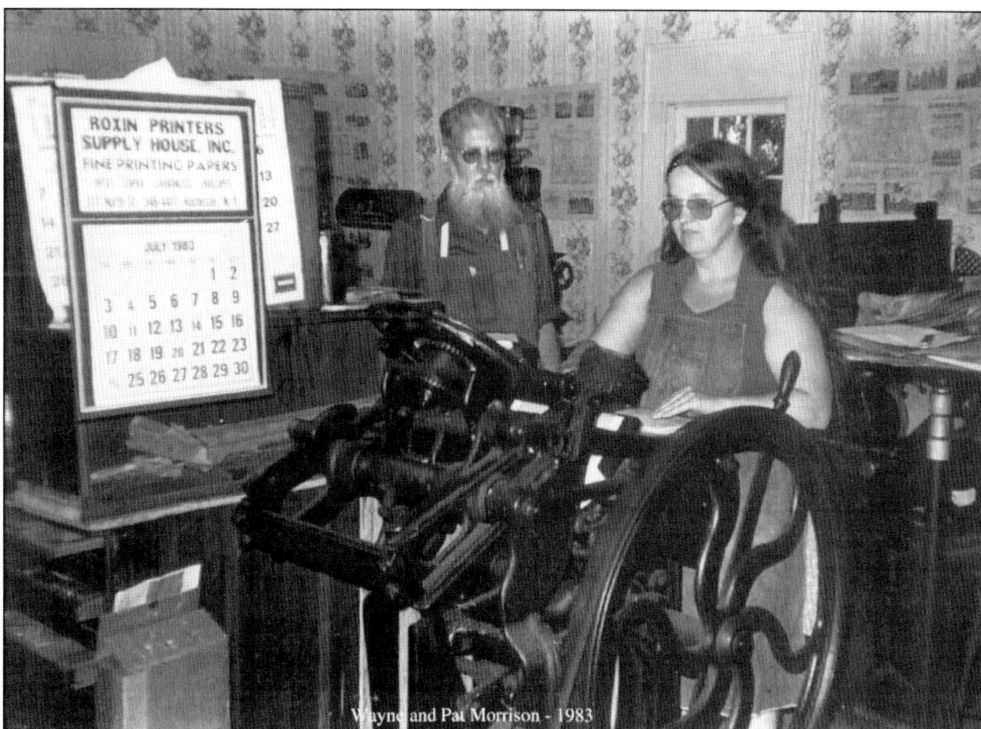

Wayne and Pat Morrison - 1983

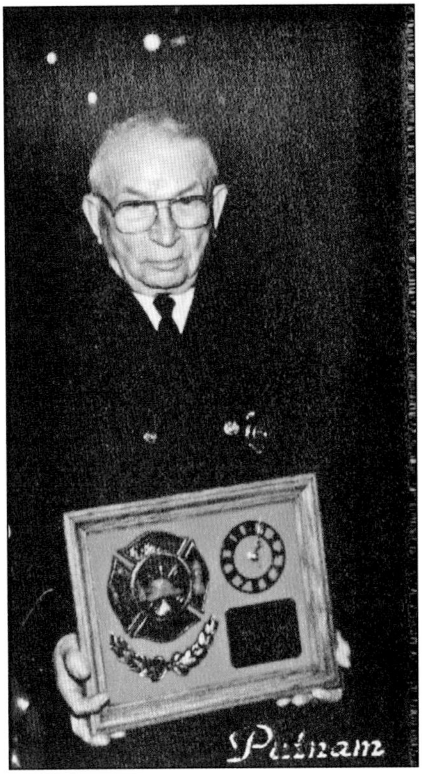

Claude Cassidy is honored by the New York State Firemen's Association as the oldest and longest-active fireman in the state. He has many other age-related honors in Ovid and Seneca County. Claude has lived in Ovid his entire life, and therefore he naturally is the oldest and has the longest membership in the church, the Lions Club, and every organization of which he was a member.

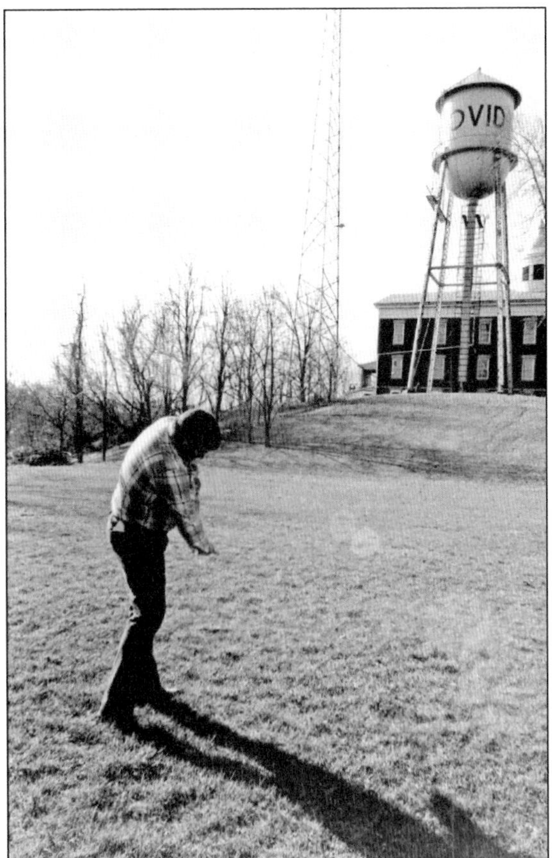

The old Ovid water tower on the hill beside the courthouse must have been there for many years. The day that it was demolished, Claude Cassidy was a spectator. He remarked, "I watched them build it when it first went up, and I am here to watch it come down!"

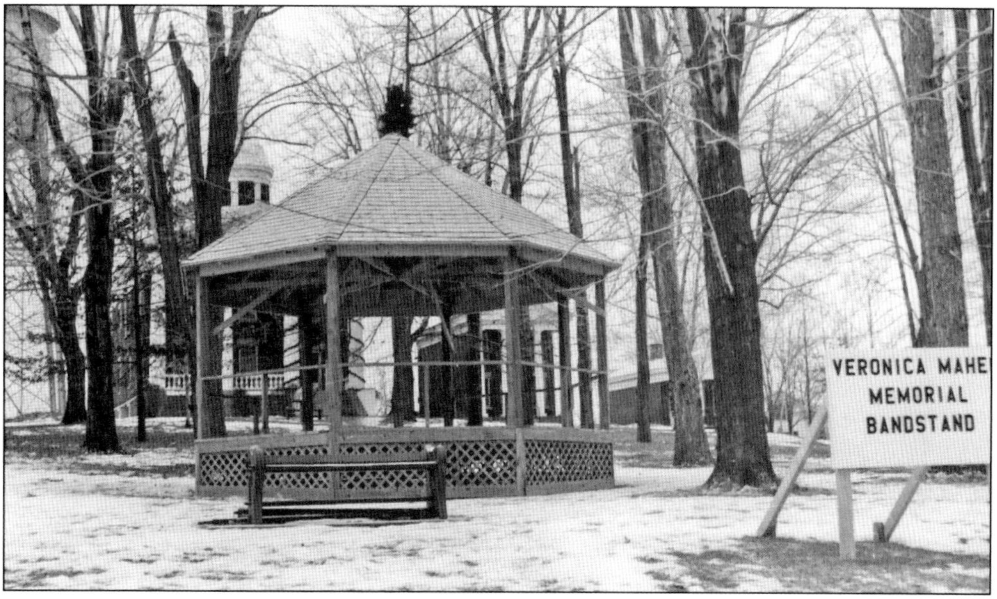

Veronica Maher graduated from college in 1919 and accepted a position with the American Red Cross in Rochester, New York. In 1941, she became the executive director of the Red Cross in Rochester and Monroe County. She held the job until retiring in 1963. Veronica founded the first National Civilian Blood Program for the Red Cross in 1948. She was the first person to donate blood. After retiring, she returned to Ovid to live and volunteered in many Seneca County organizations.

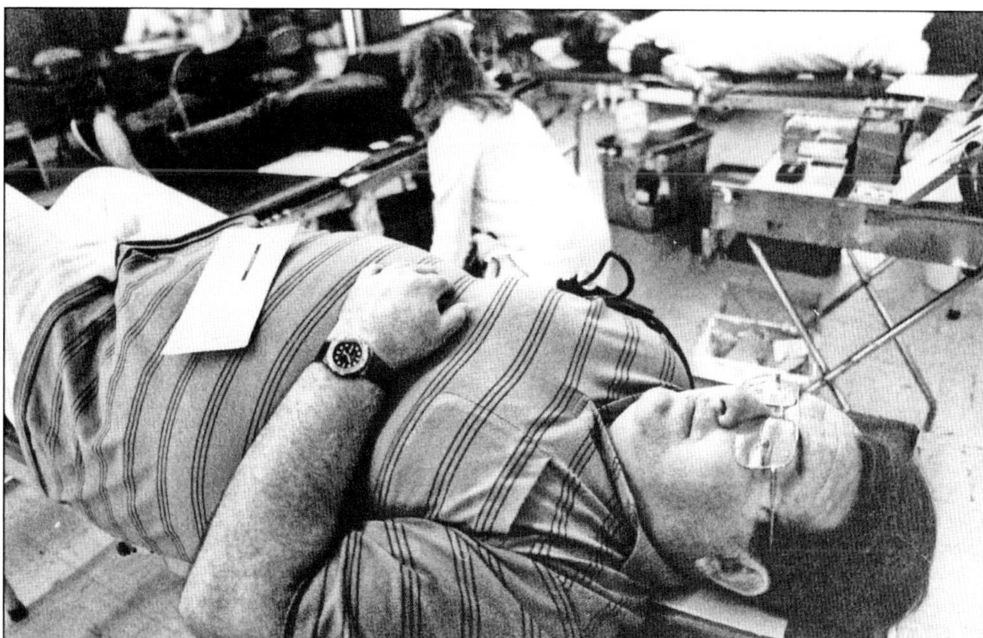

Veronica Maher would have been pleased to learn that there are frequent blood drives in Ovid. There are several residents who have donated gallons of blood during the years that the drives have been held. William Warne is pictured here attending the blood drive at the Ovid Federated Church. Warne started donating blood in the 1950s and has given over 13 gallons.

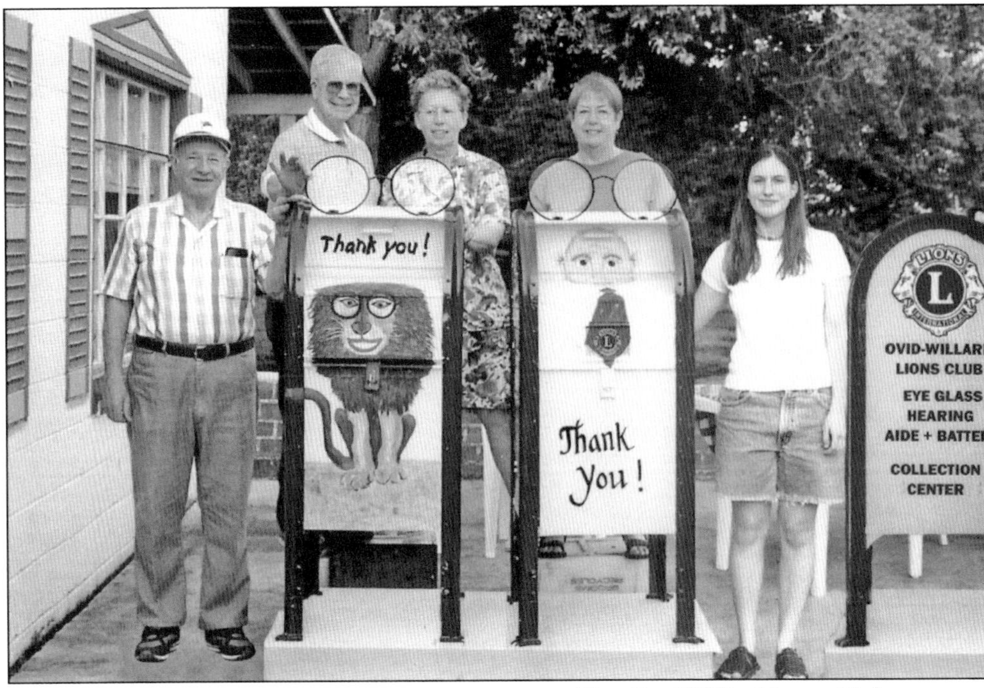

The Ovid-Willard Lions Club supports the eyeglass and hearing aid program. Local artists painted the amusing characters on old mailboxes. Placed outside business entrances, they remind everyone to donate their used items for distribution by the Lions. From left to right, chairman Howard Boyce, artists John and Frances Ratcliffe and Kathy Greule, and text artist Becky Woodard are pictured here.

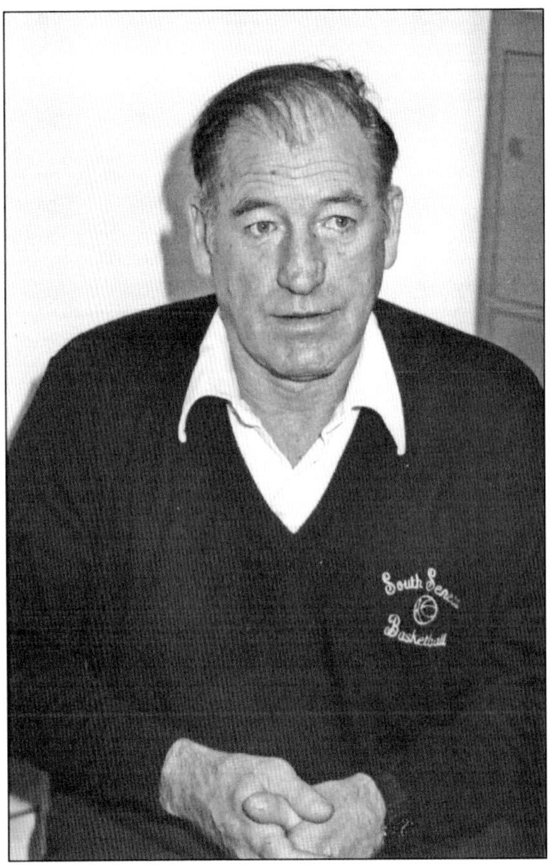

John Guinan graduated from Ovid Central School in 1952. He entered the Ithaca College Business School, went to the Naval Aviation Flight School, and received his wings in 1956. He returned to Ithaca College and received his master's degree in 1967. Guinan began teaching physical education in Interlaken, and in 1969, he moved to the South Seneca Central School, where he remained his entire career. The South Seneca Central School gymnasium was dedicated to him. He was League Coach of the Year six times and is enshrined in the Section V Hall of Fame.

Seven

MILITARY

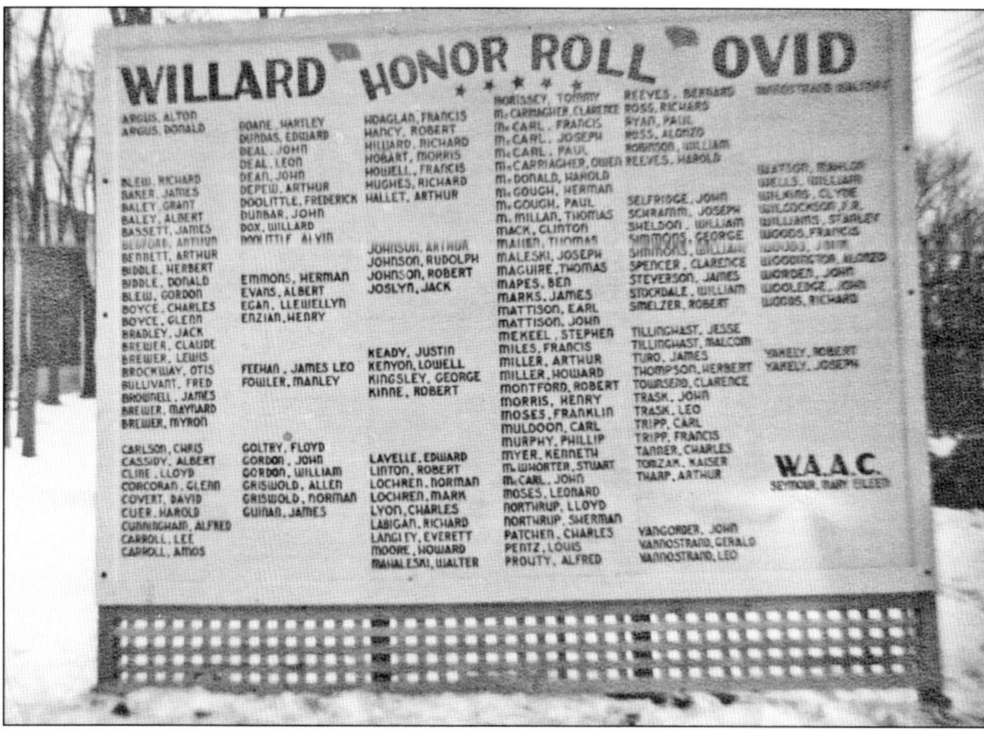

The 1944 senior class of Ovid Central School organized a fundraiser asking for pledges of $5 to make a world wars honor roll plaque. Students and teachers Clara Depew and Margaret Mannix selected the design, while Elliott Johnson assembled the 295 names. The local men and women listed served in World War I or World War II.

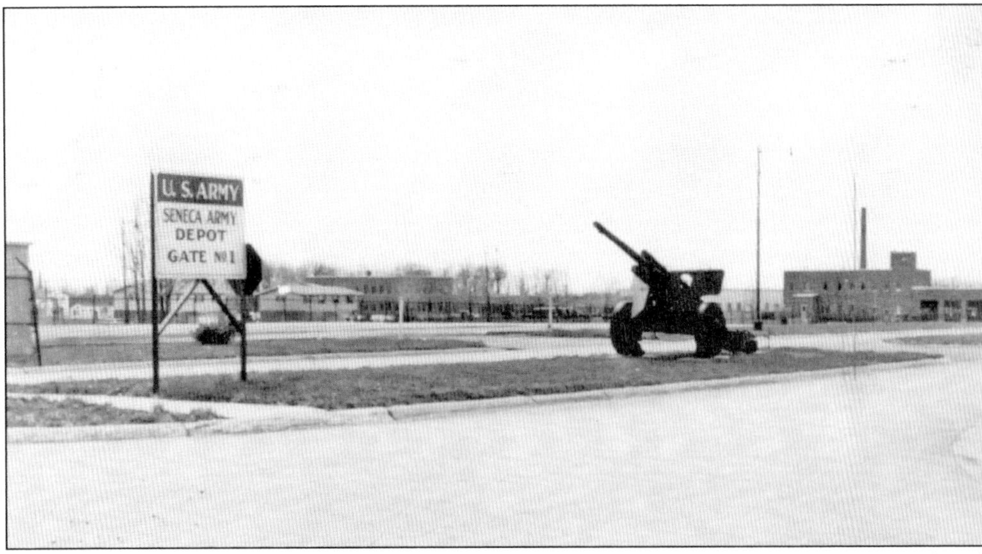

The Seneca Army Depot was just north of the village of Ovid. In documents associated with military training in the area, federal government officials refer to Ovid as "a sleepy local town that became a boom town." The 10,000-acre facility was built in 1941. Farms, homes, two churches, three schools, and 100 families were dispossessed. The depot was used for munitions storage and disposal, which required 500 troops and civilian men and women to maintain. It was finally closed on September 30, 2000.

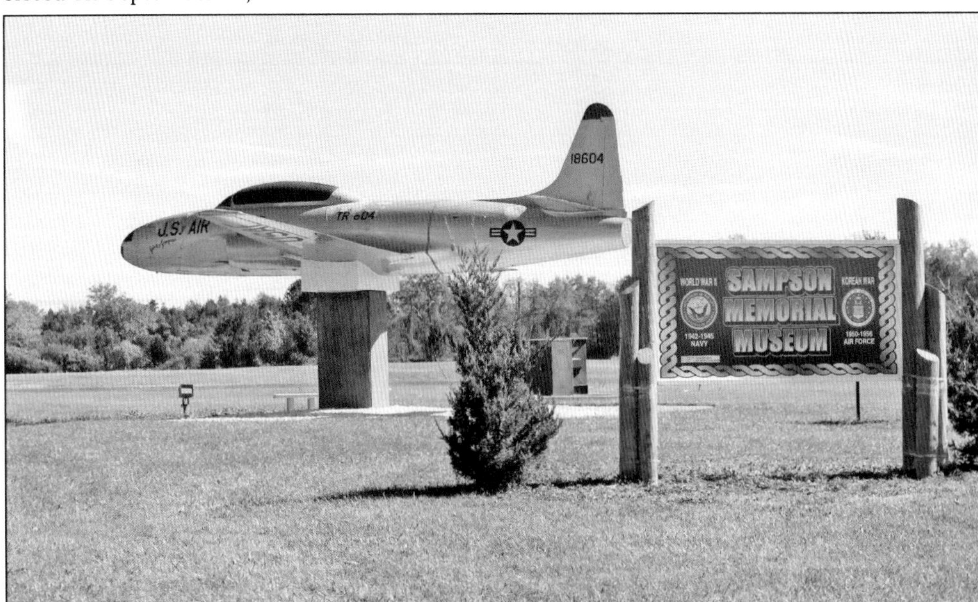

Sampson Naval Training Station was established in 1942. The property was on the shore of Seneca Lake, which was more than 600 feet deep. That made it an ideal spot for training in the water. The 26 acres were used to train 400,000 recruits during its World War II operation. Sampson Air Force Base was opened at the same location in 1950, during the Korean War. Before it closed in 1956, three hundred thousand airmen were trained. The original main gate still remains at the entrance to Sampson State Park. With those numbers from the Seneca Army Depot and the Sampson military bases, one can imagine that the once sleepy little town became a boomtown.

The Sullivan Trail marker, installed along highways by the New York State Education Department in 1926, cites the prehistory of the town of Ovid. George Washington sent General Sullivan on the expedition to clear Indians from the middle of New York State—the Finger Lakes region and where the future village of Ovid would be located. (Courtesy of the Seneca County Historian Office.)

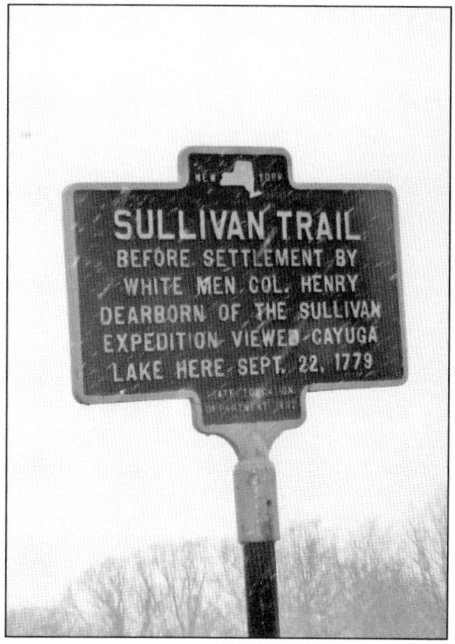

The Sons of the Union Veterans have a museum in Baby Bear, the smallest of the Three Bears courthouse complex. The Civil War organization has been meeting for more than 100 years. The official group name, since 1914, is Sons of the Union Veterans D.G. Caywood Camp No. 146. With such a long name, one can understand why the members are simply known as the Sons of the Union Veterans. The little building is decorated with banners and flags during every military celebration.

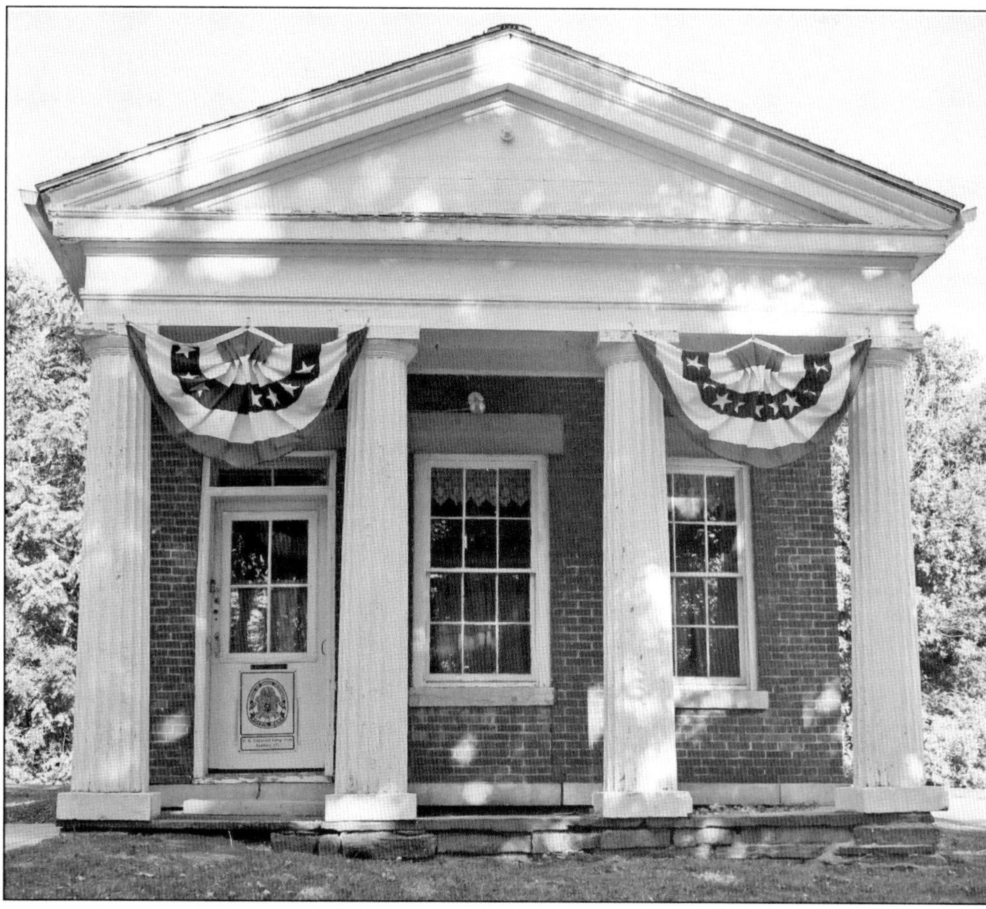

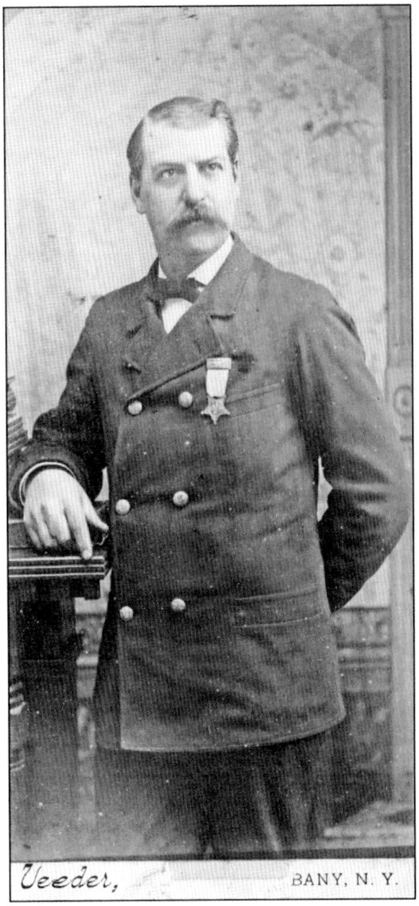

David Genoa Caywood enlisted in I Company, 3rd Regiment, on September 30, 1861. He was wounded at Fredericksburg on May 4, 1862, and was discharged on June 6, 1862. The Sons of the Union Veterans D.G. Caywood Camp No. 146 was named in his honor. When the group was formed in 1914, one of its objectives was to ensure proper burial and assist the sick and disabled. Eight veterans are buried side by side in the Ovid Union Cemetery. A six-foot cross decorated with flowers is placed at their graves every Memorial Day.

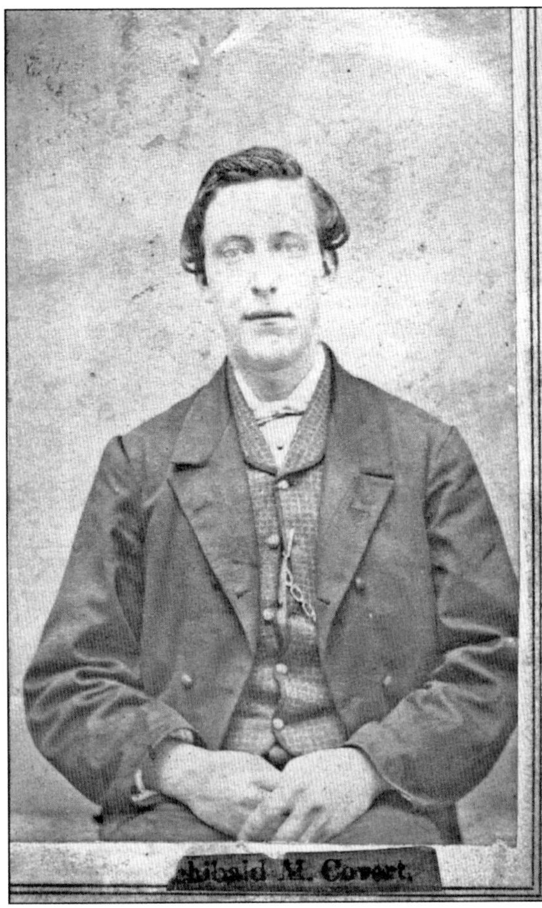

Archibald McNeal Covert enlisted in E Company, 148th Regiment, on December 21, 1863. He was discharged from fighting in the Civil War on October 28, 1864. He died on November 24, 1883, aged 42 years, and is buried in the Union Cemetery in Ovid.

Joseph M. Foster was born on June 29, 1835, in Ovid. He enlisted in the Army in April 1861, before his 26th birthday. Joseph was with Company K, 50th Engineers, in the Civil War. Following the war, he worked as a cabinetmaker until he died on June 26, 1910. He is buried in the Ovid Union Cemetery.

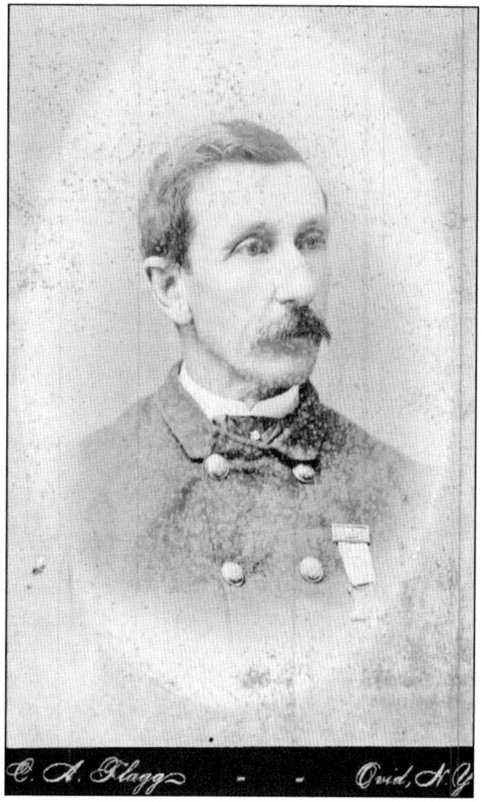

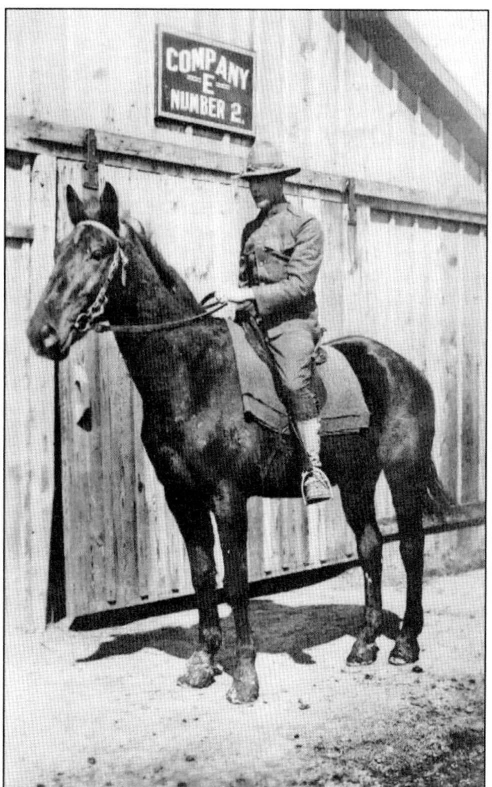

Lynn Munson served in France in World War I. He was in the cavalry, Company E, Number 2. Riding a horse was a natural for Munson, since he was raised on a farm. When he was honorably discharged on May 28, 1919, he returned to farm and raise a family. Munson later worked as a guard at the nearby Seneca Army Depot. (Courtesy of Naomi Brewer.)

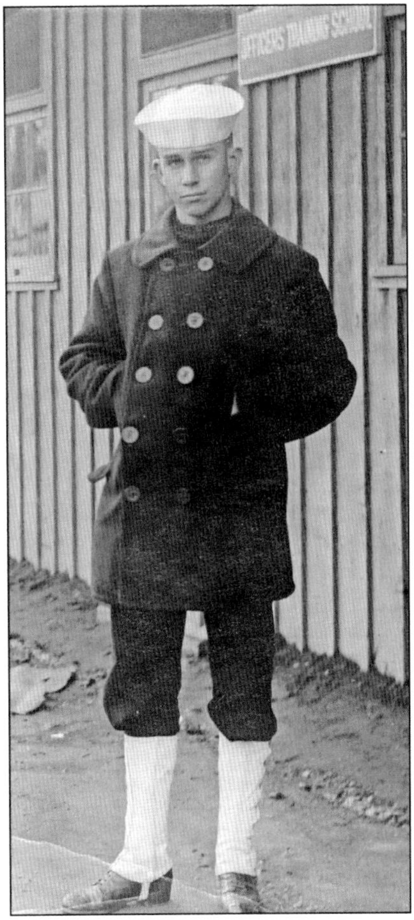

Francis McElroy graduated from Ovid High School and joined the Navy on June 1, 1918. He served at the naval hospital at Pelham Bay Park, New York, during World War I. This 1919 photograph was taken before he was discharged in June as a seaman, second class. Francis later graduated from Syracuse University with a law degree. He lived in Dewitt, New York, and served as a New York state senator. He died in 1958, leaving a wife and two children. (Courtesy of Dorothy Hicks.)

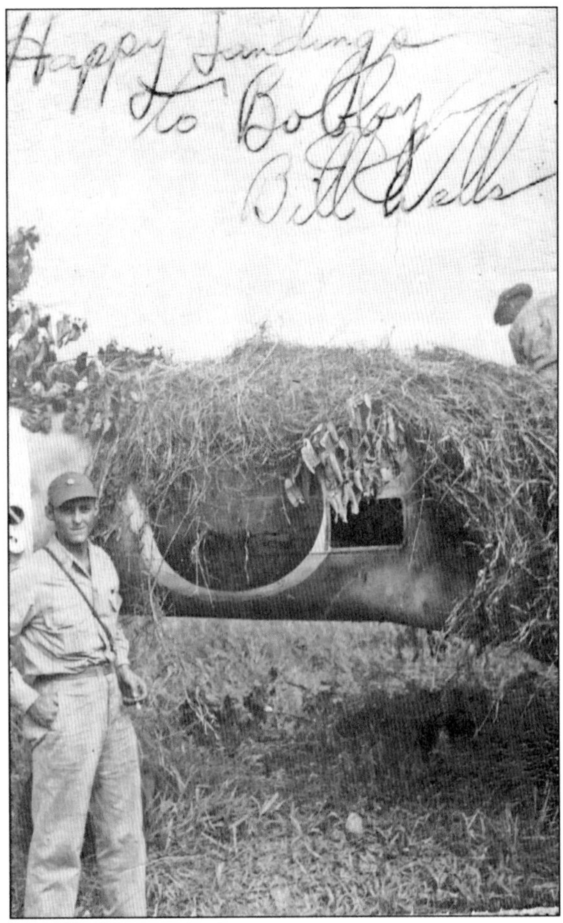

Behind Maj. William Wells is a camouflaged Japanese aircraft in New Guinea. The soldier on the right is unidentified. Wells graduated from Ovid High School in 1931 and entered the Army at the beginning of World War II. He flew C-47 transport planes, known as the "Bully Beef Express." The squadron earned the name as it carried tons of boiled beef to allied combat troops in Australia and New Guinea. Wells was mustered out as a lieutenant colonel. (Courtesy of Dr. Robert Zimmer.)

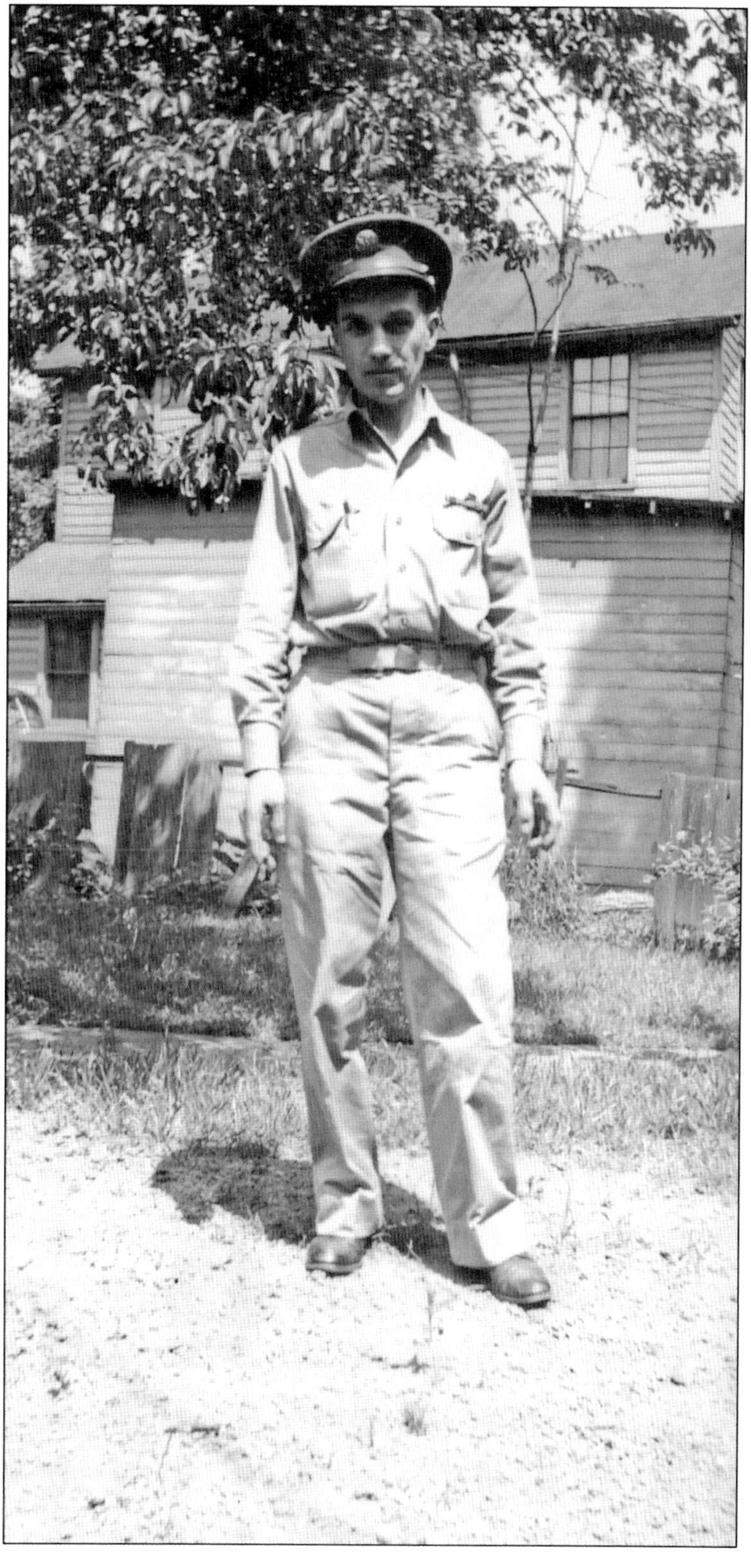

Francis Tripp served with the Army Engineers in World War II. He was in the European theater and at Normandy Beach on D-day. His ring stopped a bullet from killing him. Francis met his wife, Florence, at the base where he was stationed in England and where she was a cook. They married in England and returned to Ovid to live. (Courtesy of Pamela Tripp Coleman.)

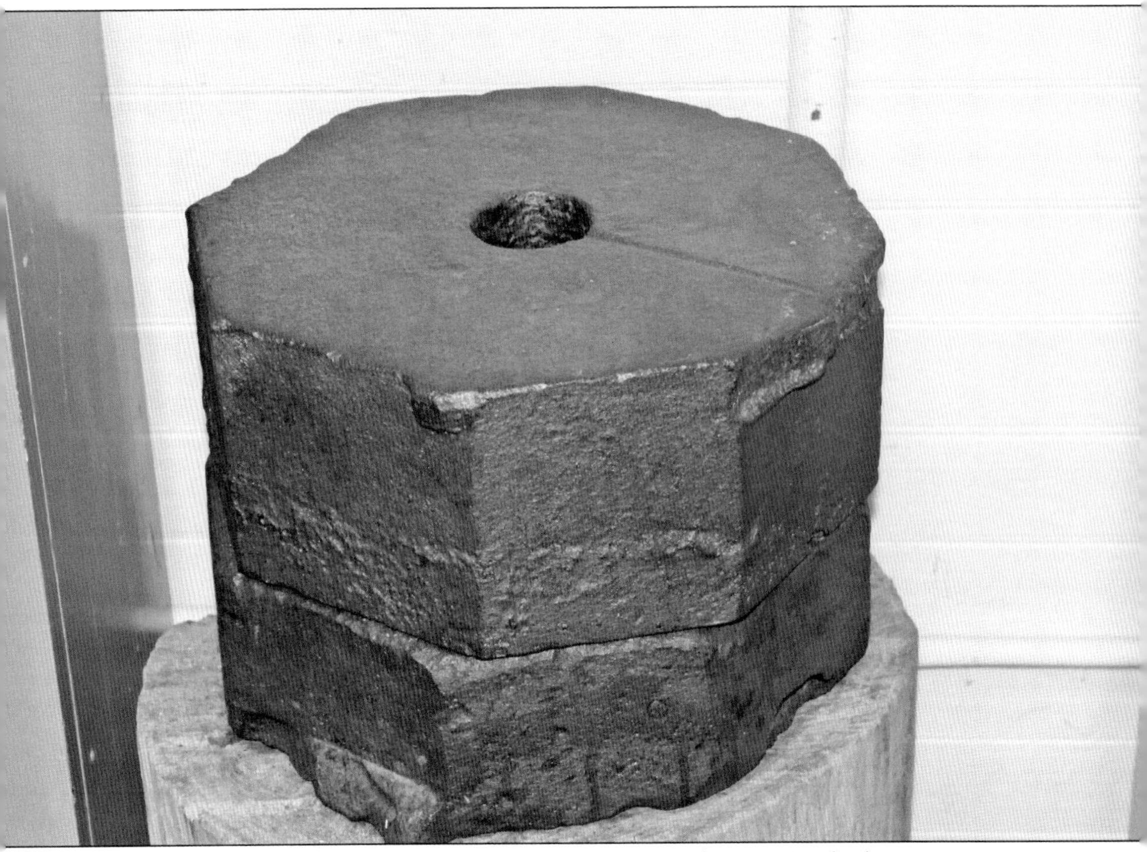

The Spit-Box Cannon was made of two pieces of wrought iron. In the bottom portion is an indentation with a channel that goes from the hole to the outside edge. Gunpowder was poured in the hole and the bottom was covered with wet paper before the top portion was placed on it. The cannon was fired by a long iron rod. When the top section blew off, it would make a terrible noise and clear the treetops. It was harmless as a weapon, but could be dangerous if it dropped on someone.

Eight

LANDMARKS

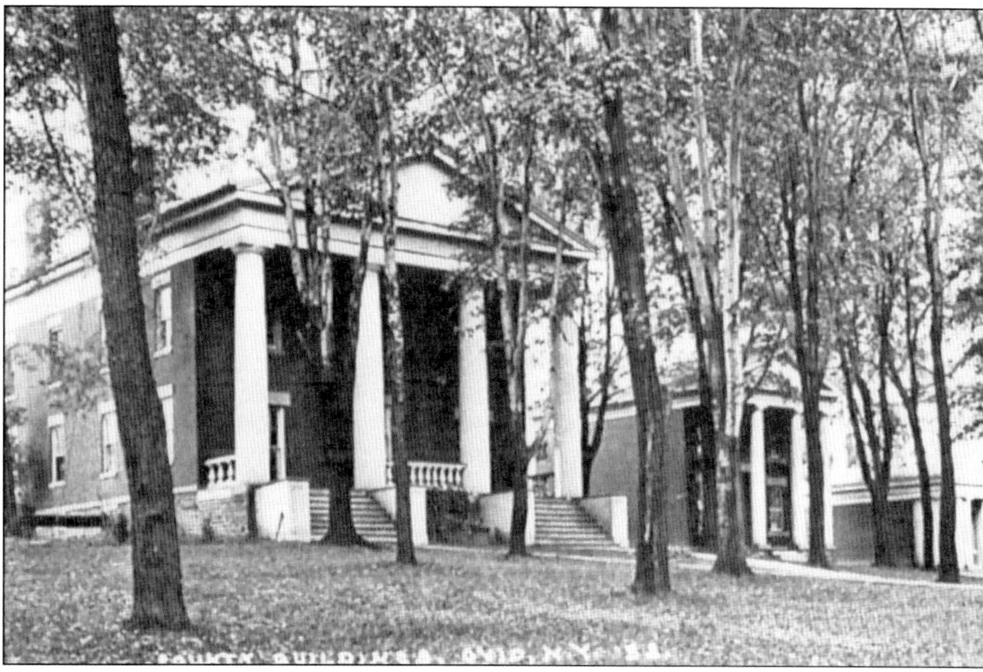

The most famous landmark in Ovid, New York, is the group of three brick buildings that sits at the top of the village green. They are in the National Register of Historic Places. The largest building was constructed in 1845 and contains the courthouse. The smallest was built during the same year and was formerly used as the office of the county clerk and the county records. When this building was unable to hold all of the records, a medium-sized building was constructed between the two in 1860. The three received "The Three Sisters" as their first label, but it was not long before "The Three Bears" became the nickname. This was most appropriate, for the graduated sizes were a perfect fit for Papa, Mama, and Baby Bear. It is believed that there is no other such group of buildings in the United States. Yolanda Scofield, Wayne Morrison, Robert Harmon, Anne Knight, and David Arkland did pen-and-ink drawings of the buildings, and tourists have taken hundreds of snapshots of the structures. Morrison printed a booklet of the history of the buildings that has been given to all the tourists who have taken a few minutes for a quick stop just to take a photograph.

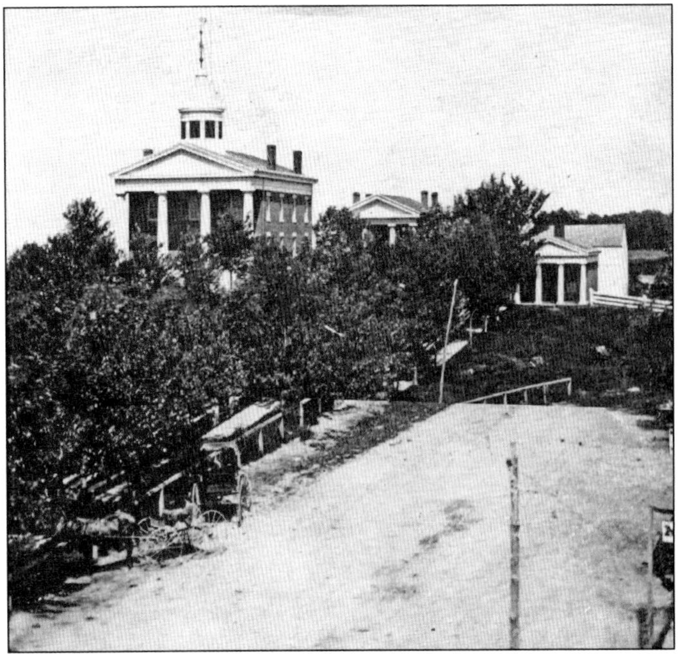

No photographs can be found of the first Ovid Court House. A huge thank-you is given to the artist who made this sketch of the building. It was built of wood in 1806 and sat on the knoll occupied by the present courthouse. The plot was bought for $5 from Ovid's pioneer settler, John Seeley. Justice was administered here for 40 years before the more substantial brick courthouse was constructed.

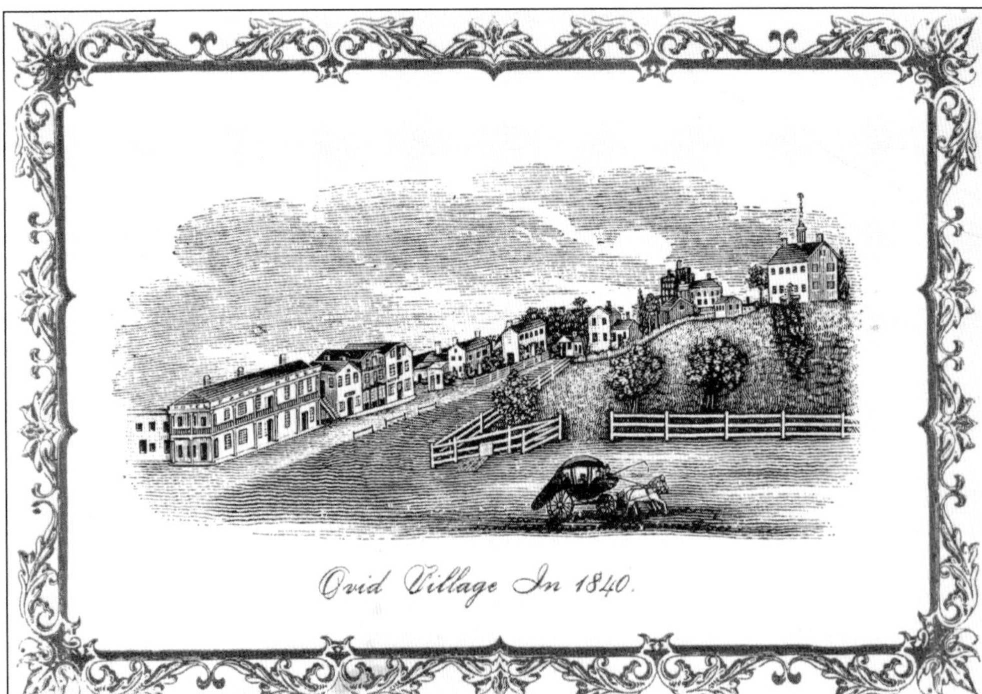

This pen-and-ink drawing shows the original 1840 wooden stores with the original wooden courthouse on the hill. The fence surrounding the village park confined the stray animals that were held until the owners claimed them. The resident sheep kept the grass at a respectful height on the courthouse lawn. The horses pulling the stagecoach were probably tied to the hotel bar made for that purpose. The ropes would be untied when the stagecoach was ready for the journey to the Cayuga Lake ferryboat.

The most prominent of the Three Bears is shown in a close-up view. The numerous large old trees in the park have made it difficult to find a good angle to capture all three buildings. The original courthouse weather vane can be seen above Papa Bear's cupola. The second pair of stairs on the left side has been removed. They have since been replaced to give a symmetrical appearance to the Greek Revival building. A portion of Mama Bear can be seen to the right of Papa Bear.

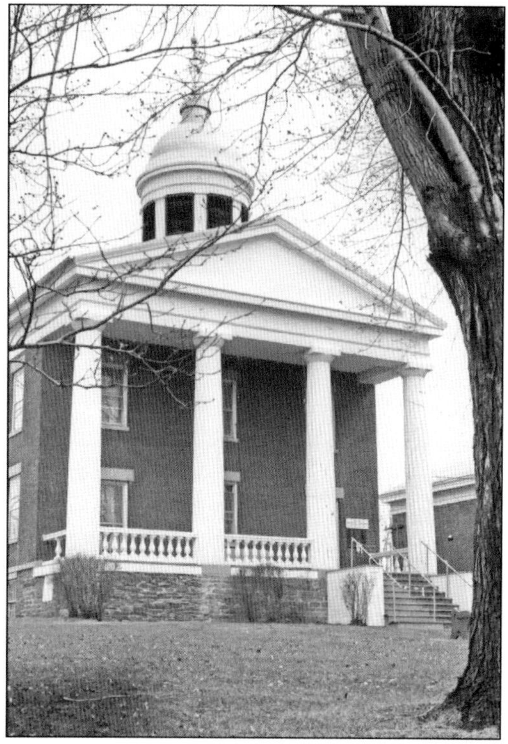

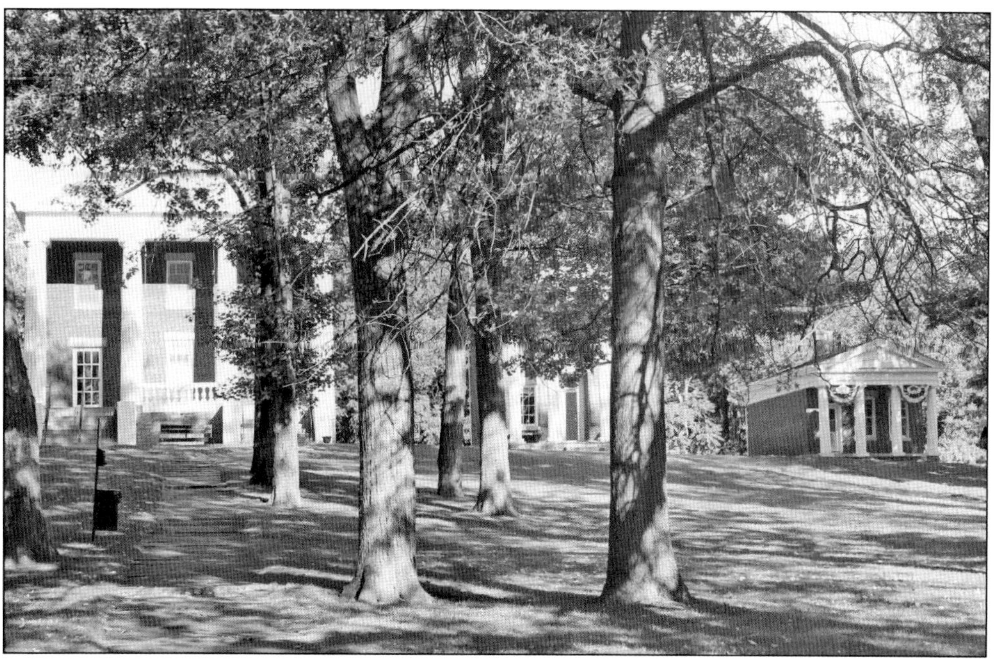

A summer scene shows the park as it appears during the months of June, July, and August. The courthouse sidewalk and steps are covered by the shade of the trees. One could walk through the parklike area. This area could be use for picnics and quiet gathering areas for conversations as well.

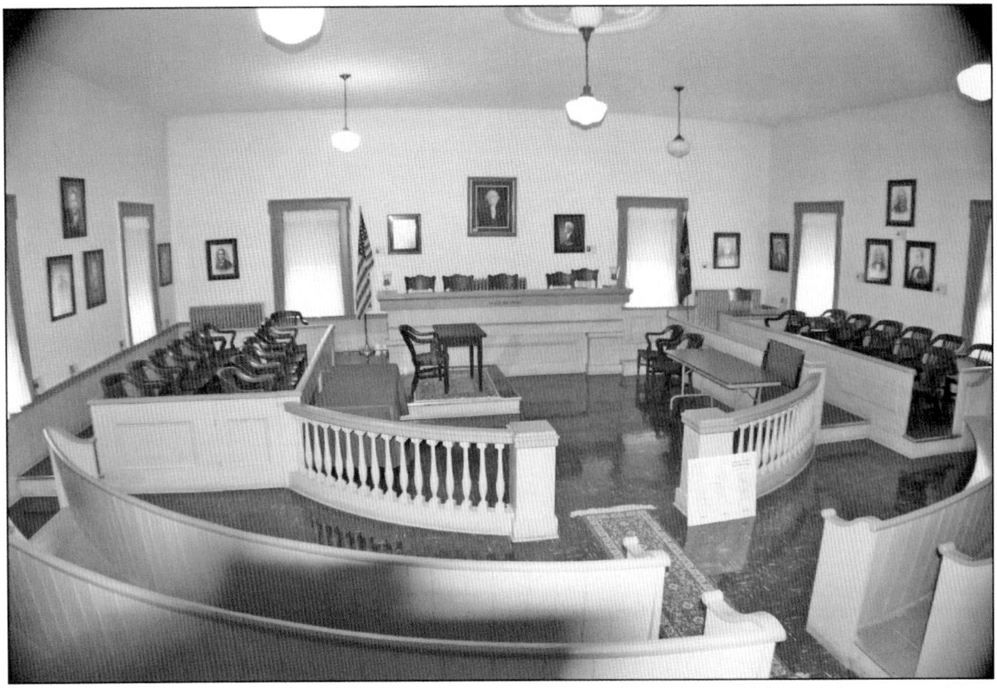

The courtroom is on the second floor of Papa Bear, the courthouse building. The original five chairs for the judge and his assistants can he seen behind the bench. The two sets of jury chairs have also remained. The jury arrangement was used when a double trial needed to be held at the same time. The backs of the curved spectator seats are so straight that no one would ever fall asleep during a trial.

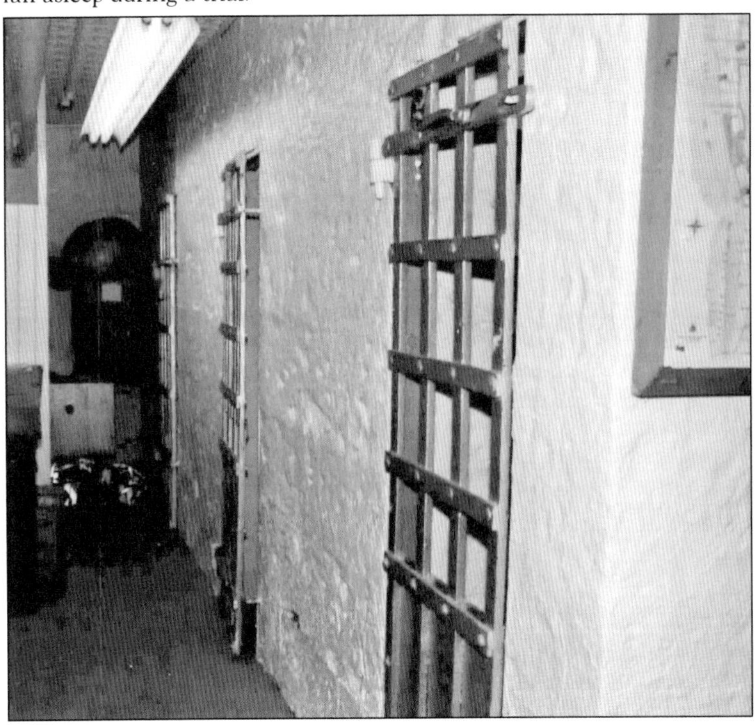

The three jail cells are built within the jail room in the basement. The prisoners could see that it would be useless to dig their way out of their cells. The doors indicate the amount of security. The first door has full lattice bars. The lattice on the second door allows only a view through the upper half. The third door has only a small square peephole. The sheriff-warden is stationed just a short distance away.

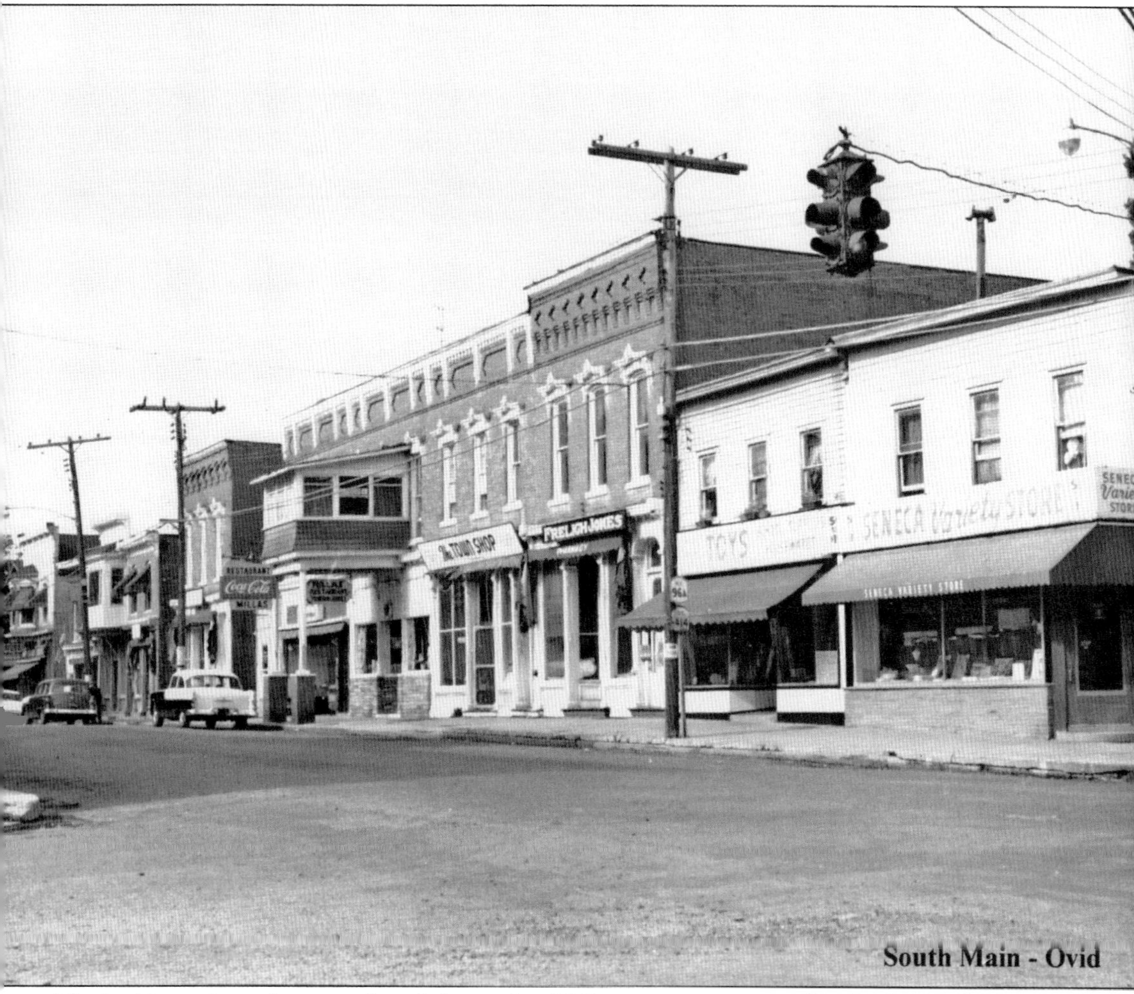

South Main - Ovid

The buildings shown here are, from left to right, A&P grocery store, owned by Arthur Hall; Elmer Burnham Store/Parish Shop; G.R. Gray Insurance; Ovid Post Office/Odomirok Realty; Potter grocery; Herman Emmons-Stanley Gorski Barbershop; Harris Shoe Store; Millas Restaurant; the Town Shop dry goods, owned by Cliff Strause and Mary Maher; Freligh Jones drugstore; toys portion of Seneca Variety Store; and Ken Keady's 5&10 and Victor Kaiser Store, which are part of the Seneca Variety Store.

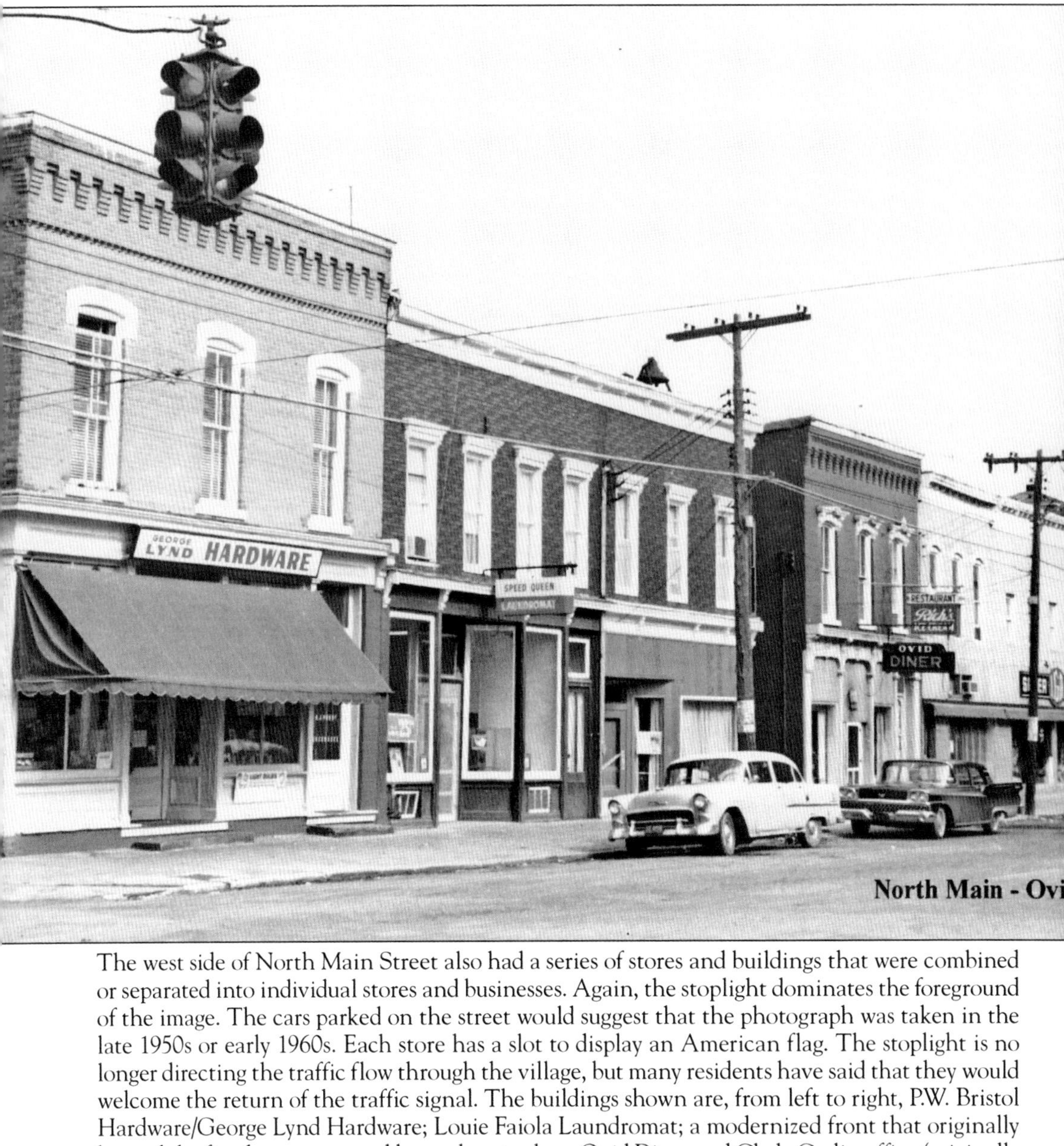

The west side of North Main Street also had a series of stores and buildings that were combined or separated into individual stores and businesses. Again, the stoplight dominates the foreground of the image. The cars parked on the street would suggest that the photograph was taken in the late 1950s or early 1960s. Each store has a slot to display an American flag. The stoplight is no longer directing the traffic flow through the village, but many residents have said that they would welcome the return of the traffic signal. The buildings shown are, from left to right, P.W. Bristol Hardware/George Lynd Hardware; Louie Faiola Laundromat; a modernized front that originally housed the fire department and later a beauty shop; Ovid Diner and Clyde Caslin office (originally the George Depew Garage); Dr. Allen office (originally Broadway Theatre); and the IGA Big M Market (originally the site of the N.R. Boyce gas station).

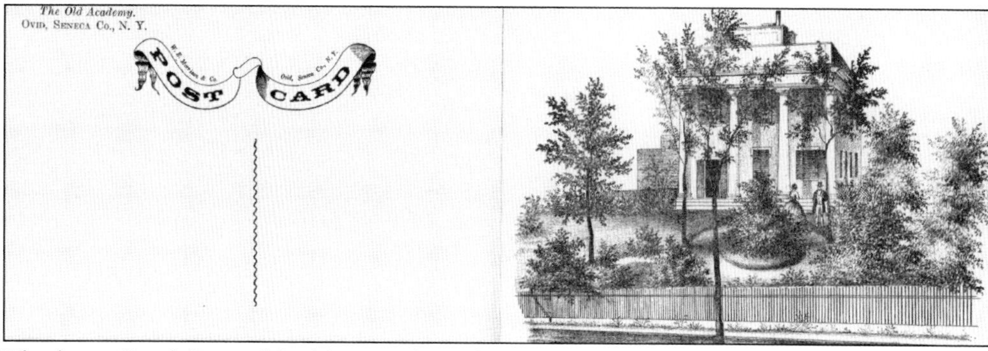

The large Greek Revival building, with its four columns, was built in 1827 for the Meridian Masonic Lodge. The building was converted into a residence by Asgill Gibbs. John Manning was the next owner, and after his death, his daughter sold it to printer George Pashley. Stephen McKeel published the *Ovid Gazette* in this building until he sold it to printers Wayne and Patricia Morrison. The huge home can still be seen at its original site on the hill.

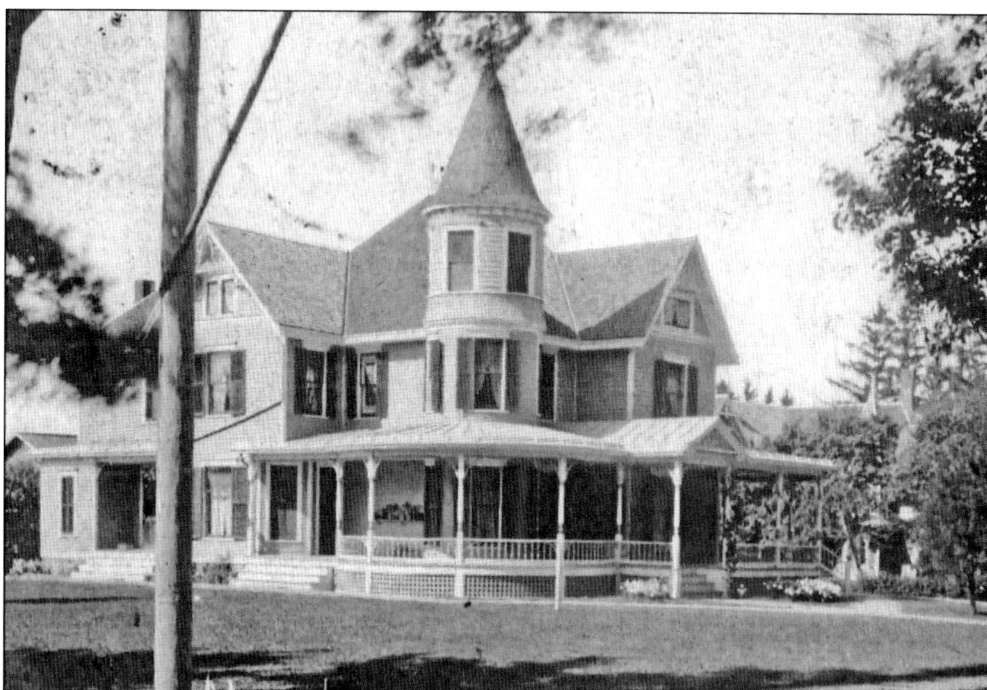

The Queen Anne house on the west side of South Main Street was constructed for Emma Kinne in 1897. It contains 13 rooms and has a prominent three-story turret. Roger and Shirley Clemenson purchased the house in 1983. Its color is reminiscent of the famous "Painted Ladies" in San Francisco, California.

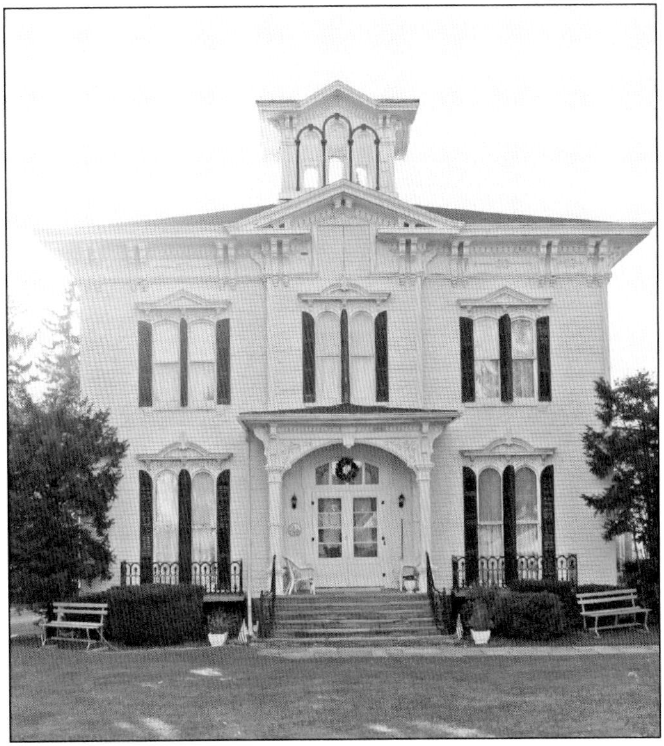

The Italianate house on the west side of South Main Street was built by George W. and Hannah Jones in 1873. George Jones was the owner of the Ovid Steam Mill, which produced the lumber for his large home. A panoramic view of Ovid could be seen from the cupola. In 1884, George was elected a member of the New York State Assembly. George and Hannah had many guests; the most famous was Theodore Roosevelt, who stayed overnight in their home. George died on October 17, 1886.

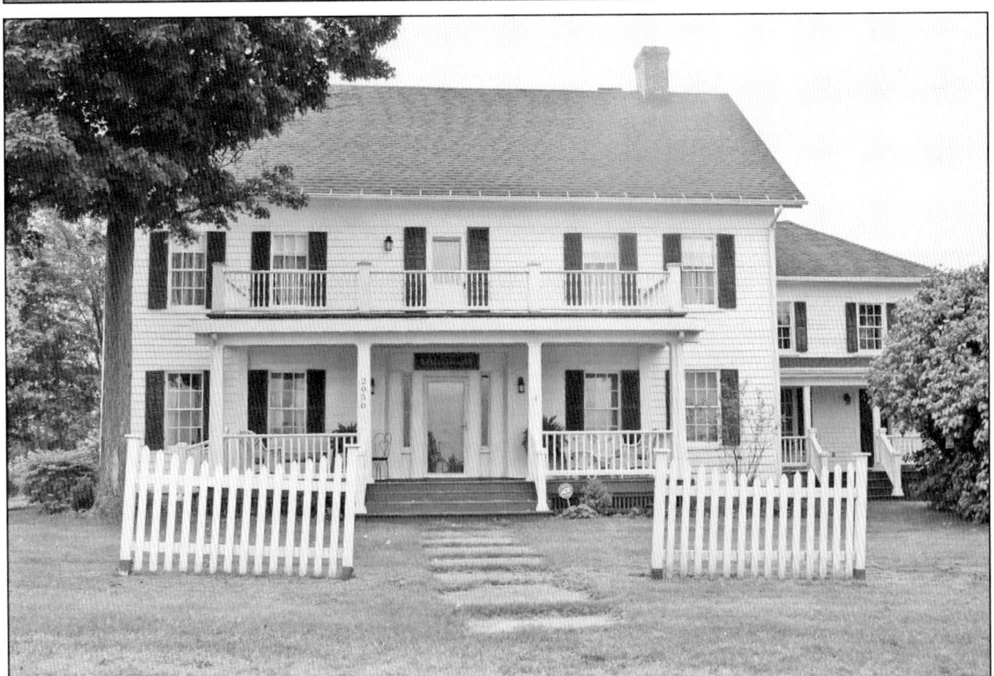

This Federal house was built in 1812 by Elijah Kinne. When he and his wife, Jerusha, came from Connecticut in 1792, they built a log cabin. Their family of 10 children prompted the building of the large house. Elijah had the first grindstone in the village, which was used to sharpen axes. He also had the first frame barn built on his property. Elijah died on February 6, 1830.

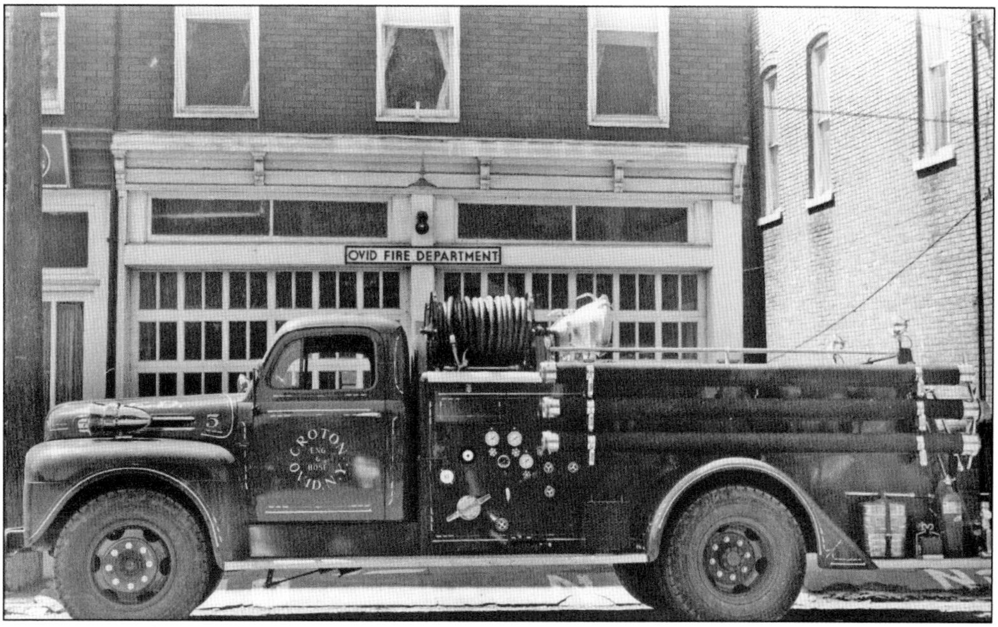

At one time, the Ovid Fire Department was housed in the second building north of the corner hardware store on North Main Street. An alley on the north side of the fire department can be seen in the picture. Two trucks were all that needed to be housed. The people in the apartment above were probably aware of every fire.

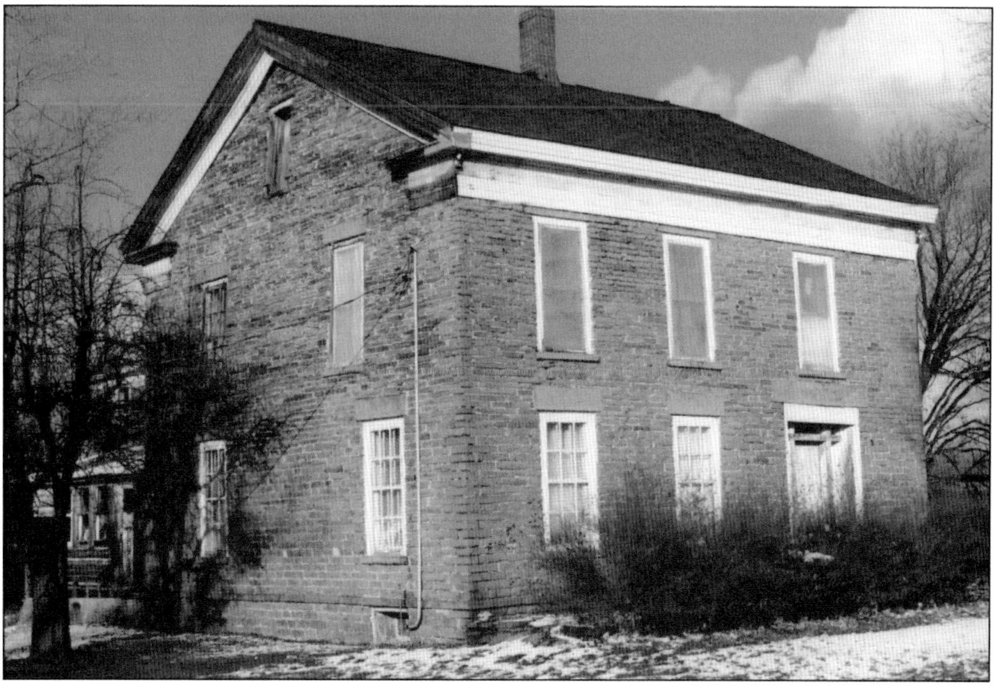

The Dr. Cornelius VanHorn Morris House, on the Ovid-Lodi Townline Road, was completed in 1857. The stones were transported from nearby quarries, and one huge slab was used for the fireplace hearth. Another slab became the lintel above the front door. This was one of seven stone houses that were built in the town of Ovid.

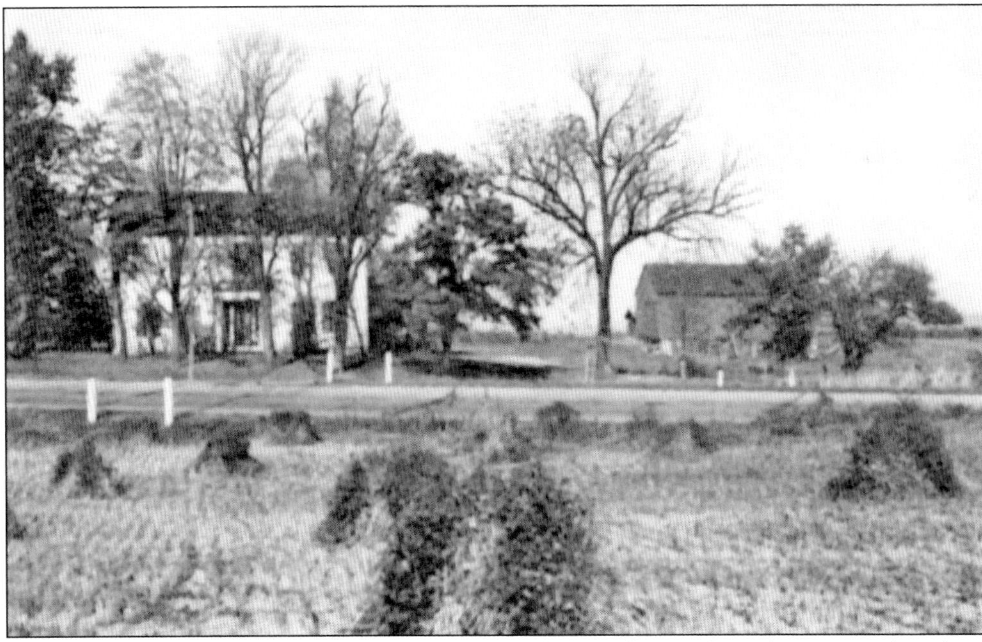

The Gideon Scott family, with eight children, settled southeast of Ovid in 1796. Their large Federal home became a tavern and stagecoach toll stop in 1810. The Ithaca Geneva Turnpike was a corduroy road. Revenues were collected until 1823, when it was declared a free highway. When descendent Donald Powell died, the home became vacant, and it burned down in 1970.

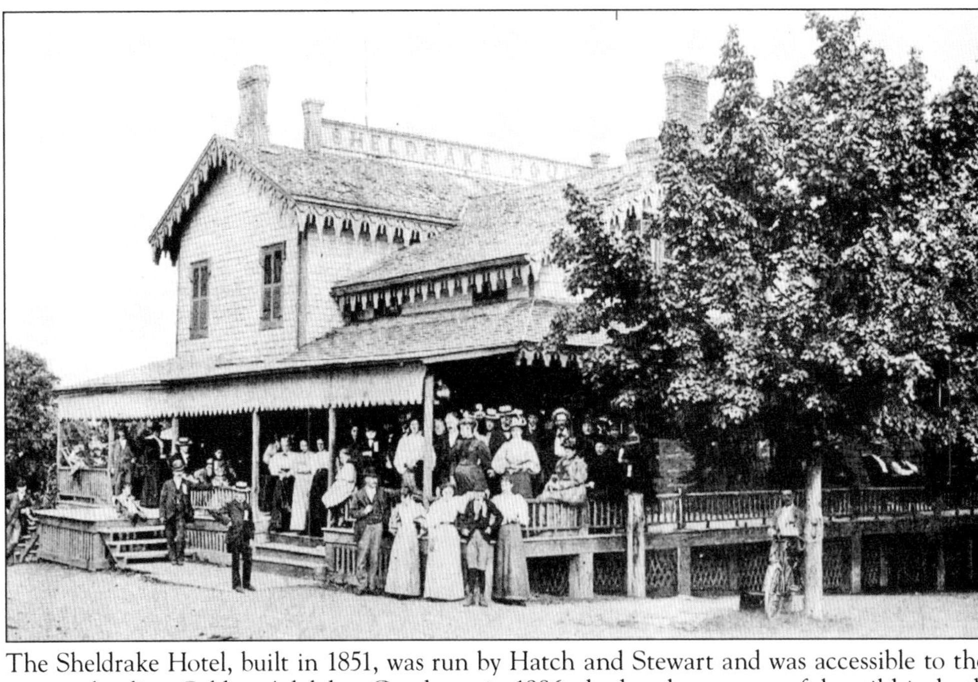

The Sheldrake Hotel, built in 1851, was run by Hatch and Stewart and was accessible to the steamer landing. Sold to Adolphus Goodman in 1886, the hotel was successful until his death in 1902. The new owner's business declined when automobiles became popular. In 1939, it was bought by the two Dunwoody sisters for use as an international camp for children. Later, it was sold and became a home.

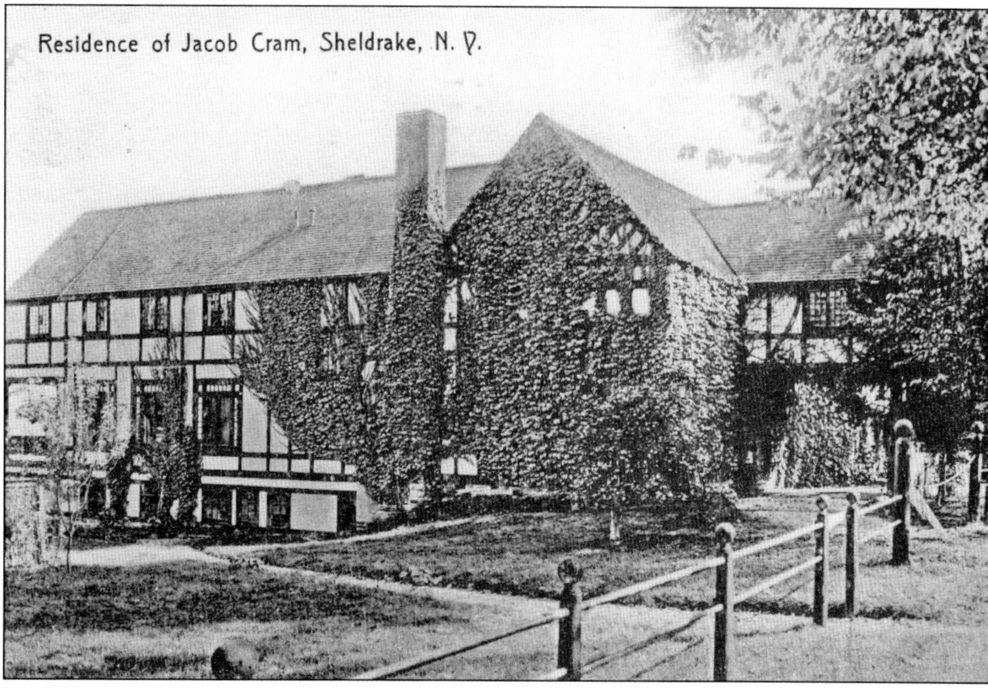

Jacob Cram came from New York City to settle in Sheldrake in 1890. He acquired land near the lake and had this English-style 22-room house built. This postcard shows the ivy-covered house where he had carriages, horses, yachts, and servants. Cram died in 1917, and soon after the house sat idle. It was torn down in 1946.

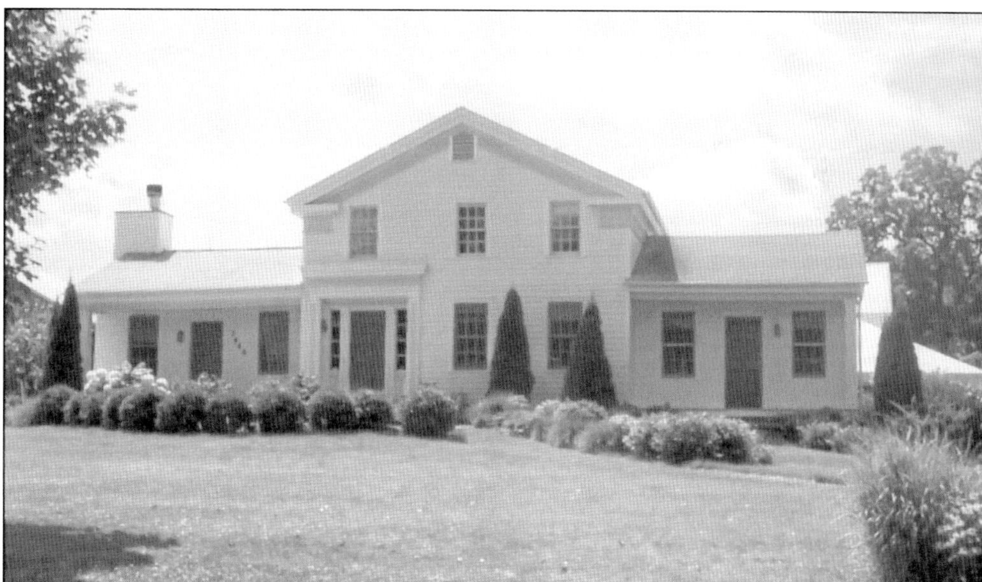

This Greek Revival house was built in 1834 by early settler John S. Blew. This was to replace his 1827 log cabin, which was no longer large enough for his increasing family. The Diamond family farmed the land for years before it was sold to the Sheldrake Vineyard Group. The wide board floors survive under the new, level flooring needed to accommodate electronic machines. The house is used for offices to oversee the growing of acres of grapes and manage the winery.

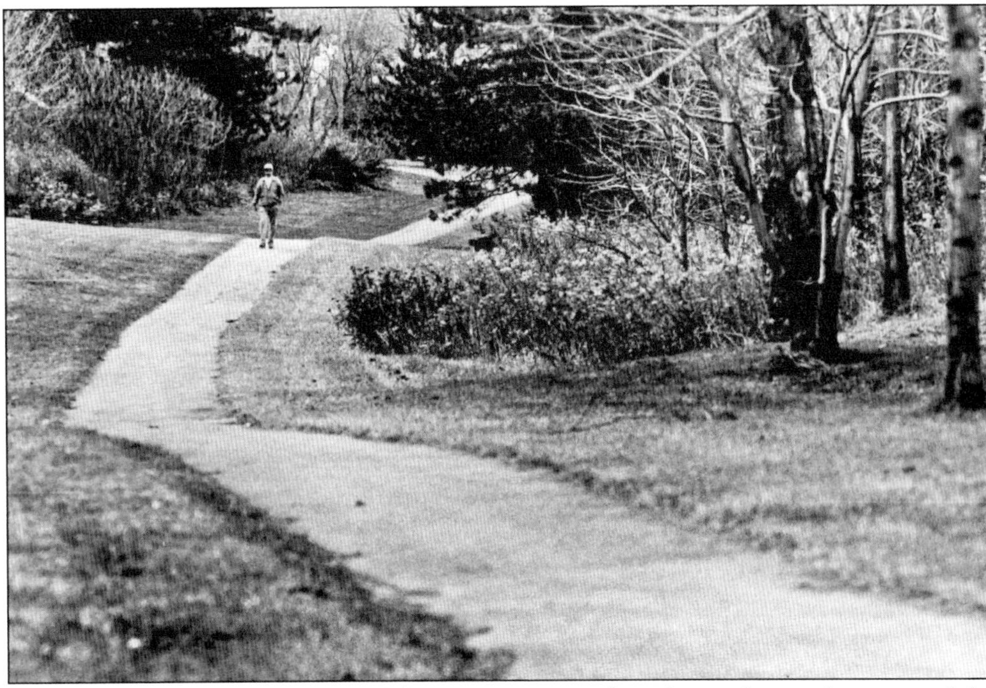

Daniel Taggerty strolls along the path between Verona Village Senior Citizens housing and the main part of the village of Ovid. The path is used by many who want the exercise it encourages. The trees provide a cool, refreshing environment. The width of the surface is excellent for riding a bicycle or using a motorized wheelchair.

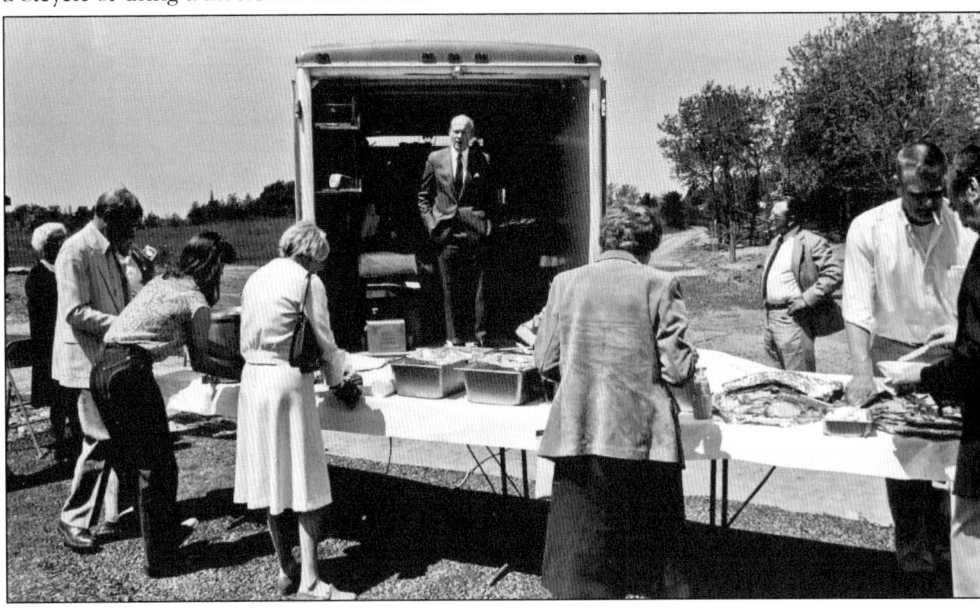

Unidentified attendants at the Verona Village ground-breaking ceremony are enjoying the food that is provided. Congressman Gary Lee is answering questions from his vantage point in the van. Wisner Kinne, the facilitator of the event, is seen standing at the right of the image. Attractive senior apartments were built and have been occupied through the years since this May 19, 1982, ceremony.

Nine

Recreation

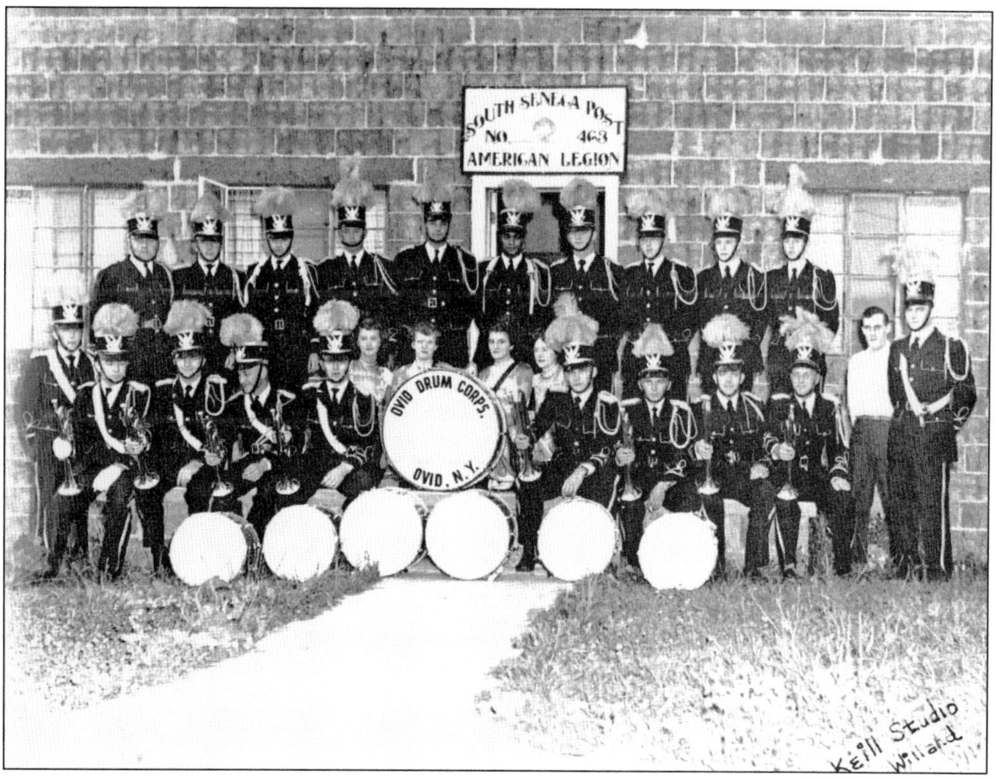

The Ovid Drum and Bugle Corps was organized in 1946. There were 45 members during the years that the group was together. They marched in parades and performed at New York pageant competitions. Where ever they went, they were recognized by their theme song, "Blue Moon." The group disbanded in 1958, when many of the members left to serve in the Korean War.

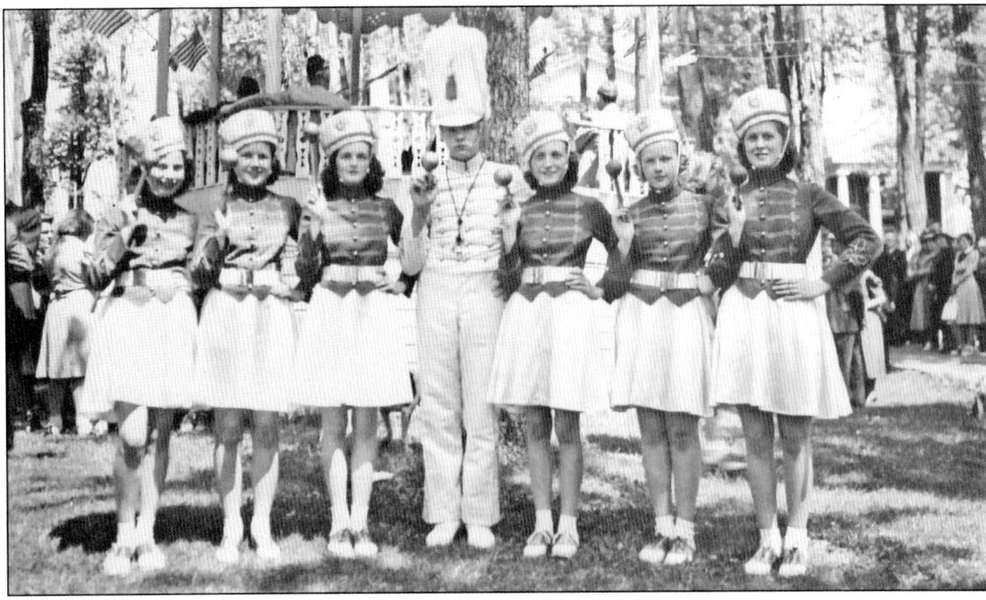

The majorettes that marched with the drum and bugle corps stand at attention while the song "Blue Moon" is played. The Ovid Central School Band must be the next in line, for the drum major is patiently waiting to march. Among those pictured are drum majorettes Bette Lou Conklin (far left), Eugenia Kaiser, Carol Rowers, and Margaret Woodington. The other majorette and the drum major are unidentified.

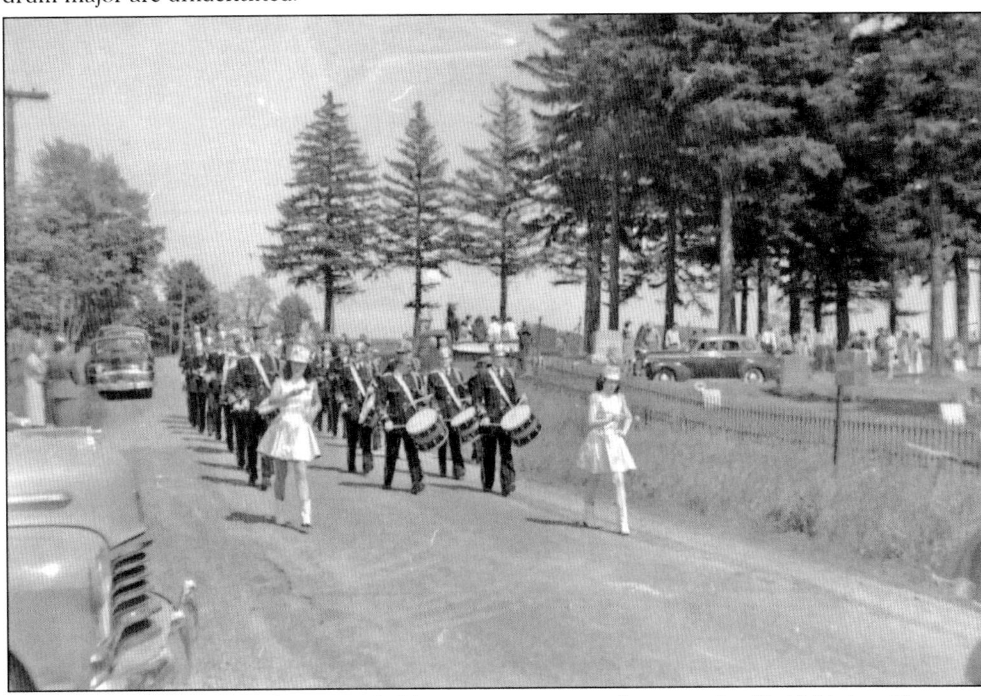

The Ovid Drum and Bugle Corps, led by majorettes, marches past the Ovid Union Cemetery on Gilbert Road. The corps is officially known as the Seneca Chiefs. It will enter the cemetery gate and proceed to the Veterans Memorial by the US flag. A tribute is made to the veterans each Memorial Day.

The Ovid bicentennial play in 1994 was one of the many plays that were held during the summer. Chad Eastman and Shelley Williamson portray the young boy and girl standing in the village park. The play was written by Mark Brown, a graduate of South Seneca High School in Ovid. He directed all of the other plays, but for this one, he tried his hand at writing and choreographing as well as directing. Local artist Sandra Tascarini painted the Three Bears on the back wall of the auditorium stage.

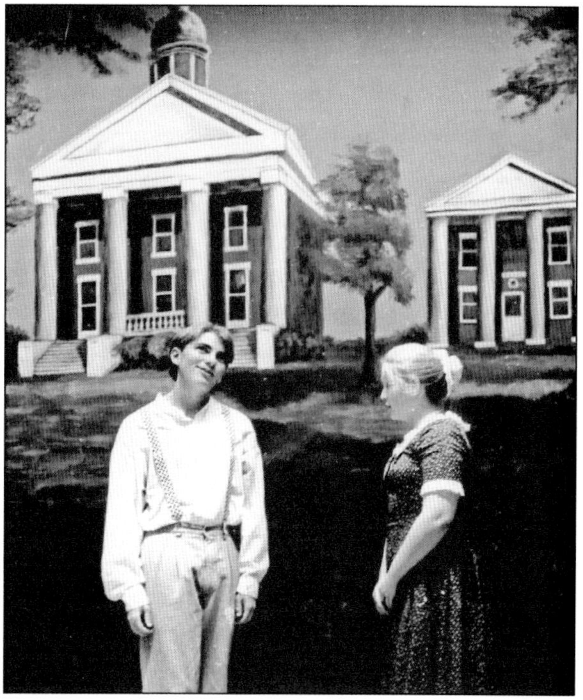

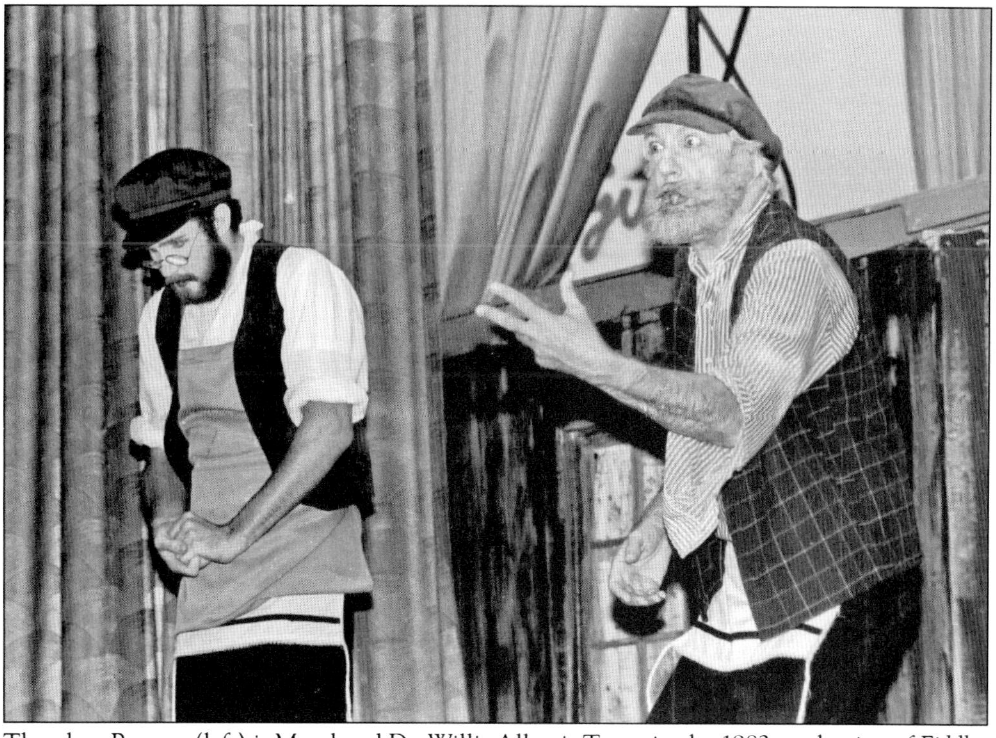

Theodore Benson (left) is Motel and Dr. Willis Allen is Tevye in the 1983 production of *Fiddler on the Roof.* Dr. Allen, an Ovid general practitioner, was in nearly every play that was produced, but it was difficult to recognize him in his costume and makeup. The moment Allen spoke, there was no denying to whom the voice belonged.

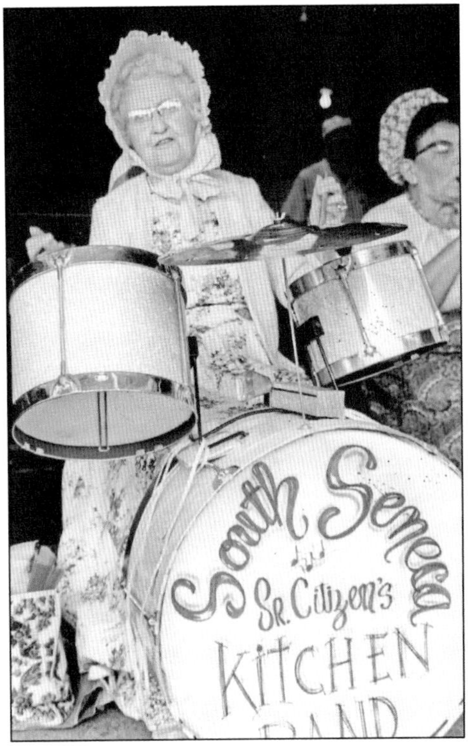

The South Seneca Senior Citizens Kitchen Band played for Ovid events as well as for organizations in Seneca and neighboring counties. Members in their fancy old-time costumes played every instrument imaginable. They ranged from kazoos to cigar-box guitars. Playing the snare and bass drums along with the cymbal is Georgiane Sharp. The wood block would indicate that they may have played "Syncopated Clock" or some song like "Jingle Bells" that required the sound of trotting horses.

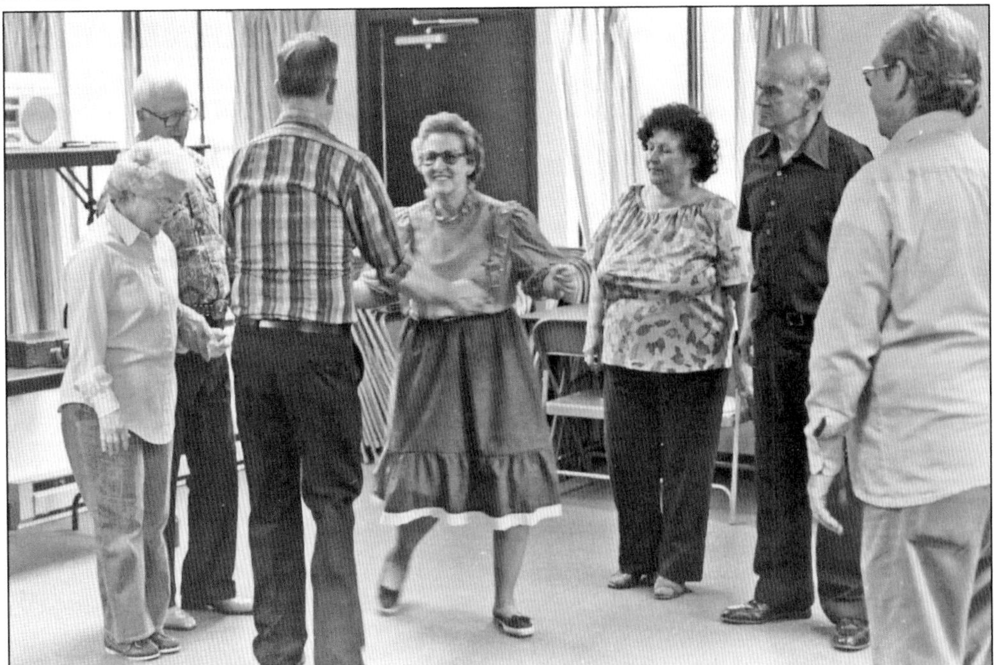

Square dancing was an activity enjoyed by many local groups. A 1940s poster advertises a barn dance to be held on Wednesday nights from 9:00 to 11:00. Gents paid 60¢, and ladies were charged 40¢. Hopefully, couples would pay $1 to round and square dance to the music of the Woodhull Old Tyme Masters. They were popular square dance recording artists for Victor Records.

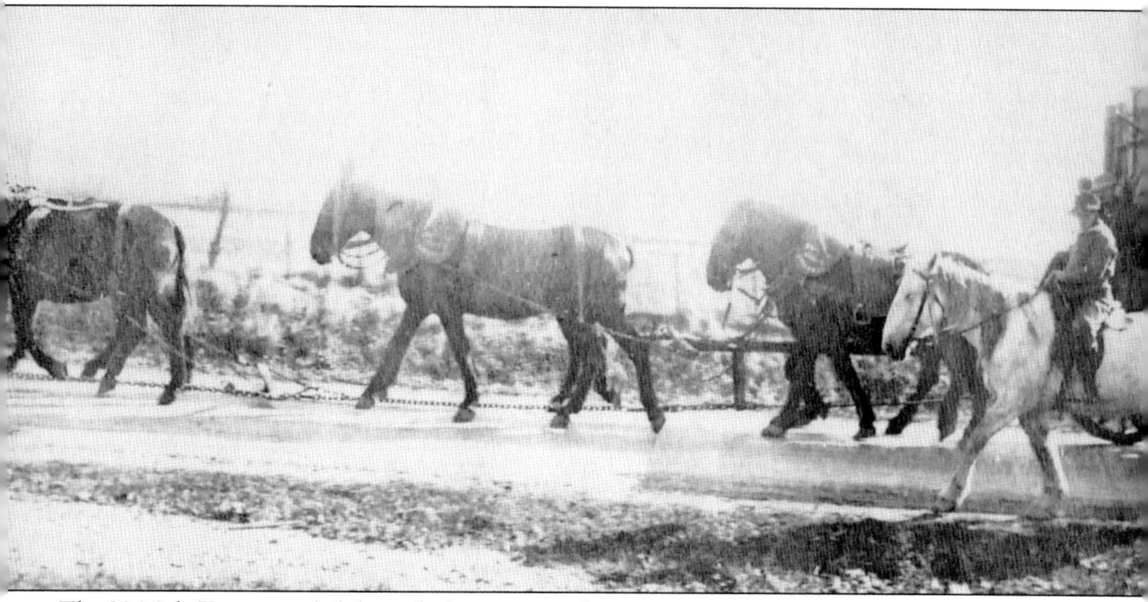

The 20-Mule Team traveled through the country advertising 20-Mule Team Borax, an all-natural laundry booster. This photograph was taken by Esther Eastman in 1919, when the team went by her home south of Ovid. The long procession must have slowed traffic on Route 414, for it required the entire width of the road for horses and wagons.

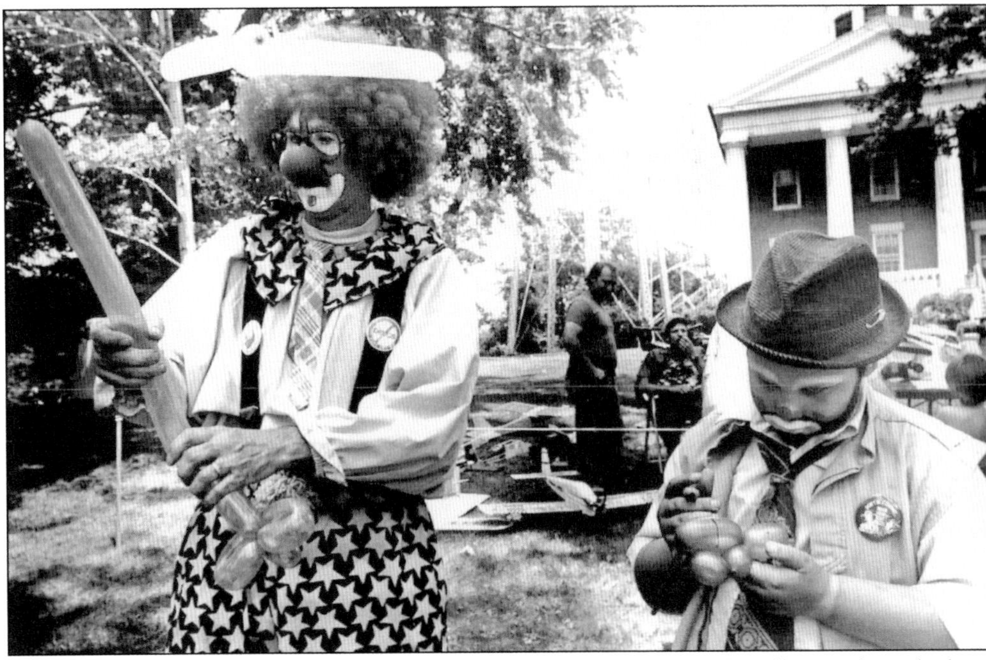

The Strawberry Festival was an annual tradition in Ovid. It was held in the village park on the lawn leading up the hill to the Three Bears. A parade, led by the high school band, concluded with the area fire department members and their equipment. In the middle of the parade were representatives of various Ovid organizations. Following the parade, the carnival completed the remainder of the day. Clowns could transform a balloon into a poodle or anything one desired.

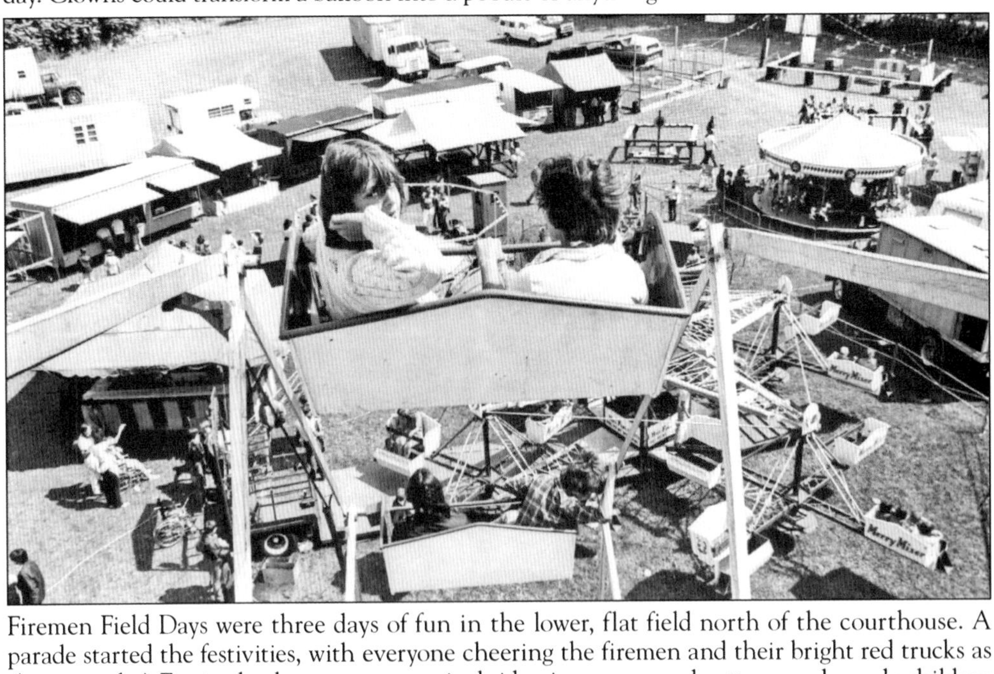

Firemen Field Days were three days of fun in the lower, flat field north of the courthouse. A parade started the festivities, with everyone cheering the firemen and their bright red trucks as they passed. A Ferris wheel, numerous carnival rides, ice cream, and cotton candy made children and adults enjoy a great time at the fair. Food tents supplied the hot dogs and hamburgers that everyone bought.

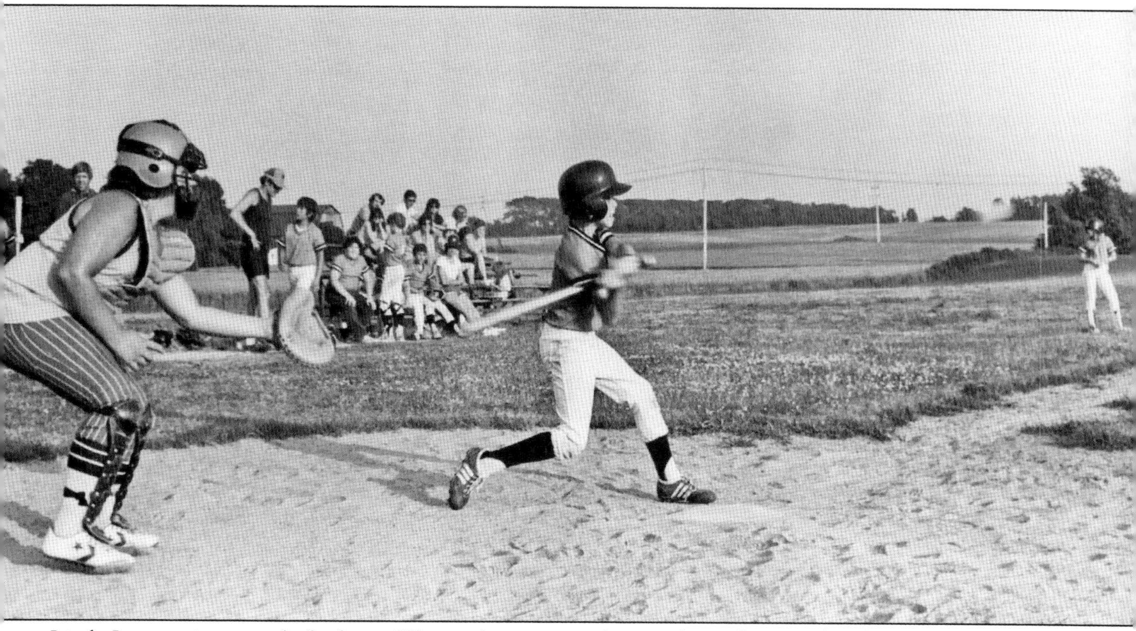

Little League is not only for boys. This girl appears to be as talented as any brother she may have had. The proper equipment assured players that injuries were not likely to happen. This built confidence and encouraged all players to perform better than they may have otherwise.

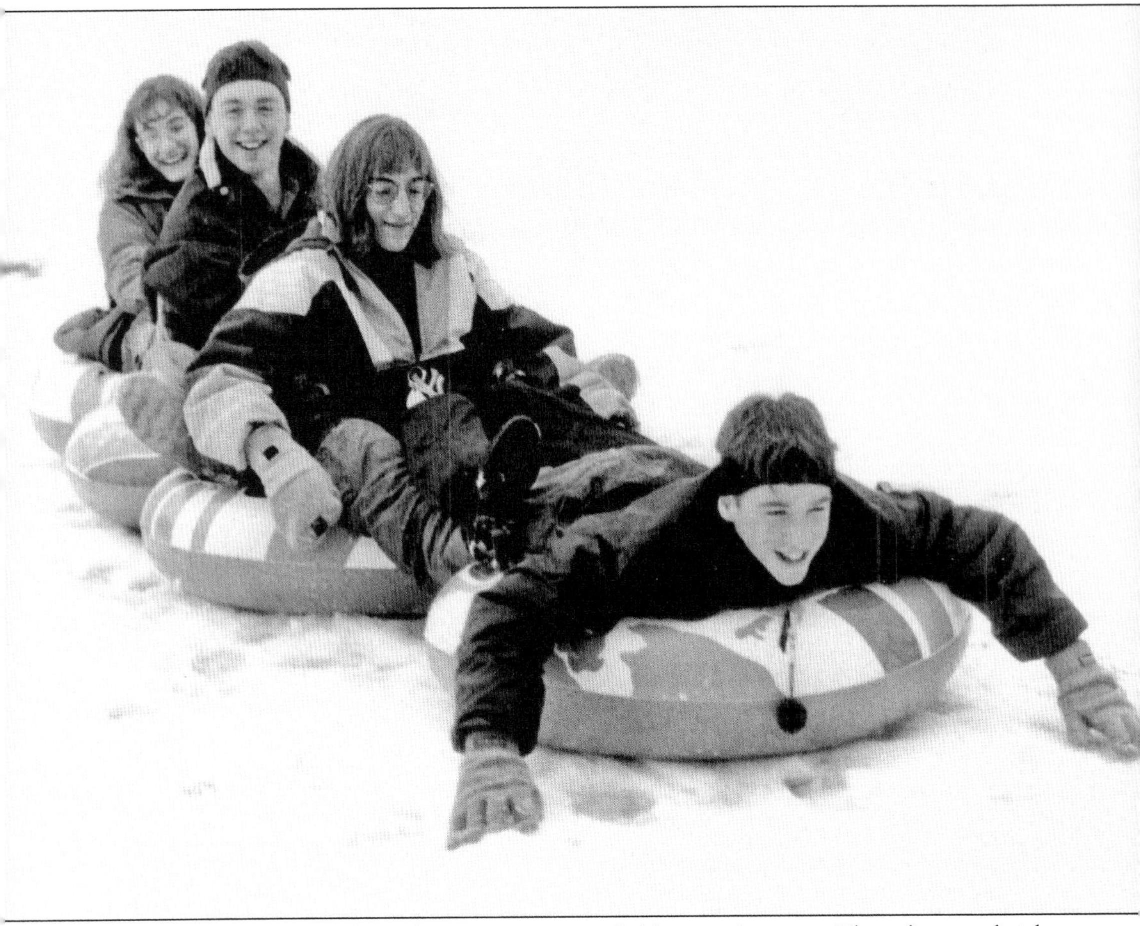

During the winter months, a favorite pastime is sledding in the snow. These boys and girls are teaming with one another on their tubes. Sometimes, the level terrain and lack of snowfall curtails sledding in Ovid. This snowstorm provided lots of snow for the young folks. After digging out from the recent storm, they found a more entertaining use for the white stuff.

The annual Easter egg hunt on the front lawn of the school was a favorite for all ages. The older recreation counselors hid the regular and special prize eggs very early in the morning. The very youngest boys and girls were allowed to hunt for the eggs first. This little girl appears to be happy about the amount of eggs she was able to find.

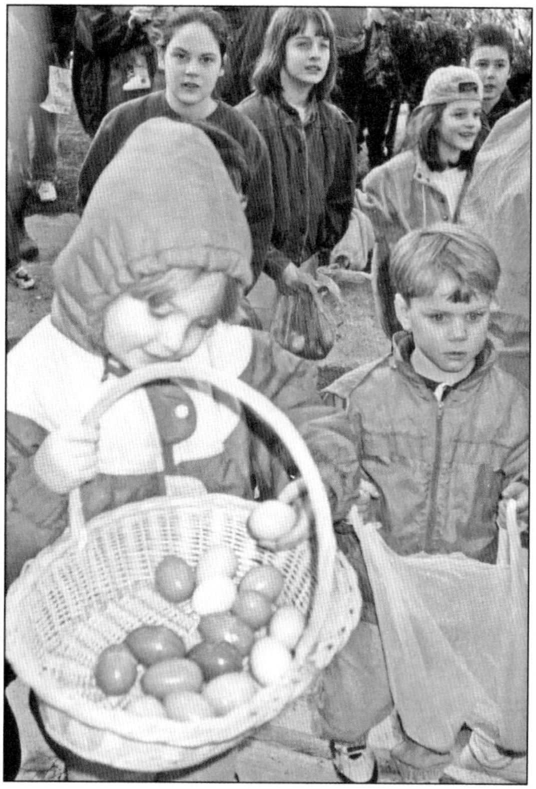

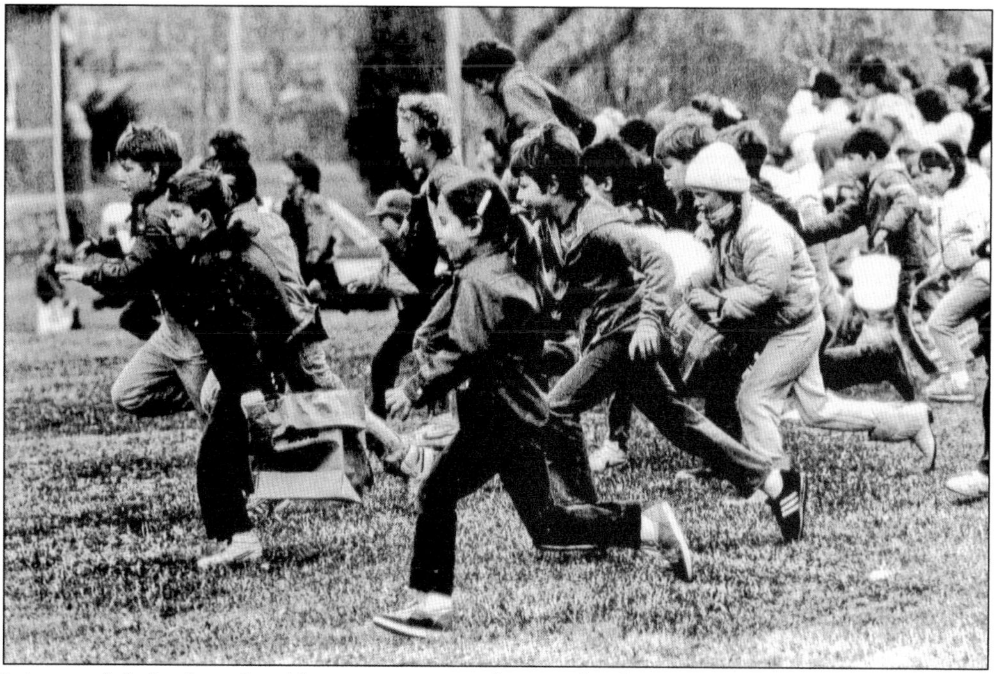

It is a mad dash when the older group is given the signal to begin its search for eggs. The size of the bags and buckets is an indication of the expectation of success that each child has in mind. No child goes away unhappy, for there is Easter candy for everyone.

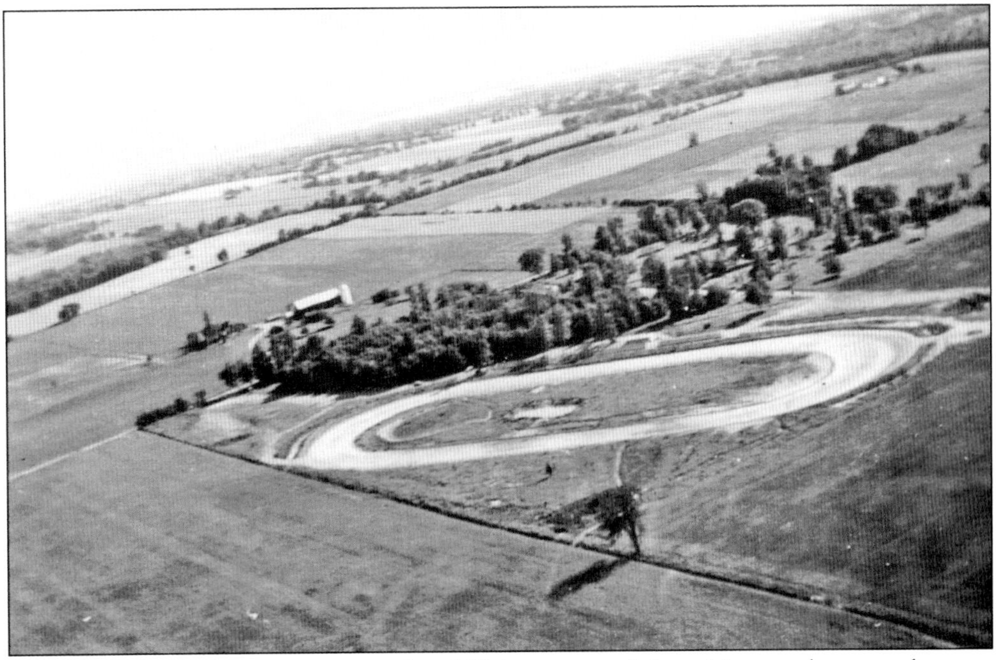

South Seneca Speedway was conceived in 1951 by a group of about 15 men who wanted to race their cars. The parents of Charles, Howard, and Gordon Boyce gave their sons permission to make a track on the farm property southeast of Ovid. The first stock car race on Sunday, June 29, 1952, had 20 cars entered and 1,000 spectators. In September, there were 60 cars in the races and 2,000 fans. The death of Bert Boyce was a contributing factor in the closing of the track in 1954. The boys had to concentrate on the farm, leaving no one to operate the racetrack.

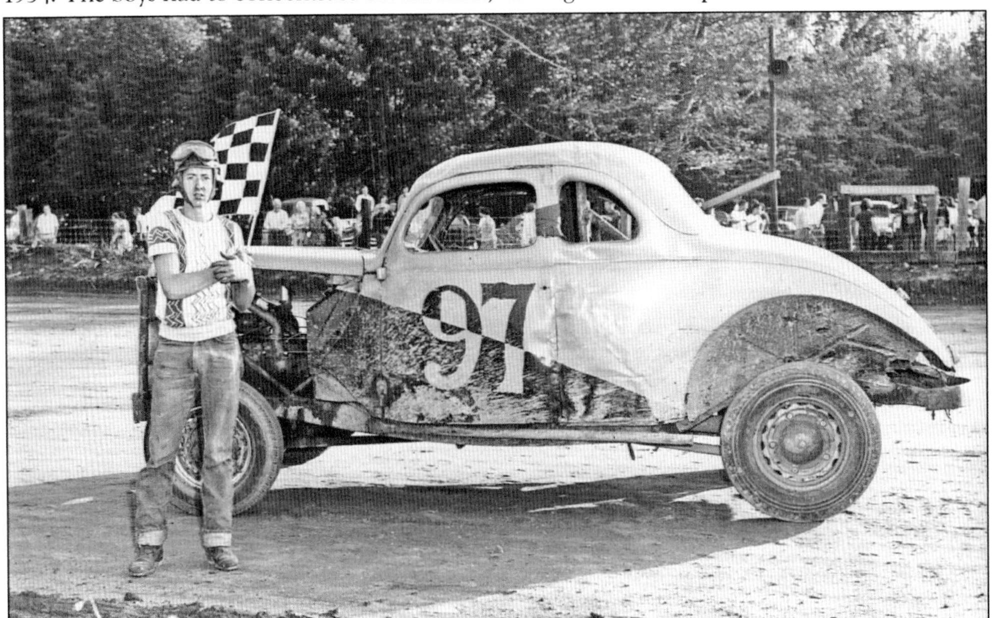

This unidentified young man was only 16 when he started helping around the track. When he turned 18, he drove his first race and won. The track closed, and he moved away and hopefully on to another racing track to win many more races.

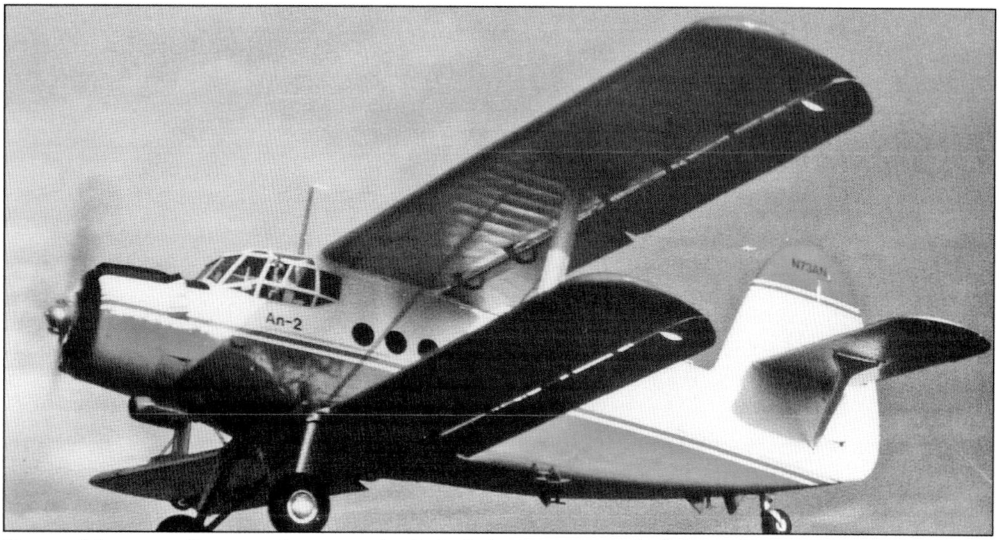

Pictured here is a Russian Antonov An-2 Cole biplane typical of those flown by the pilots of the Ovid Flying Club.

. . . The World's Largest Single Engine Biplane . . .

Russian Design ANTONOV AN-2 "COLT" Polish Built

TYPE: Two-Crew Utility Transport

ENGINE: One 1,000 Hp. Shevetsov Ash-621R

PERFORMANCE: Maximum Speed 160 Mph. Initial Climb Rate 689 Fpm. Range 559 Mi.

WEIGHTS: Empty 7,606 Lbs. Maximum Takeoff 12,125 Lbs.

DIMENSIONS: Span 59 Ft. 7.75 In. Length 41 Ft. 9.5 In. Area 770.72 Sq. Ft.

PAYLOAD: 12 Passengers Or 2,866 Lbs.

Owner & Pilot - **COMRADE PETER DEPEW** - *Ovid, NY 14521*
607-869-5425

An identification is shown for the Antonov An-2 Colt. Materials like this were used to promote events and air shows at the local "international" airport. Oftentimes, these daredevil pilots were homegrown.

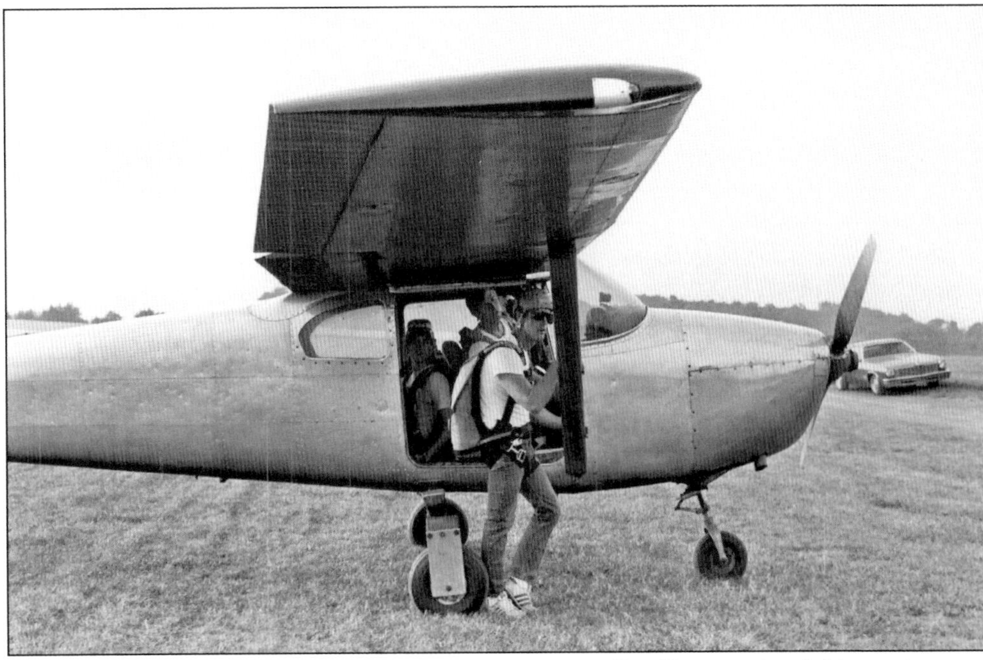

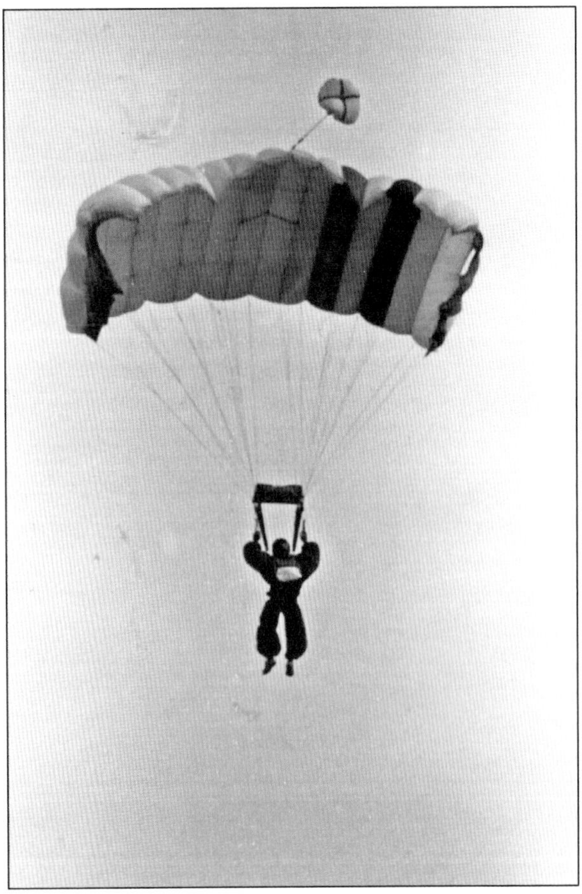

Ovid International Airport is located southeast of Ovid. The small airport uses the word "international" with tongue in check. The name was assumed because Canadian pilots often flew into the airport. The Ovid Flying Club was started by Robert Parish and several flying friends—George Pentz, Cory Trout, Keith Wickham, Stanley Graber, Charles Patchen, and Elmer Porter.

The New York State Parachute Center, the first one in New York State, opened on August 29, 1967, at the Ovid Airport. It was owned and operated by Robert Parish. There were 14 male and female jumpers. Clifford Mayo from Newark, New York, was the pilot. On sunny days during the summer months, one to four colorful parachutes could be seen drifting down with the blue sky as a background.

Fishing is a very popular recreation around Ovid, as witnessed in this 1940s photograph. George Depew (left) and son Chauncey Depew were very successful on their fishing trip, with each catching a nice-sized lake trout. They proudly display their fish at Chauncey's drugstore on the comer of South Main and East Seneca Streets. George had a garage on North Main Street in a space that later became the Ovid Diner.

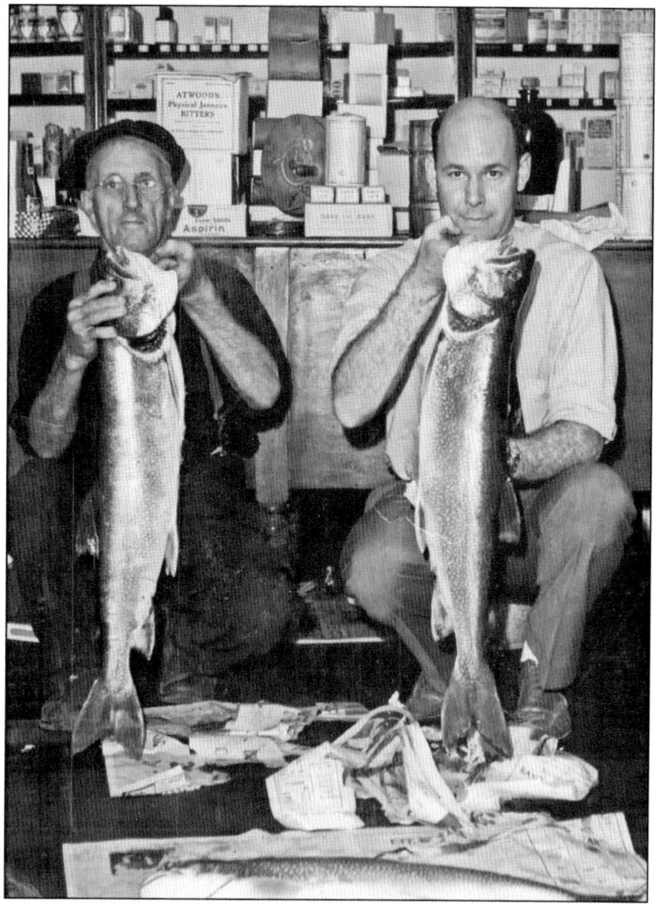

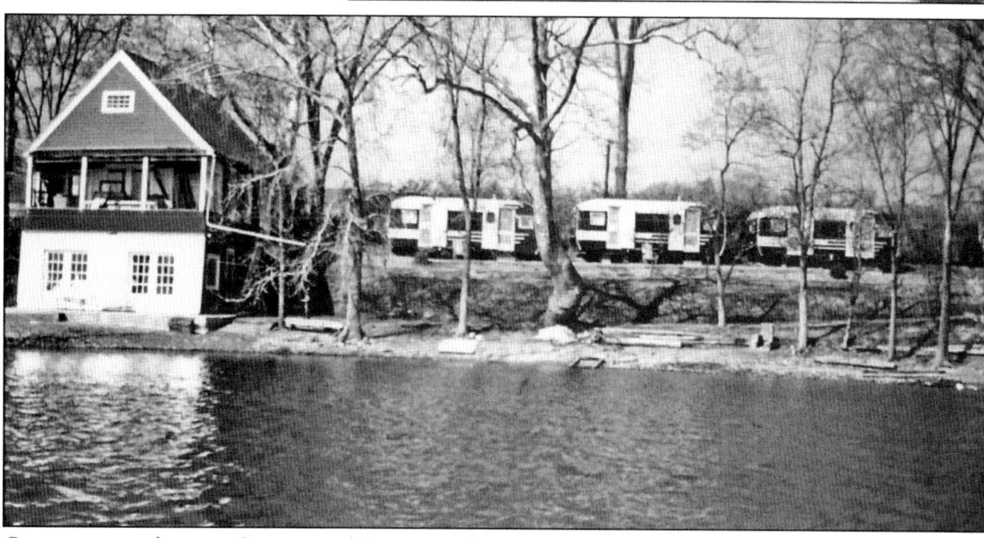

Camping was done on Seneca and Cayuga Lakes. Originally, people used tents for their weekend vacation. When mobile trailers were produced, individual families and groups of campers frequented the lakeshores for a weekend or longer. Eventually, trailer parks were established where campers could rent space for an entire season.

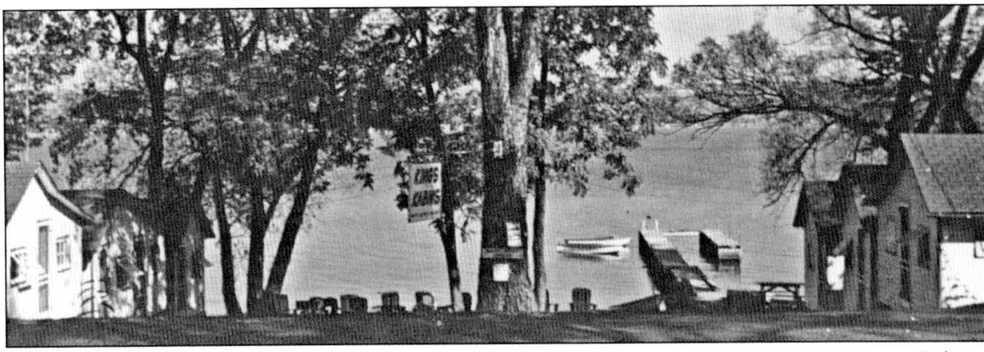

These lakeside cabins were owned by Kingsley and Pearl Brodhead. Known as Kings Cabins, they were rented to tourists each summer in the 1940s and 1950s. By 1963, "Kings Kabins—Only Kabins on Cayuga Lake Shore" was the new spelling in the advertisements. A double bed per night cost $9; per week, it was $55.

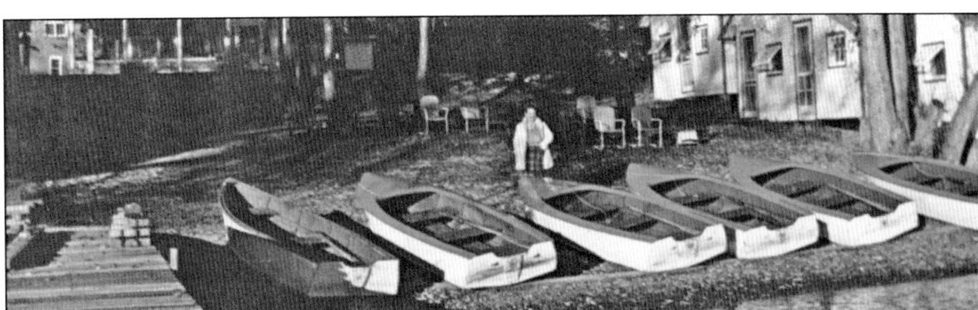

Boats were available for those who wanted to be on the lake. Outboard motors could be rented for waterskiing. Swimming was enjoyed near the shore, or one could dive into the water from the dock. Picnic tables and chairs were on the lawn to be used for picnics.

Ten

Odds and Ends

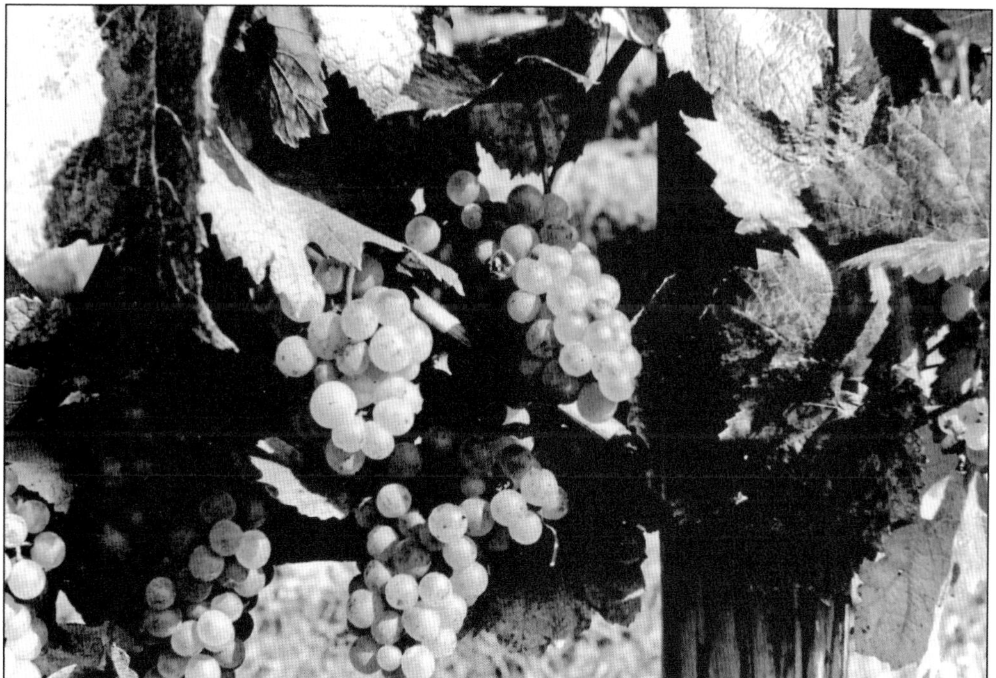

Ovid is in the Finger Lakes grape country. There are more than 30 vineyards on the road that passes through the village. The sloping hills that lead down to Seneca and Cayuga Lakes provide the best land to grow grapes. The cool temperature of the lakes in the spring delays the growth until the air is warm. In the fall, the warmth of the lakes extends the season until after the grapes are harvested. White and red grapes are grown, which produce sweet and dry wines. The wineries have greatly contributed to the tourist business in the area. Large tour buses and long limousines are seen daily at the wineries and restaurants.

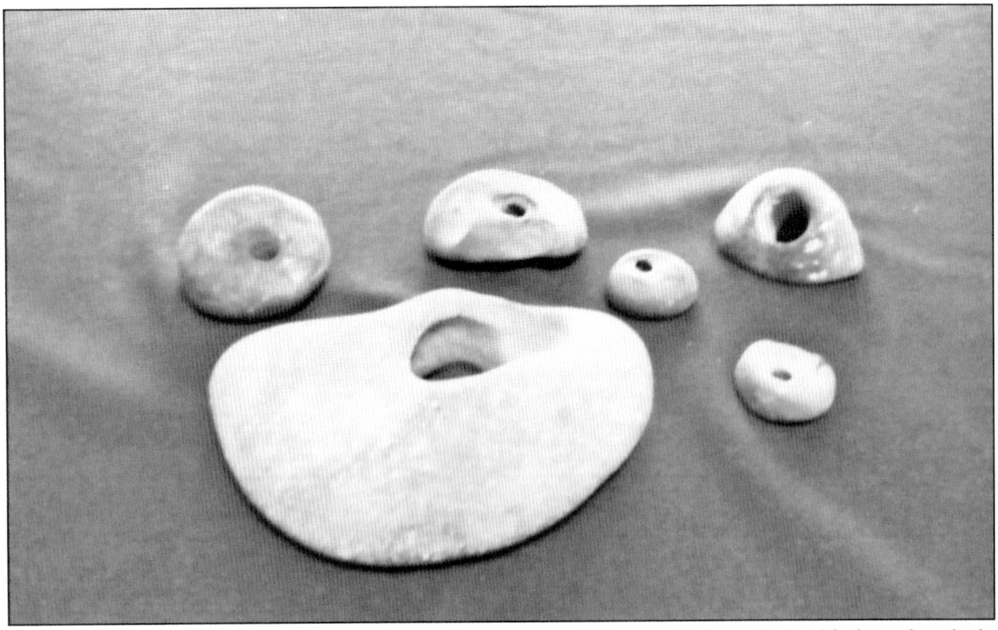

Lucky stones are found on the lakeshore of Seneca and Cayuga Lakes. Embedded in the shale are concretions or blobs of limestone. Over time, these concretions fall out of the parent rock, leaving a hole. It is considered good luck when a person finds one of these rocks. There must be many lucky people, for the stones are found by residents as well as visitors.

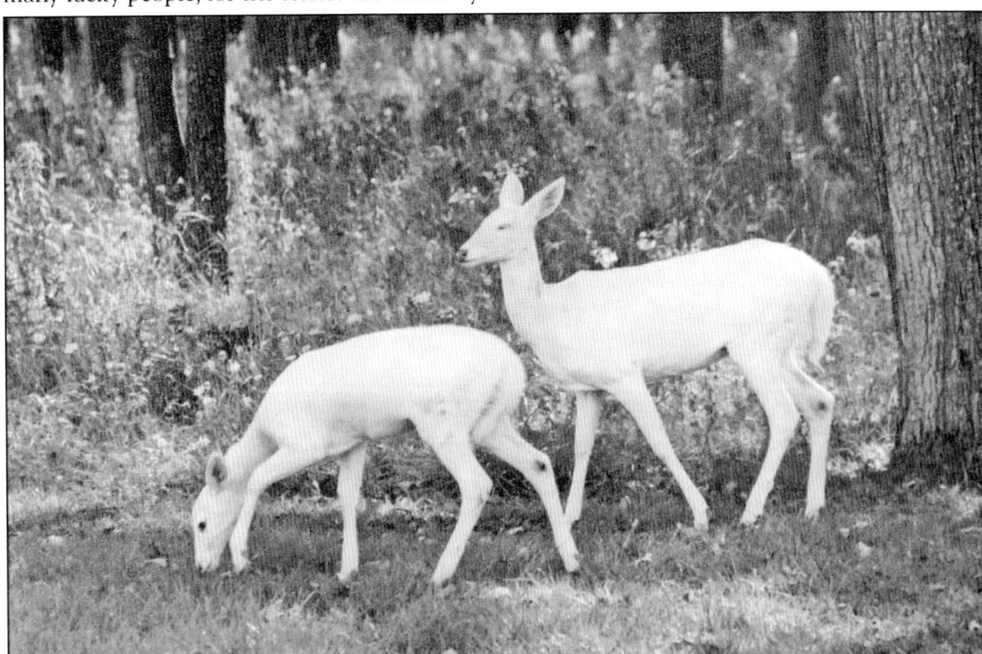

These all-white deer are confined within the surrounding fence of the former Seneca Army Depot. It is the largest herd of white deer in the world. They appeared after the fence was installed in 1941 and were isolated inside. The white-tailed deer carry a recessive gene for all-white coats. These deer have brown eyes, as opposed to the pink eyes of albino deer.

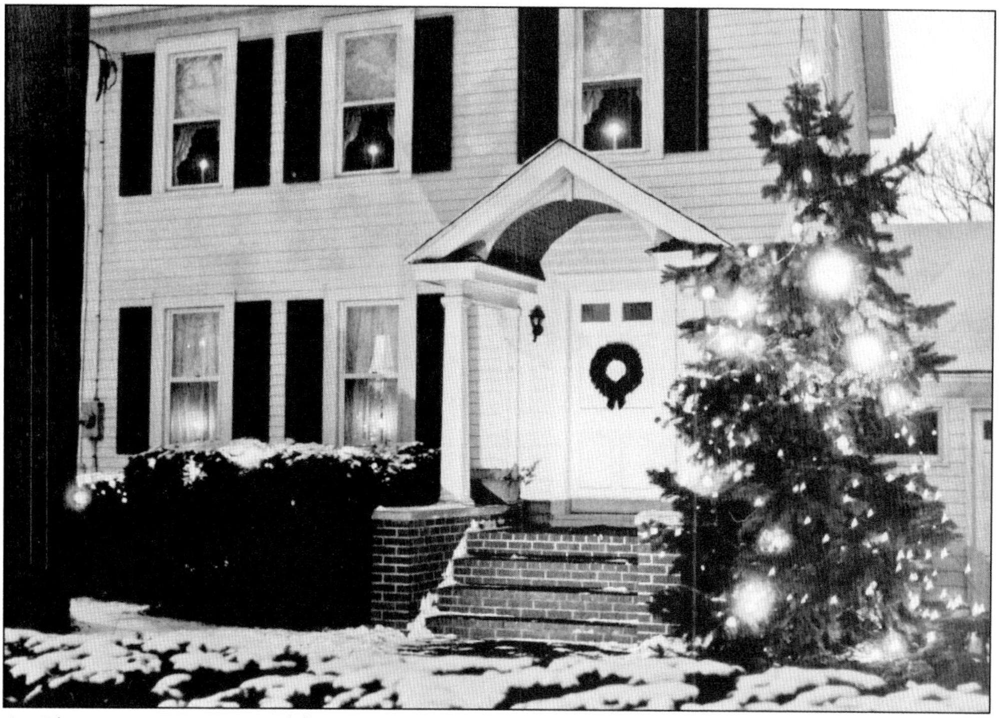

At Christmastime, many of the houses are decorated with candles in the windows and wreaths on the doors. Hedges and trees are brightly lighted with white or colorful strings of lights. Everyone wishes for a covering of newly fallen snow to add to the season. It is not always forthcoming, so residents often have to be content with green grass.

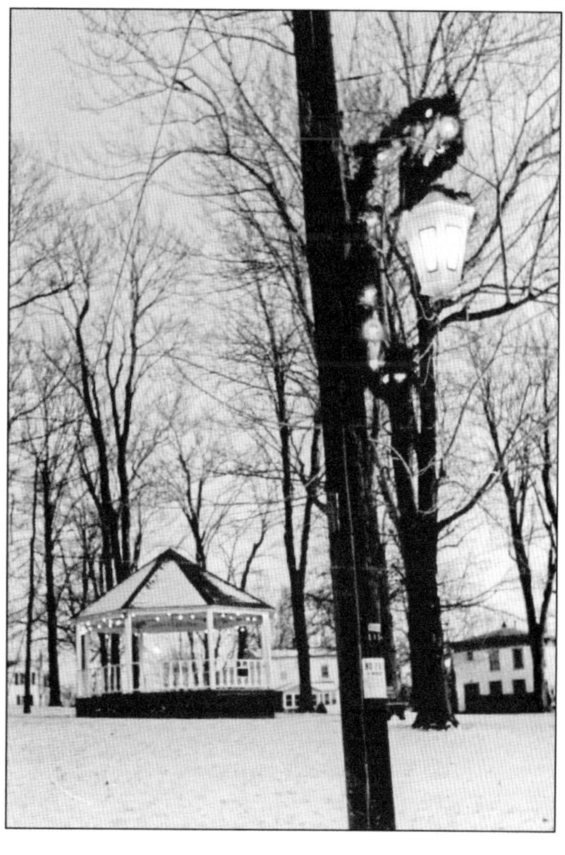

The street and the park are aglow with holiday lights in early December. Garlands of lights are hung on the gazebo in the village park. The lanterns with their arched wreaths are connected to each pole on the main and side streets. All of the village decorations are lighted each night at dusk.

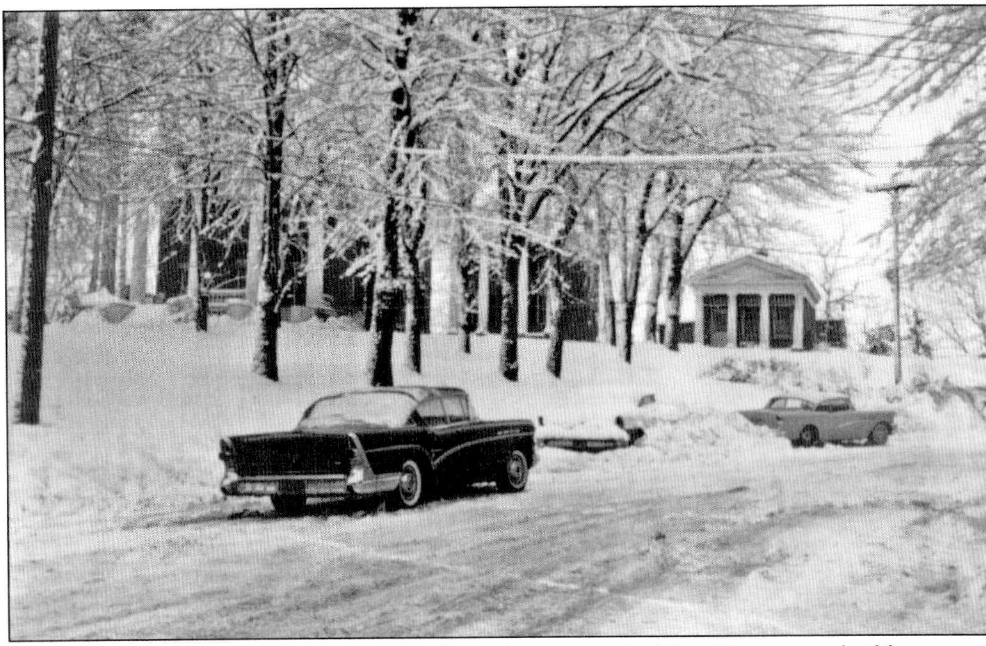

Sometimes, the amount of snow is more than what was wished for. The streets, buildings, cars, and trees are covered with clinging, wet snowfall. When it is too heavy, tree limbs are broken, and there is a great deal of shoveling that has to be done. The bright side of all of the snow is that it is beautiful to see, especially at night when the lights shine on it.

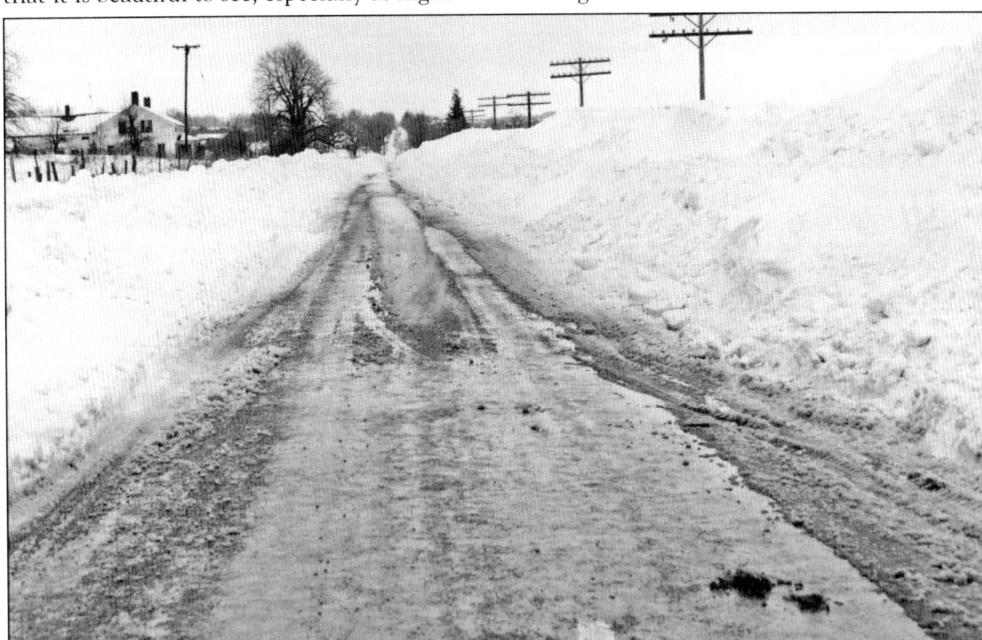

When this photograph was taken, years ago, the amount of snow was not appreciated. The snowplows were unable to clear the roads. Piles of snow are nearly as high as the telephone poles. Two-way traffic was difficult, because the path is not wide enough. Farm horses were often called upon to pull cars out of ditches or carry a rider to the store for supplies.

The moment snow fell, everyone rushed outside to try a variety of activities. These skis are not running smoothly, but there is a good reason. A little more snow is needed to completely cover the grass. When it falls, the snowsuit, hat, and mittens will really be needed to keep warm.

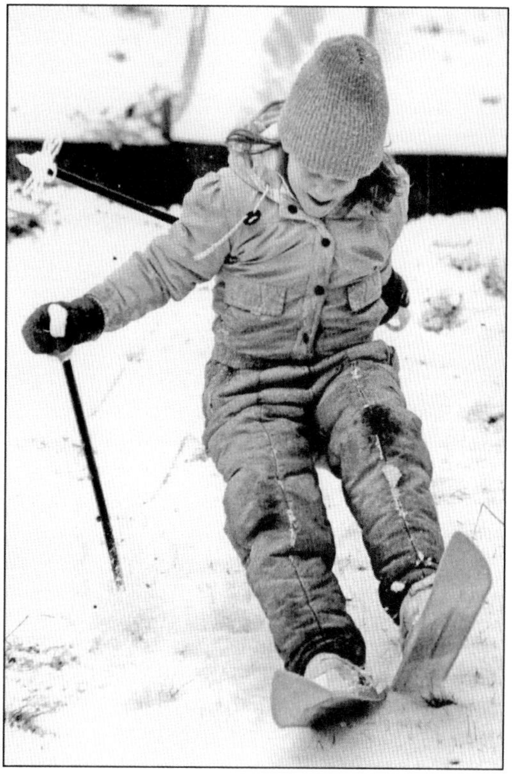

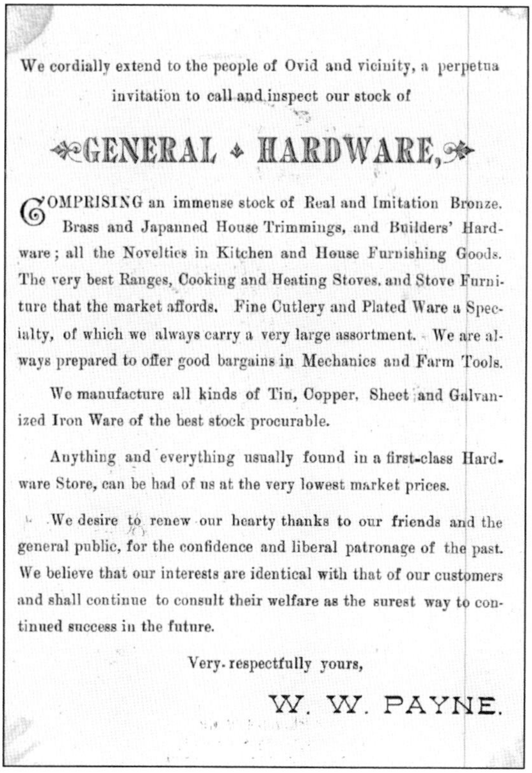

We cordially extend to the people of Ovid and vicinity, a perpetua invitation to call and inspect our stock of

GENERAL HARDWARE,

COMPRISING an immense stock of Real and Imitation Bronze. Brass and Japanned House Trimmings, and Builders' Hardware; all the Novelties in Kitchen and House Furnishing Goods. The very best Ranges, Cooking and Heating Stoves, and Stove Furniture that the market affords. Fine Cutlery and Plated Ware a Specialty, of which we always carry a very large assortment. We are always prepared to offer good bargains in Mechanics and Farm Tools.

We manufacture all kinds of Tin, Copper, Sheet and Galvanized Iron Ware of the best stock procurable.

Anything and everything usually found in a first-class Hardware Store, can be had of us at the very lowest market prices.

We desire to renew our hearty thanks to our friends and the general public, for the confidence and liberal patronage of the past. We believe that our interests are identical with that of our customers and shall continue to consult their welfare as the surest way to continued success in the future.

Very. respectfully yours,

W. W. PAYNE.

A trip to the hardware store in the winter can be delightful. The shelves are stocked with all sorts of interesting products. The most-wanted items at that time of year are listed in the advertisement: "The very best ranges, cooking and heating stoves, and stove furniture that the market affords." Many are noticing the phrase "all the Novelties in Kitchen and House Furnishing Goods."

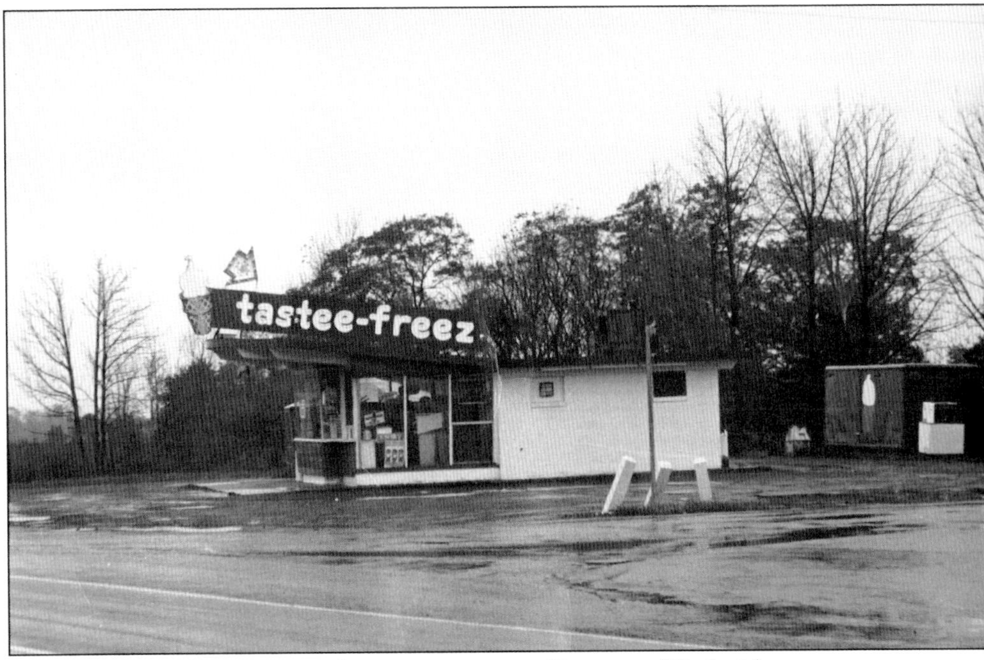

Nearly everyone likes a trip to the ice cream store. Cones are filled with one or two scoops of favorite flavors. There are so many sprinkles and toppings that it is difficult to make a choice. A hot summer evening becomes much more pleasant when one is licking as fast as possible. The Tastee-Freez shop on the northeast corner of Route 96 and County Road 139 is the destination for many drives on hot summer evenings.

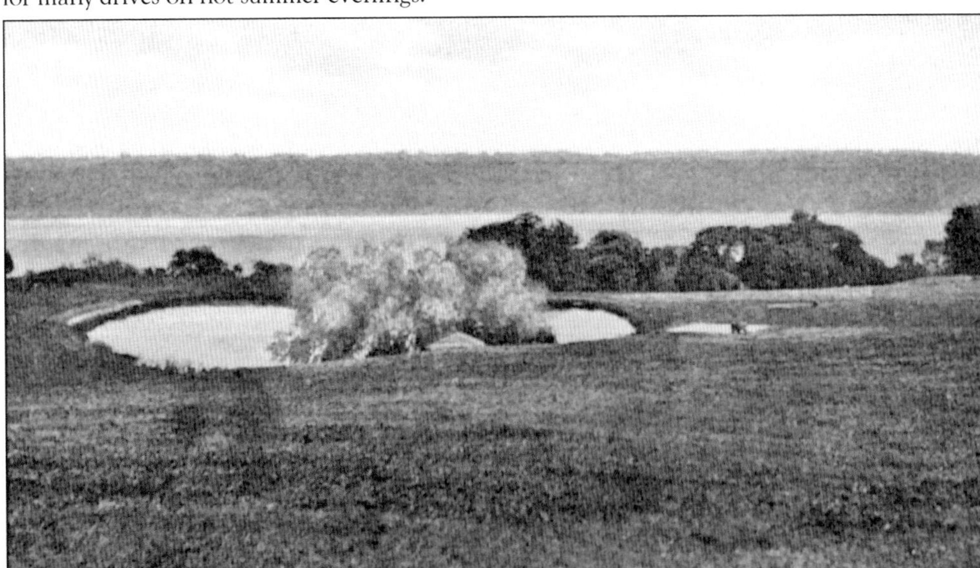

Golf is a great pastime for young and old, beginners and pros, workers or retired. The golf course in Ovid was located by the Willard Psychiatric Hospital. The staff and employees enjoyed the distraction from daily work. When the psychiatric hospital closed, it became the Bona Vista Golf Course. The course pond is shown in the foreground, and Seneca Lake is viewed from the second hole.

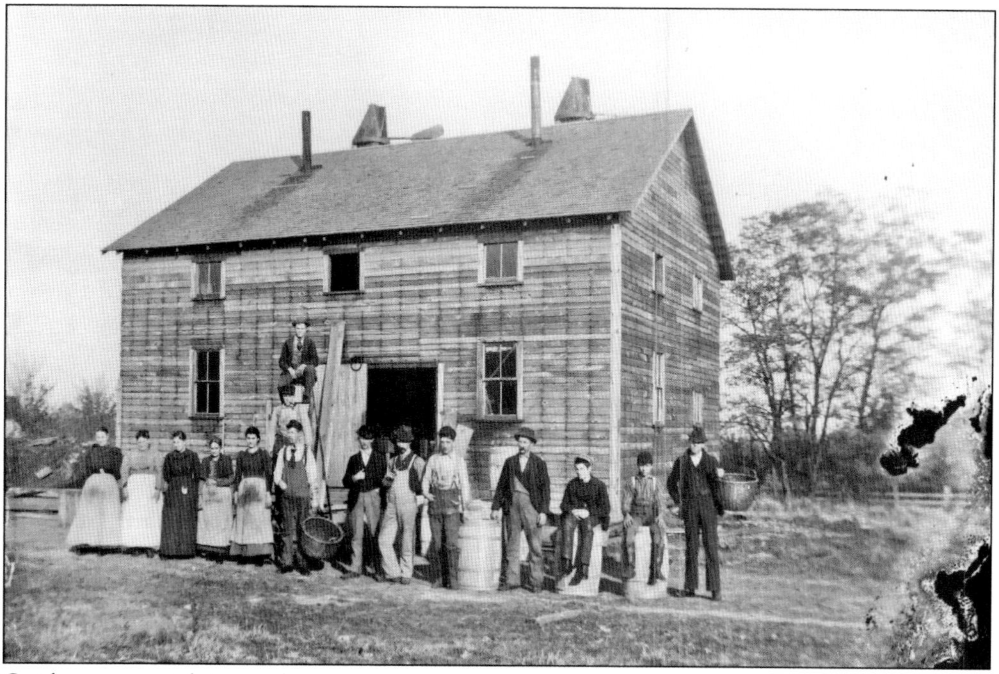

Ovid is a town rich in rural and agricultural history. This evaporator and its crew likely represent the livelihood of a local family and a valuable cog in the town's economy. In the early years, Ovid's borders were significantly larger, and this evaporator was once located in town. Due to changes in municipal boundaries, the evaporator is now in the town of Interlaken. (Courtesy of the Interlaken Historical Society.)

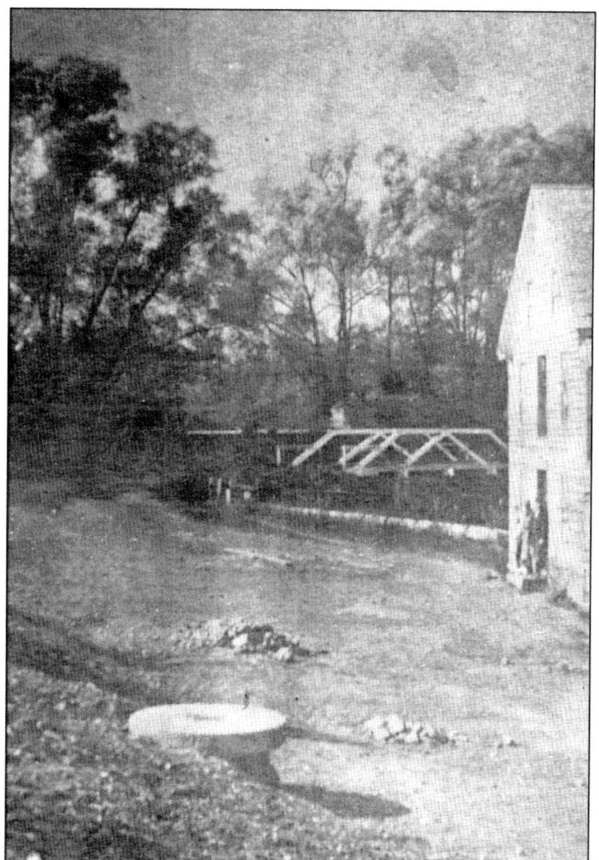

An early postcard shows Edwin Barry's gristmill, located on Morgan Road along Sheldrake Creek. The flood of 1935 destroyed the wooden bridge over the creek. West of the bridge was the Quigley Pond, where ice blocks were cut during the winter months. Men used horses and wagons to fill icehouses.

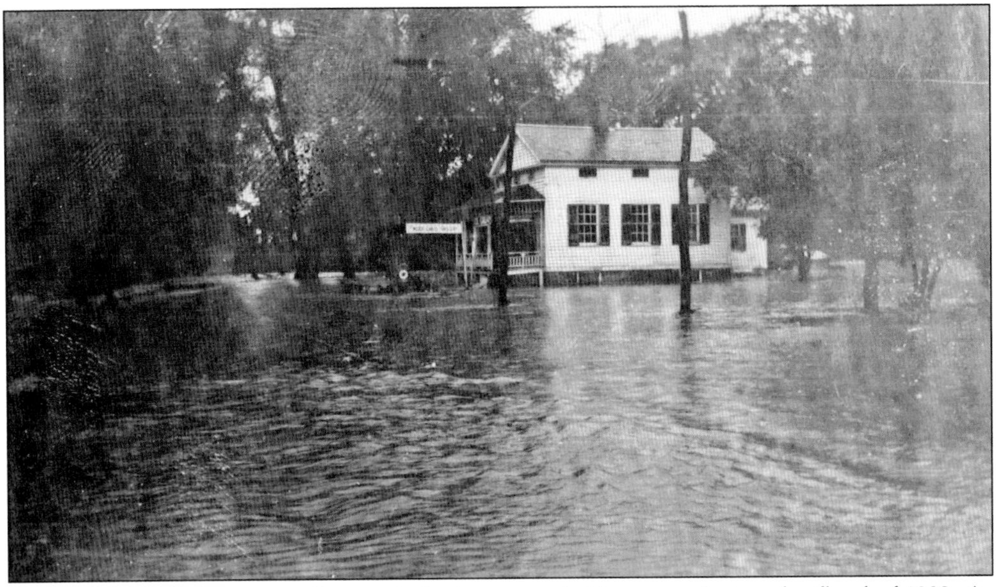

The Finger Lakes Store near Cayuga Lake is surrounded by water during the flood of 1922. As the streams overflowed and the lake water rose, there was much damage from the flood. Roads were covered, which made travel very dangerous or impossible.

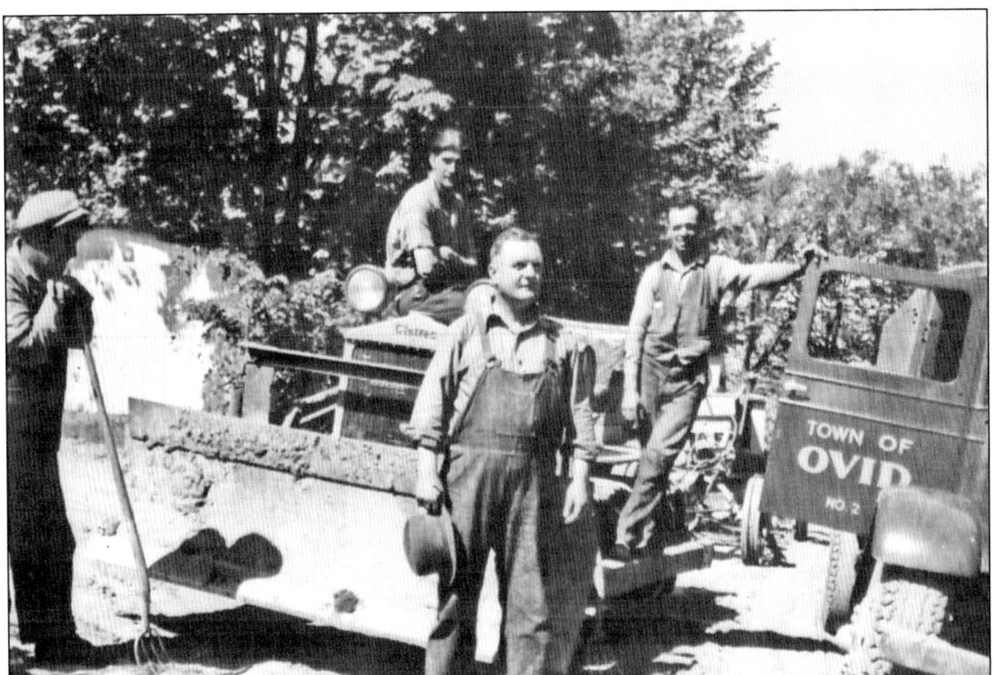

The Town of Ovid highway crew repaired the Wyer's Point Bridge after the flood of 1935 washed it away. The water carried trees and debris into Cayuga Lake. Pictured are, from left to right, (first row) Carl Craft, Arthur Depew, Kenneth VanNostrand and Jerry Fowler. (Courtesy of Naomi Brewer.)

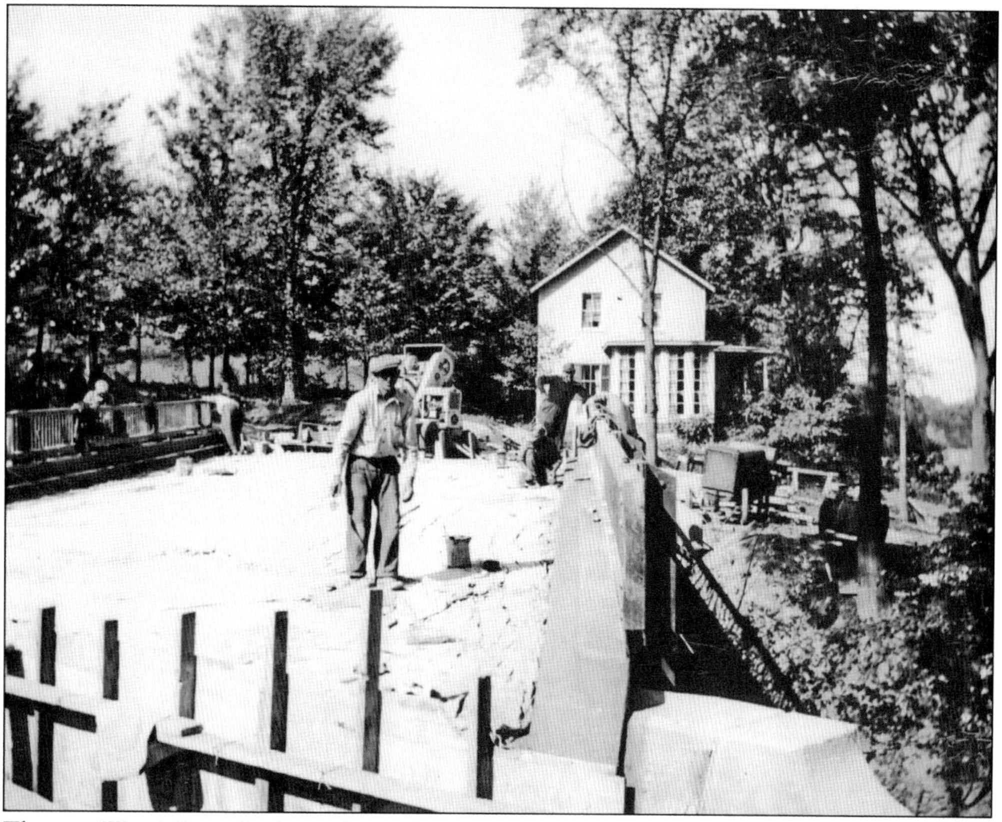

The new Wyer's Point Bridge is shown during construction. While the bridge was being rebuilt, there was no road for Wyer's Point residents to reach Sheldrake. The route to the corner store was the long way around, using the main highway. The contractor is shown in the foreground, and the workers are unidentified.

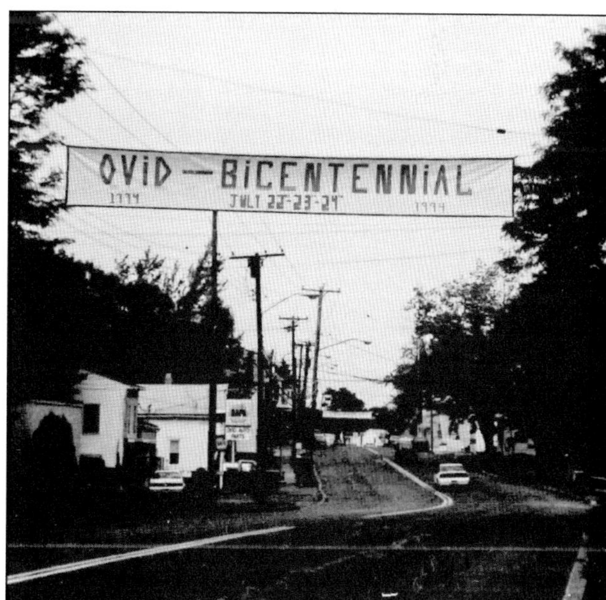

The Ovid bicentennial celebration was held July 22–24, 1994. Two hundred years made a great difference in the village and town of Ovid. The three days were filled with speeches, parades, and fireworks. The tour of the Three Bears introduced many residents to the buildings they had never entered. Reunions were held that reacquainted friends who had not seen one another in years.

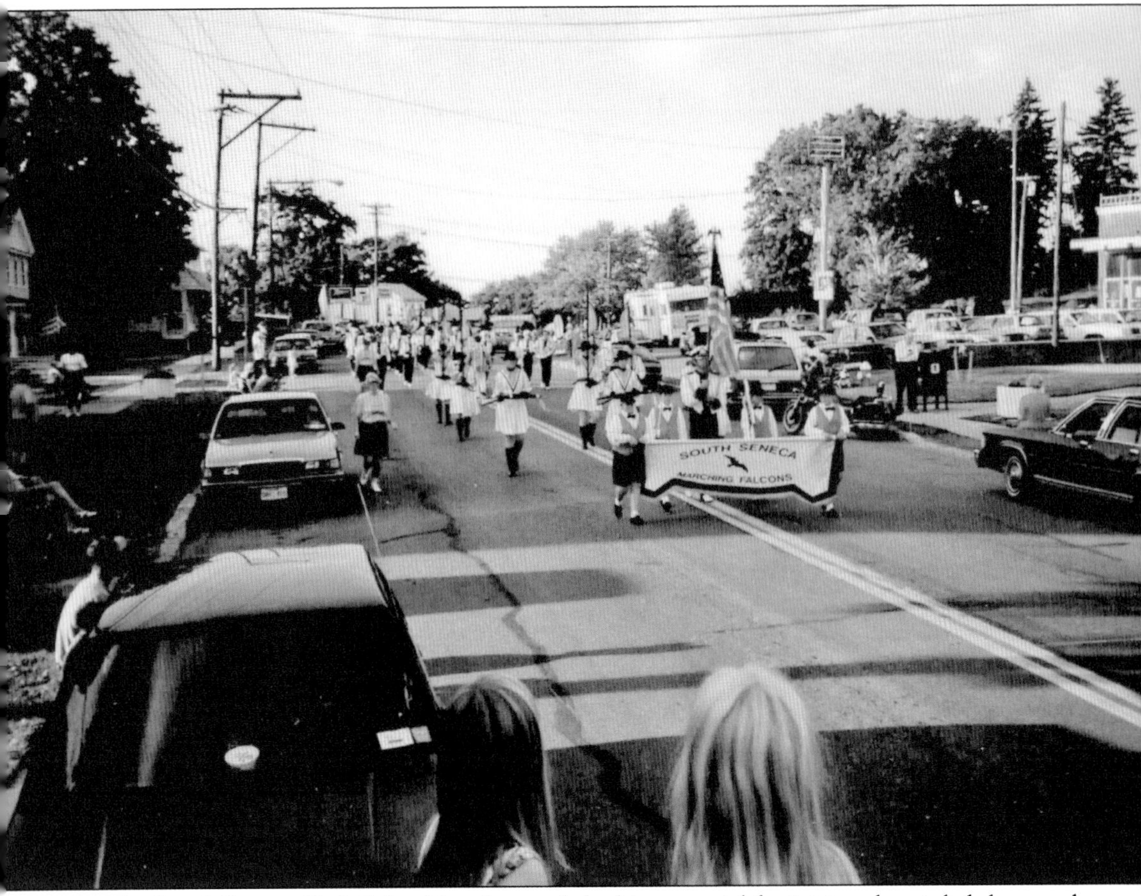

The South Seneca High School band started the bicentennial festivities when it led the parade down Main Street. The jackets of the black-and-gold uniforms were removed, because very warm weather blessed the whole celebration. No umbrellas were needed, but the use of suntan lotion was recommended.

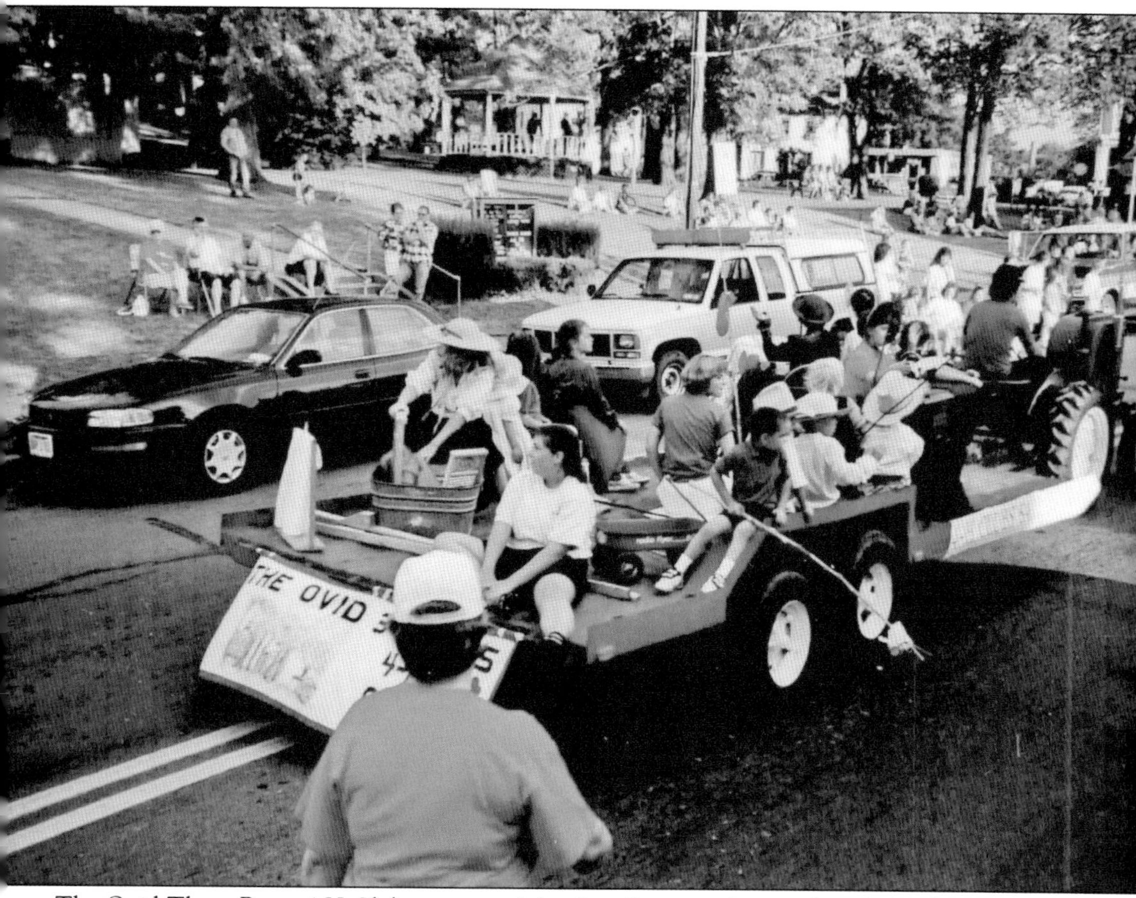

The Ovid Three Bears 4-H Club was one of the first floats in the parade. The washerwoman launders the clothes in an old metal boiler tub. The washboard is leaning against the end of the tub, ready to be used on the dirty overalls. People are lined on the sidewalk and steps to watch the parade.